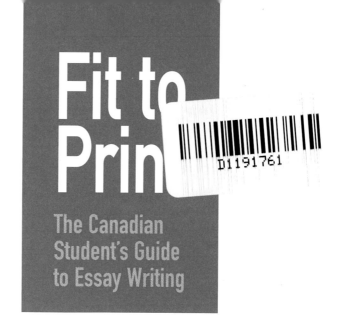

Fit to Print

The Canadian Student's Guide to Essay Writing

Eighth Edition

JOANNE BUCKLEY

McMaster University

NELSON EDUCATION

NELSON / EDUCATION

Fit to Print: The Canadian Student's Guide to Essay Writing, Eighth Edition

by Joanne Buckley

Vice President, Editorial Higher Education:
Anne Williams

Executive Editor:
Laura Macleod

Senior Marketing Manager:
Amanda Henry

Senior Developmental Editor:
Sandy Matos

Permissions Coordinator:
Carrie McGregor

Production Service:
Cenveo Publisher Services

Copy Editor:
Gail Marsden

Proofreader:
Erin Moore

Indexer:
Andrew Little

Senior Production Coordinator:
Ferial Suleman

Design Director:
Ken Phipps

Managing Designer:
Franca Amore

Interior Design:
Dianna Little

Part Opener/Chapter Opener Image:
© ronstick/Shutterstock

Cover Design:
Peter Papayanakis

Cover Image:
© Intoit/Dreamstime.com

Compositor:
Cenveo Publisher Services

Printer:
RR Donnelley

Library and Archives Canada Cataloguing in Publication Data

Buckley, Joanne, 1953-
Fit to print:
the Canadian student's guide to essay writing / Joanne Buckley.—8th ed.

Includes index.
ISBN 978-0-17-650387-1

1. Report writing. 2. Exposition (Rhetoric). 3. English language–Rhetoric. • I. Title.

LB2369.B83 2012   808'.042
C2011-907338-2

ISBN-13: 978-0-17-650387-1
ISBN-10: 0-17-650387-0

Contents

Preface

The Eighth Edition of *Fit to Print*, like its predecessors, is aimed at the problems students encounter when they write essays in a scholarly environment. This book may be used as a textbook in writing courses or as a supplementary guide in the humanities or social sciences in universities, colleges, and secondary schools.

The Eighth Edition continues the tradition of teaching students how to organize and write an essay and how to overcome specific difficulties of grammar and style. It also includes some features that improve its coverage for contemporary students and instructors:

1. A list of learning objectives to accompany each chapter.
2. A new structure that allows students and instructors to work through the writing process more completely.
3. A more thorough discussion of patterns of development, argument, and logical fallacies.
4. A more thorough treatment of thesis statements, topic sentences, and paragraph development.
5. An updated discussion of research methods, including accessing the Internet and using the library.
6. Some new, varied, authentic, and interdisciplinary sample essays by students.
7. New exercises.
8. The most recent changes to documentation styles of MLA, APA, and University of Chicago.
9. More focus on student revision and a sample essay to demonstrate the process.
10. A complete Instructor's Manual with additional exercises and answers for use as test materials.

Canadian in authorship and in much of its content, *Fit to Print* is a readable guide that is aimed at helping students gain mastery of the writing process and improve their grasp of the particulars of style and documentation. It may be used as a self-help guide or as a classroom text. Its examples are frequently drawn from student work and essay assignments across a variety of disciplines.

Acknowledgments

The Eighth Edition of *Fit to Print* owes its existence to a number of editors, students, colleagues, reviewers, and friends. I would first like to thank Sandy Matos, Senior Developmental Editor at Nelson, for being so quick and so dedicated to helping me get through the revision process. I would also like to thank those students whose work I used in this edition, especially April Beresford, Dan Rosenfield, and Dustin Manley. Dustin Manley also provided valuable assistance and suggestions. I extend my great appreciation to the following reviewers for their comments and suggestions during the development of this edition:

Dr. Jeoffrey Bull, Humber College

James Doelman, Brescia University College, U.W.O.

Dana Hansen, Humber College

Dr. Nigel Joseph, University of Western Ontario

Additionally, I would like to thank Anne Williams and Laura Macleod for their support and inspiration. Neither *Fit to Print* nor I would exist without the continuing steadfast support and patience of Mary Buckley.

A Note from the Publisher

Thank you for selecting *Fit to Print*: *The Canadian Student's Guide to Essay Writing*, Eighth Edition, by Joanne Buckley. The author and publisher have devoted considerable time to the careful development of this book. We appreciate your recognition of this effort and accomplishment.

Introduction—Defining the Essay

The essay is a literary device for saying almost everything about almost anything.
—ALDOUS HUXLEY

If at First You Don't Succeed...

As any dictionary will tell you, the essay is an attempt. This definition ought to be reassuring if you have ever worried about how to write an essay. You can't fail as long as what you write is a sincere attempt to come to terms with a particular subject. The finished essay succeeds if it is an honest attempt to elucidate some aspect of your topic.

An essay will not fail if you treat your ideas fairly, honestly, and in a spirit of thorough and intensive investigation. You must communicate these ideas to the reader! If the essay seems an especially burdensome assignment, it may be because most of us are not accustomed to independent thought. Try to think of the essay as an opportunity to stretch your intellectual muscles and to think your own thoughts.

To write an essay is to engage in a creative process, to bring an idea to life. The essay itself, however, is a finished product, not a record of the process that you used to write it.

Whether you are writing an expository essay that explains something or a persuasive essay that argues something, the essay's chief purpose is to present a thesis or sometimes just to consider a question in an exploratory way. The essay focuses your ideas and conveys them to the reader in a way that shows their worth and their validity. Depending on the occasion, an essay may be formal or informal; however, academic writing usually demands formality. Depending on the nature of the assignment, the essay may be a product of reasoning or a combination of reasoning and research.

This text deals with the essentials of essay writing and the variations that different kinds of assignments demand. Skim its contents first to acquaint yourself with the most important steps of essay writing. If you are unfamiliar with the basic requirements of the essay, pay special attention to Parts One, Two, and Three. If you are unsure of the specific guidelines for a particular kind of essay, check the pertinent section in Part Five. Then, as you write your next essay, use this book as a step-by-step guide. It will provide helpful suggestions on how to organize your thinking and how to present your material in the most effective manner.

Remember that the essay is an attempt to think through your ideas in a structured way. Each attempt will teach you more about how the process works for you.

Try, Try Again

As you plan and write the essay, you will try on various ideas for size. The process of writing an essay involves finding some part of a large topic that fits your attitude toward, and interest in, the subject. Compromise is essential. The essay must fit both you and the topic: it will show you and the reader what you know and what you have yet to learn. For best results, choose a topic in which you have some personal stake. Make sure that you can treat the topic satisfactorily within the required word limit and within the time constraints of the assignment.

Overcoming Your Fears

Writing is hard work, even for those who write for a living. A glance at some of the epigraphs that begin each chapter of this book illustrates this point. You may find it difficult to get your thoughts down on paper, or even to feel that you have any important thoughts to record. Here is some advice that makes starting to write easier:

1. Divide the writing process into smaller steps; don't try to do everything at once.

   Look again at the table of contents in this book. It suggests that your first task is finding some central focus; your next task is building an outline; your third task is writing a preliminary draft; and your final task is revising the whole. Don't skip any of these steps.

2. Don't ignore your real questions about a topic because you feel they reveal your ignorance.

   The essay is meant to be an exploration of something; if you knew everything about the subject before you began, you wouldn't need to write. In large part, the writing process is meant to help you and your reader discover something.

3. Pay attention to your real interests in, and your real objections to, the subject matter.

   Let the focus of your conversations and your wondering become the focus of your essay.

4. Don't approach the assignment in a perfunctory manner.

   Ask yourself why the assignment is a good one and what connections it makes with the course, with other courses, or with other things you have read.

5. Don't expect too much from an essay.

   An essay is not meant to provide a definitive answer; instead, it explores what you think, and why you think it, in a clear way.

6. Gather information and ideas, and write them down as you go along.

   Remember that you need to keep good track of your findings, particularly of ideas that are not your own. Things you encounter on the Internet, or in your reading, need special acknowledgment. Keep track of authors, titles, page numbers, and URLs so that your steps may be retraced as your ideas gel.

7. Ask questions of your instructor and other experts who can help you delineate your topic.

   Online and off-line reading can help you accomplish this task. Preliminary reading is an essential step to getting a feel for your topic and your take on it.

8. Try not to think of your instructor as an enemy who seeks to trip you up.

Think of your reader as someone engaged in the topic and deeply interested in your point of view.

9. Explain your ideas to a friend.

The transition of your ideas to paper should then involve the detailed work of careful documentation and editing. Be a writer first, then an editor. To do both together is to set an impossible standard.

10. Learn from your mistakes.

Diagnose what went wrong with previous assignments and resolve not to make the same mistakes again. Reflecting on your own work is an important part of the process of writing.

Part One
DEVELOPING THE ESSAY

CHAPTER 1

Devising a Thesis

A person with a new idea is a crank until the idea succeeds.
—MARK TWAIN

In this chapter:

- How to get started on your essay
- How to write a thesis statement
- How to evaluate the effectiveness of your thesis statement
- How to write a "route map" to direct your essay

Usually when you begin to write an essay, you will have in mind a broad area of concentration or a fundamental topic that you mean to explore. To write a successful essay, you must find the focal point of your discussion—the centre of your thought from which the points you make may radiate outward. This focal point is the thesis statement.

Topics are only the starting point for your thinking. They tell you only the general area of investigation. Whether the instructor gives you a topic or you find your own, you must narrow down the topic to serve as the focus of your paper. Like the bull's eye in the middle of a dartboard, the thesis statement is the centre that holds your argument together. An essay succeeds because the point to be made is directly on target, and the significance of the point is firmly established.

Discovering a Topic

If your instructor has not suggested areas for exploration, you will have to create your own, usually subject to his or her approval. This process need not be drudgery; it gives you the opportunity to explore your own interest in the subject. The following suggestions will help you find a general topic or area of interest:

1. Skim the index and table of contents of any book mentioned in class as a useful source.
2. Skim through class notes and texts for ideas that catch your imagination.
3. Ask questions about the meaning and value of the subject.
4. Look at class assignments and essay questions, and ask yourself what points they make. Ask yourself why these questions are particularly fitting to the subject with which you are dealing.

5. Listen to yourself to determine what issues and matters of concern come up in your conversations outside of class.
6. Allow yourself the chance to express your real puzzlement about something you have read. If you don't understand something crucial in your area of study, make finding out more about it one of the goals of your investigation.
7. Always write down ideas as you go along.

Starting to Write

This book began with the assumption that instructors assigned topics, partly because that was the usual practice and partly because invention is the most nebulous and frightening part of the writing process. It is still true that inventing a topic is a challenge; what has changed in the classroom is the expectation of what a topic is and how best to arrive at it. While you may still be given a specific question to answer, and the answer will constitute your essay, you may also be expected to write in a more exploratory way before, during, and after your essay or other writing assignment.

This section will discuss some ways of exploring your ideas in order to arrive at a good topic. This process is sometimes called pre-writing, though perhaps it should simply be called writing. Those who teach writing and study the psychology of writing tend to agree that the best way to learn to write is by writing. Even the attempts to discover a topic are forms of writing—exploratory forms—meant to help you access your own deeper ideas, your own thoughts and interests. The best way to avoid a boring B on an essay is to make sure that you don't skip this early, messy, inventive, and provocative part of the process.

Here are some suggestions of how to arrive at something suitable to develop further in an essay:

Timed Writing

Not only does this help you discover possible topics quickly, but it also forces you to put pen to paper and eliminate the anxiety of procrastination. Decide to give yourself ten minutes to write down topics as they occur to you. Try not to censor yourself. Just keep writing. Put down anything, even crazy things that occur to you. You don't need to be neat, organized, or careful; this kind of freewriting is meant to loosen you up and remind yourself that you can do it, especially if you feel rusty or insecure. For a starting point, consider an important word in your classroom study, a point of argument, a question you have, or a summary of what you remember from today's class. Focus on the "edgy" issues. Ask yourself what bothers you about some element of course content. Consider what untruths or misconceptions you would like to see cleared up. Ask a tough question and then try to answer it, even if your answer is ludicrous. At this point, you are playing with ideas and words, and nothing is subject to judgment.

Here is a student example that shows how freewriting can develop your thinking and help you overcome writer's block:

John Stuart Mill's utilitarian principle advocates the greatest good for the greatest number. Obviously, though, that kind of principle applied too rigorously would have devastating effects on the rights of the individual. How does Mill come to terms with the rights of the individual? How does he safeguard them? One way is his insistence on liberty if that liberty does not harm others. This idea, by itself, goes a long way toward protecting individual rights in a political state. For example, if I write something that slanders those of another race, Mill would judge that to be an infringement of others' rights because it has potential to do them harm. For that reason, he would argue against my individual right to do it. On the other hand, if I want to drink alcohol in the privacy of my own home, Mill would likely determine that I have the right to do so. My liberties are safe as long as I pursue them with a sense of responsibility toward others.

Start with a Stimulus

Rather than inventing something out of whole cloth, start by "borrowing" a sentence from a source, a writer in the field you are studying, a title, or an interesting statement. Comment on it, or see if you can figure out what the next sentence might be, and the next, and the next, and the next. This technique works well when it is timed. The whole idea does not spring from you, and you are at liberty to take your cue from a learned written source, an inspiration, or a reference in the classroom. Writing from a prompt can get you started, even when you are stuck.

Dialogue

Make a point of listening to yourself. If you and other students engage in any discussion of your course of study, keep track of what is being said on both sides. Because this is not yet a formal piece of writing, you can jot down ideas in a notebook or summarize them at the end of the day. You don't need to commit yourself yet; feel free to discuss both pros and cons of an idea, perhaps by remembering a dialogue you engaged in with a friend. See where this process of writing down your thoughts leads. Many online courses and tools take advantage of this human urge to communicate our thoughts by encouraging discussion over the Internet. The dialogue helps to clarify thinking and to address objections. Having an audience, whether on paper or online, has the benefit of making us conscious of an audience wider and different from an instructor alone. Instructors can be intimidating because they are focused on grading and not usually on dialogue. It is also more fun than writing just to oneself. Consider participating in an online discussion group with other class members when you are trying to structure your thoughts for an essay.

Reading Journals

When you begin to examine sources, including library and online materials, keep track of your comments as you read. One good way to do this is to summarize in your own words, and on one page or less, each article or chapter that is pertinent. Leave some space, perhaps in a different colour, for the questions, comments, and quarrels that the piece incites in you. Finding words for the concepts you are dealing with is the first step to becoming fluent enough to write a paper that you can be proud of. If you are comfortable sharing your thoughts, consider the idea of a blog that may invite others to participate. Writing can be a lonely occupation; a blog may open up the world for you by helping you find others to read and respond to your work in progress. The Internet allows a vast opportunity to exchange thoughts and to participate in conversation about current issues. With pictures, audio, and a swell of words, it can chronicle the books you have read, the movies you have seen, and the events in your life in a way that allows others to comment.

Mapping Ideas

Draw your ideas. This process—commonly called clustering—might be as simple as putting the names of concepts in balloons and figuring out where on the map they belong. For visual thinkers, this process of mapping out thoughts may be more helpful than words alone. Don't hesitate to use images that help you visualize your thoughts and see their relation to one another. In these days of Web design, images tell a lot of the tale, and some kind of storyboarding may be the most effective way to get your first thoughts on paper.

Test Anxiety Mind Map

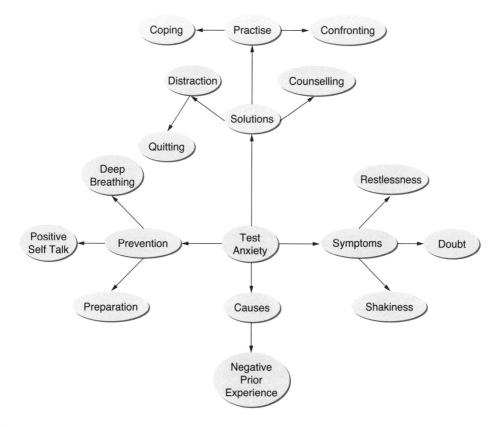

Writing as an Activity

Writing may occasionally seem like inspiration, but most of it involves perspiration first. Don't wait for inspiration; start doing your writing, in whatever form initially feels comfortable, and inspiration may well come. Even if it doesn't come, you will have something written to show for your efforts.

Shopping for a Thesis Statement

Often, your instructor will give you a general topic and tell you how to narrow it down. Remember, though, a topic is only a general idea in need of development. Suppose you were asked in a political science course to write an essay of 2500 to 3000 words about American–Canadian border relations. Obviously, this is a broad subject that could yield several promising thesis statements. By itself, however, it is just a phrase that makes no meaningful statement. Keep this example in mind as you read through the following tips on developing a specific thesis statement.

When You Develop a Topic, Keep These Determining Factors in Mind:

1. your interests, strengths, and weaknesses
2. the reader's expectations
3. the restrictions of the assignment

Use Whatever You Have at Your Disposal

1. supplemental bibliographies you may have been given
2. advice from the instructor
3. material from the course itself
4. your own skills, knowledge, and background
5. library resources—books, journals, and audio-visual materials
6. the Internet

Ask Questions about the General Topic

Your first question with regard to our sample topic might be "What about it?" Your in-class and out-of-class sources may have revealed to you that American–Canadian border relations have changed drastically since the tragedy of September 11, 2001.

Your next question might be "Why?" suggesting a cause-and-effect development, or even "How?" suggesting an argument based on classification (the breakdown of ideas into categories) or on process (the orderly presentation of steps). Refer also to Chapter 6 for some suggested approaches to topic development. A good way to begin might be to ask the six journalist's questions: Who, What, When, Where, Why, and How.

Consider Your Topic in Conjunction with Something Else

Try joining your topic to these conjunctions: "and," "or," "but," and "so." These linking words should give you some idea of what might be productively attached to your topic to yield interesting results.

"And," for example, might help you think of things that can be compared (or contrasted) with your subject: variations in attitudes toward the defence of the Canadian–American border at different periods in our history, for instance.

"Or" might lead you to consider a controversy about the causes of the change in Canadian–American border relations: national perceptions or ongoing trade hostility, for example.

"But" might allow you to refute the position of a particular authority on the subject, or to prove that the change in American–Canadian border relations was a political change based on government defence attitudes rather than fear of terrorism.

"So" Americans have tightened up border defence to demarcate less friendly terms with Canada than was previously the case. Because Canadians have long had a different policy toward immigration than Americans and because the Canadian–American border is the longest undefended border in the world, America is within its rights to step up security.

Your exploration need not be limited to these coordinating conjunctions. To build logical connections into your exploration of a topic, try dealing with subordinate conjunctions and your topic. A word like "because," "although," "unless," or "since" may lead you to new provocative connections with respect to your topic. You might argue, for example, that border crossings are more complicated and evidence of less trust between the countries, even though at this time the U.S. has agreed to accept a simple photo I.D. rather than a Canadian passport.

Consider Key Words That Form Part of the Topic

Ask yourself about the nuances of the question or topic for discussion: is there ambiguity or potential for development in the wording of the question? When setting questions, instructors usually have only a sketchy idea in mind; try to see in the topic as much as, or more than, they have seen.

In our sample general topic, one phrase to which this tactic might apply is "drastic change." To develop your topic, you might investigate what particular areas have most drastically changed to find a clue for your response. You might also want to explore exactly what is meant by "border relations" and how they are defined and characterized in the popular press.

Consult Your Own Taste

You should consult your taste in topics before you settle on anything. About the only serious mistake you can make is to choose a topic simply because it looks easier than the others. A challenge is often the best choice because it allows you to ponder the topic rather than assuming, probably incorrectly, that the main point is clear or the answer obvious.

Try On the Topic Before You Decide

Always play with the topic before you work on it. Play with ideas by scratching them down haphazardly on a sheet of paper without regard (for now) to problems of order or clarity. This kind of unstructured thinking will open up the possibilities of the question or the topic in a way that no amount of tidy compartmentalizing can.

Brainstorm by Writing Ideas Down

1. Try clustering ideas together according to their associations for you.
2. Try drawing diagrams, connecting various ideas.
3. Check the meanings of words in the topic, and perhaps their etymologies, for clues to the direction you should take.

A Working Thesis versus a Polished Thesis Statement

If you follow the guidelines, you should be able to arrive at a narrow focus for your paper. But even a thesis statement should be subject to revision. Because it is normally part of the introduction to a paper, writers often mistakenly assume that it should be written first. In fact, your real thesis statement may emerge only after you have made several false starts.

Since you have to start somewhere, begin with a working thesis. It will allow you to consider your material from a tentative point of view. If you find that the evidence begins to contradict it, or you no longer consider it the centre of your discussion, redefine your statement to suit the new circumstances. Many writers need to compose a fair amount of their essay before they are able to state their thesis clearly. Just make sure to go back to your original working thesis and adjust it when you finally come to the end of your work. It can be useful to focus your thoughts on a subject by imagining a letter to the editor that you might write on the subject. Such engagement with a topic helps to develop your voice as a writer and ensures that you choose a topic that you care about and can justify. As with a letter to the editor, any point you make needs to be clear, backed up by authoritative facts or figures, cool-headed and polite, and expressed as succinctly as possible. While the letter or the thesis is based on your opinion, it is your educated opinion and your ability to persuade others of its truth and validity that count.

The thesis statement that appears in your finished introduction will be the best description of what you are trying to prove and of how you propose to do it. For example, your thesis statement on the subject of American–Canadian border relations might look like this:

Example   Changes in border relations between America and Canada can be understood in terms of political changes and an increasing mistrust between the two countries, quite apart from any fear of terrorism on the part of the Americans.

This thesis statement prepares the reader to expect a discussion of the political changes that have led to mistrust between the two countries. The route map or preview might then go on to list what these changes have been.

Look Before You Leap

Once you have formulated a contention, that is, some idea of what your approach to the topic is going to be, you must formulate a thesis statement, along with some sense of the essay's ultimate direction. The sense of direction, or method statement, is a route map for your thinking. It provides a preview of the steps you will go through in order to show that your thesis is strong and defensible. Sometimes this route map will be part of your simple thesis statement, implicitly or explicitly. Sometimes it will appear directly after the thesis, but like the thesis, it is a structural foundation for your essay. To help you see your path clearly, you may want to visit the library to take note of what relevant books and journal articles are available on your specific subject, and whether they support or contradict your working thesis.

To write a good thesis statement, you need to remember that a strong thesis is a contention that forms the basis of your argument. It is what you are trying to show the reader. A good thesis statement takes into account the purpose of the writing and its audience, but it does more than that. For instance, your purpose might be to define for a beginner the perfect golf swing. Although this idea shows promise, it is not a thesis statement. To transform it, you need to make a claim. Look at this statement:

A perfect golf swing demands a proper grip, delicate balance, and excellent timing.   **Example**

It is a strong thesis statement because it makes a claim that the rest of the essay, presumably, will go on to support.

Suppose, now, that your topic is "learning a foreign language." Your purpose is to tell your reader what you consider the best way to learn a foreign language. You must not, however, leave the topic too vague. Instead, you might compose a thesis statement like the following:

The best way to learn a foreign language is through active practice and immersion   **Example**
among native speakers.

This thesis is stronger than one that argues that learning a foreign language is difficult because this thesis is contentious. Some individuals might, after all, disagree and claim that studying and reading are more important than practice and immersion. It is your job to make your case convincingly.

What to Look for in a Thesis Statement

Purpose

Whenever you write any document, you need to ask yourself questions about what it is intended to do and you need to show your reader why the point you are making matters to them. We have established that essays are often informative or persuasive and aim to teach or to persuade readers about a subject of interest to you and to them. Hence, it is vital that you know when you begin to write what you intend your audience to think by the end of the paper. Do you wish to change their thinking, beliefs, or actions, on a subject like the environment and the need to combat the greenhouse effect? Or do you wish to give them all the information they need to improve their understanding and appreciation of modern art? Having your purpose firmly in mind will ensure that you keep your contract with the reader. When you complete a draft, you will be in a good position to assess whether you have been as thorough and as convincing as you need to be to make your case to the reader. The purpose is the reason behind your thesis statement, that is, the reason behind your convictions. Establishing your purpose clearly at the outset will help you gauge why your topic matters.

Personal Conviction

No writing of any power is ever possible without commitment to the subject. No motivation is ever as pressing as the need to say something on a subject that matters urgently to you. Your first task is to find an approach to the topic capable of moving you to care and to work and to write. If you can find such an approach, the process of writing—the reading, the thinking, even the reworking of your thoughts—will be carried along by the desire to know and not only by the need to complete the assignment. Your thesis is one point that you wish to make about the topic, one point that you can make clearly and support with good reasons.

Pertinence

An essay should not be a trivial pursuit. It should matter to you and to its reader. As you shape your thesis statement, keep the *value* of your subject in mind. When selecting a point of view, allow yourself to think about its broader implications, even if there is no place to include all of these in the essay itself. You don't have to tell readers how relevant your topic is, but you should believe it, and you should be able to show that you do. Ensuring that your perspective is new and making your point of view matter to your reader are fundamental requirements.

Proportion

The thesis statement indicates what size the essay will be in its finished form. A well-measured thesis statement is snug, not loose, in its fit. If it does not fit properly, the arguments that follow will not seem convincing. To ensure a good fit between thesis statement and essay, ask questions. Ask yourself if there is room in a 1500-word essay to discuss all the implications of unemployment in Canada. If not, then trim the topic to fit: for example, unemployment among students seeking part-time jobs in Canadian cities. A good thesis statement might argue that "Students seeking part-time jobs in Canadian cities are given many incentives and have an excellent chance of finding work, unlike students in rural areas."

Precision

As in a legal contract, the essay is the delivery of promises made in its thesis statement. With such a contract, the issues to be dealt with must be clarified at the outset. Make sure before you develop your thesis statement that you have made clear to your readers both what your essay will do *and* what it will *not* do. Feel free to announce (without apologies) in or near the thesis statement the limits of your treatment of the subject.

Point

Not only should your thesis statement make a point, but it must also point in a particular direction. A useful addition to the thesis statement itself is the "route map." The route map informs readers of the highlights of the journey they are about to make. For instance, in a sociology essay comparing the changing attitudes toward women in advertisements from the 1940s to the 1990s, as reflected in two issues of the same magazine, you can briefly outline the steps in your discussion:

> Three major changes can be noted in the presentation of female figures: women are shown less often in domestic situations; women are more often featured as authority figures; and women are more often shown in active, rather than passive, roles.

Example

Such a statement contains the direction of the entire essay in miniature and points toward the arguments to follow.

How Can You Tell a Good Thesis Statement from a Bad One?

A good thesis statement is credible, relevant to the course you are taking, narrow enough to be treated in the space you have available, and specifically focused on the point you are making.

Here are some bad thesis statements. Can you tell why they don't do the job they were intended to do?

> Canadians with disabilities are still an overlooked minority.

Example

The problem with this attempt at a thesis statement is that it doesn't go far enough. It leaves us wondering what exactly the word "overlooked" means. You could improve this statement by continuing with a precise route map. You could, for example, write this:

> Canadians with disabilities need legal protection of their rights comparable to those enjoyed by Americans since George H. Bush passed the *Americans with Disabilities Act* in 1990. The weaker Human Rights Commission in Canada, while well-intentioned, does not give timely solutions to pressing problems.

Example

Now consider this unsuccessful thesis statement:

> Myths of creation reveal a great deal about the philosophy of a people.

Example

The chief difficulty with this statement is that it leaves the reader asking "So what?" And the thesis in this case could be the subject of an entire book. Better to say something like the following:

> Myths of creation, like the story of Prometheus's theft of fire, sometimes illustrate the dangerous consequences of humankind's attempts to create something that imitates the gods.

Example

This second example narrows down the topic from the outset, leaving the reader in no doubt about the ultimate direction of the paper.

What is the problem with this next example?

Example   Why does Canada need to provide more protection for some endangered species?

What makes this thesis statement inadequate is that it is not, in fact, a statement at all. Resist the temptation simply to ask a question at the beginning of your paper. Essays demand a clear statement of the results of your thinking and findings.

Finally, look at the following thesis statement:

Example   Technology is a threat to human life.

This thesis statement fails to get its point across because it is too general. First, the reader needs to know what kind of technology is so threatening. Is it airplanes or X-ray machines or computers? Next, it is too strongly stated to be entirely credible. Try this revision instead:

Example   Computer technology is dangerous to initiative because it encourages too much dependence on something external to the human mind: trust in computers is gradually replacing trust in common sense.

This thesis statement is doubtless still controversial, but at least now it identifies which technology and what kind of danger are meant.

One caveat: occasionally, you may write a paper whose purpose is to record the research process without settling the question with a specific thesis at the beginning. For this kind of paper, sometimes produced in an inquiry course or problem-based learning course, you need to keep the introduction open and not settle on a specific thesis statement. The object of the paper is different with this kind of essay: you are meant to explore the topic and ask your own questions about it, rather than to conclude anything definitively. Your instructor will inform you if you should be using this approach, rather than devising a standard thesis statement.

Now That You Have a Thesis Statement...

Use your thesis statement as the springboard for the outline. Keep it in mind as you develop your thought. With your thesis statement on paper, you are now ready to set the tone for the readers you have in mind.

How Much Time Should Preparing an Essay Take?

The answer is, of course, that it depends. For a typical student paper in college or university, you ought to spend about three weeks, at least if the essay is intended to include research materials. Your tentative schedule should allow about one week for library and Internet research, one week to write up your results in essay form, and one more week to let your essay get cold and to give you time to revise it adequately.

Approach your revision both in terms of small details, like checking notes and rewriting to ensure effective word choice, and in terms of larger elements, like the solidity of the argument and the reliability and completeness of your facts. You probably won't devote the entire three weeks to the paper, but that length of time should allow you the leisure to procrastinate a bit and the opportunity to double-check details. It will also give you a chance to recover if things go wrong.

Writing a Method Statement or a Route Map

An essential outgrowth of a thesis statement is a route map, which in many ways acts as a method statement. The thesis statement explains what you are going to show in your paper, and the route map shows how you are going to get there. It explains the paper's direction or methodology, and consequently acts as a preview of coming attractions meant to structure and delimit the reader's expectations of your treatment of the topic.

> The transition from print to film is one that many novels undergo, but few do so without significant modification. Timothy Findley's *The Wars* is no exception, but a study of its presentation in these different media is particularly interesting since Findley, the author of the novel, also wrote the screenplay for Robin Phillips's film. While much of the book is vividly realized on-screen, it has necessarily been compressed, and many aspects of the novel have not made the transition. That said, the novel itself is highly cinematic; as Margaret Atwood comments in *Second Words*, Findley "cuts the novel like a film, so that one taut scene follows another, with little filling or rumination" (293). The novel is nonetheless characterized by a narrative intricacy that has been sacrificed in the film. This comparison of the novel and the film will focus on some of the notable modifications to and omissions from the story in its on-screen presentation. First, this paper examines changes to the perspective from which events are viewed, and second, it examines changes in the use of natural elements as a structural and thematic device. Finally, the dramatic impact of these changes will be explored in detail.

Example

The last two sentences of this paragraph explain what methods the author will use to explore the differences between the film and the novel.

> Psychology involves the scientific study of all behaviour, for both animals and humans. The debate over the use of animals in psychological research has centred on charges of abuse in the laboratory. Such allegations have been made by animal rights activists who seek to abolish all laboratory research on animals. Although some animal activists work to improve conditions in the laboratory for animals, most activists would like to abolish any biomedical and behavioural research with laboratory animals. This paper will demonstrate how beneficial and important psychological research on animals is to society. Such research has not only led to tremendous improvements in the human condition, but also has been directly responsible for advances in veterinary procedures, improving breeding and conservation methods, and increasing our understanding of the nutritional, environmental, and social needs of many animal species. To eliminate all animal research would drastically impair

Example

progress, especially in the field of psychology. Research on animals is very important, and any discomfort or pain suffered by animals is severely minimized through
the interventions of ethics committees and regulations. It will be demonstrated that
the benefits of behavioural research with animals are substantial, and that the costs
and the benefits are scrutinized intensely before any research on animals is done.

Here the route map is in the last sentence of the paragraph, where readers are prom-
ised a recounting of benefits of animal research and assured that the process is regu-
lated and controlled beforehand. We thus come to expect the essay to have a two-part
structure that justifies and explains the use of animals in psychological research.

You may find that the route map is the most important structural component of
your essay. It gives readers something to base their expectations on. An essay, in
many ways, is like a contract, and a clearly delineated route map gives the reader a
clear understanding of what to expect from your investigation into a particular field
of study.

CHAPTER 1 EXERCISES

1. Draw a "concept map" for any one of the general topics listed in Exercise 2 below. Try
   to visualize different aspects of the topic before you commit yourself to focusing on one
   aspect for an essay topic.

2. Develop a focus for one or more of the following topics, using some of the techniques
   listed above. Use the Internet to do some preliminary research if a topic is unfamiliar.
   Each is meant to be the subject of a 1500-word essay in the discipline suggested.

   a. the treatment of the Muslim faith in the press (Globalization)
   b. positive psychology and its effect on treatment methods (Psychology)
   c. public health care and growing privatization (Health Sciences)
   d. news reporting and the Internet (Multimedia)
   e. part-time work and its effect on employment (Sociology)
   f. the homeless problem in large cities (Urban Geography)
   g. the graying of Canada (Geriatrics)
   h. Canada in the 21st century (History)
   i. smoking and public areas (Law)
   j. poverty among children (Economics)
   k. the *Youth Criminal Justice Act* in Canada and its implications (Sociology)
   l. gay marriage and the church (Religious Studies)
   m. Olympic scandals (Physical Education)
   n. international management styles (Business Administration)
   o. women's suffrage in Canada (History)
   p. racial differences in Shakespeare (English)
   q. access and accommodation of special education students (Education)
   r. artificial intelligence and its moral implications (Philosophy)
   s. Canada's peacekeeping role in the Middle East (Political Science)
   t. the effect of immigration on Canadian cities (Sociology)

3. Examine some of your past essays to see if the thesis statements you have written have narrowed the topic down sufficiently. Try rewriting them to give them more focus.

    Develop a thesis statement for each of the following topics:

    a. the shortage of health care and its effect on a graying population
    b. a critique of Leonard Cohen's *Book of Longing* as a self-portrait
    c. palliative care and the *Canada Health Act*
    d. HIV incidence in injection drug users
    e. learning styles and their application in the classroom
    f. attitudes toward reality TV
    g. styles of dressing among students
    h. the role of examinations in higher education
    i. corporations and accountability
    j. approaches to studying
    k. reconciling with an enemy
    l. your attitude toward your physical body
    m. the nature of happiness
    n. finding your vocation
    o. choosing a place to live

4. Evaluate these thesis statements. Make them more specific by inventing a route map for each.

    a. The fast food industry is a symptom of the health problems in this country, not a cause.
    b. Reading fiction is important for the development of human feelings.
    c. Steroid use in sports is acceptable in this age of medical technology.
    d. Part-time work interferes with higher education.
    e. There are pros and cons that must be considered when one decides whether to apply for a student loan.
    f. Shakespeare's romances explore the development of the self.
    g. Arts funding in Canada would benefit from more corporate sponsorship.

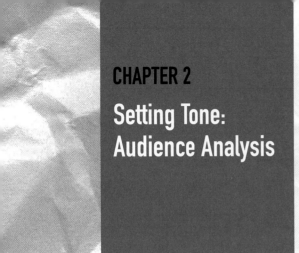

CHAPTER 2

Setting Tone: Audience Analysis

All the fun's in how you say a thing.
—ROBERT FROST

In this chapter:

- How to set the right tone, whether formal or informal
- How and when to use personal pronouns

Tone, whether your own or someone else's, is one of the most elusive features of a writing style. The tone of your essay writing, if it is to avoid clashing with the reader's expectations, should be neither too loud nor too soft. Harsh tones may antagonize your readers. Conversely, gentle tones may make your arguments seem too weak or too bland.

Tone in writing may be compared to tone of voice. It is the personality of an essay. What follows will show which tones to avoid and which to emulate. When you read your paper aloud to check for errors at the revision stage, you will listen for potential problems. But even before you write, it is important to think about the impact of your ideas on the readers.

The tone you choose must fit the purposes of your essay. If the assignment is a formal research paper, the tone must be appropriately formal as well. If, on the other hand, you are writing an informal, more personal paper, your tone may be correspondingly more casual. The expectations of your readers define the tone for you.

In large part, setting tone is a process of audience analysis. In order to communicate with your audience effectively, your writing must show that it takes the reader's reactions seriously. Some of the preparation you go through to write an essay necessarily involves anticipating how your audience is likely to react to your subject. When you have thought about the potential problems, you are ready to set the tone of your paper.

Tones to Avoid

Avoid Whispering

A tone that is too "soft" suggests that the writer is unsure of the words and the thoughts behind them. Words that are too tentative, too hesitant, are one sign of a whispering tone. Phrases like "it seems to be," "perhaps," or "it could be that" are indications of this problem. Another signal is the overuse of qualifying phrases such as "however" and "to some extent." Similarly, watch for wording such as "in my opinion," which weaken an argument unnecessarily. Although some qualifications are a good idea, too many may cause the reader to doubt your confidence in your own position. Watch too for words that may be added to bolster an otherwise weak argument, such as "obviously," "definitely," and "truly." Using words like these to build up an argument may indicate that the argument is logically weak to start with, and no amount of verbiage will save it.

✗ It seems that many stockbrokers may have been too willing to believe election promises when they advised their clients to buy income trusts. **Example**

Avoid Chatting

A chatty essay is most often the result of incomplete planning and outlining. If your paragraphs or your sentences seem to trail off or to lead to unexpected conclusions, if your ideas seem linked by random association, if your language seems too colloquial or offhand, and if you treat the reader as a friend rather than as an interested observer, you may be accused of chattiness. The cure for chattiness is care, revision, and a polite, though distanced, regard for the reader.

✗ What was the main cause of the War of 1812? Well, let's look at the question as carefully as we can to see if we can scout out an answer. **Example**

Avoid Emotiveness

An emotive tone is struck when a writer attempts to describe his or her feelings in a high-flown, exaggerated way. Often, what results sounds falsely sentimental or hackneyed. Such a tone is often found in introductions and conclusions, particularly when a writer tries to wax poetic about his or her opinions. Although opinions are warranted in an essay, it is not necessary to praise Shakespeare as a great playwright at the end of a paper analyzing the structure of *Macbeth,* or to tell the reader of an essay on nuclear disarmament that the issue is a matter of life and death for the human race. Show your feelings by supporting your opinions; don't just declare them.

✗ Michel Marc Bouchard is a brilliant Canadian playwright whose works, such as *The Coronation Voyage* and *Written on Water,* have been very successfully produced at the Shaw Festival and in other venues throughout Canada. **Example**

Avoid Declaiming

Treat your reader as an equal. Though you may well be playing the role of expert, your role is to reason with your reader and to assume his or her rationality. Any style that repeats points too often, goes on too long, or explains more than the reader needs is declaiming. This tactic, in combination with a pretentious vocabulary, is disastrous. When you revise, check to see that your writing is transparent, that it does not need to be deciphered to be understood. Avoid words that intimidate the reader because of their length or their obscurity. Choose instead the word that will most clearly express your meaning. Check also to see that the essay is within the required word limit.

In a formal essay, it is also wise to limit the use of rhetorical questions, or to avoid such declamatory devices altogether. Your job is to tell the reader something, not to ask questions.

Example ✗ Isn't it true that teachers like you go on strike without regard for the consequences for your students?

Avoid Shouting

Make sure that your essay does not inadvertently antagonize its readers. Even though it is your job to defend your viewpoint, you must not assume that your readers are opponents. This problem with tone is especially prevalent in essays that attempt to refute someone else's position. In these cases, the force should be in the logic of your argument, rather than in the tone of your writing.

Example ✗ Only an idiot would argue that capital punishment is a humane solution for the problem of life-threatening crimes.

Use Personal Pronouns with Discretion

Avoid directly addressing your reader in formal essays. "You" and "your" may alienate the readers if your assumptions about their knowledge or their attitudes are incorrect. It may even sound threatening or overbearing. If you can, keep the readers on your side; if you know they disagree, keep them at a formal distance.

Example ✗ You should have learned from this essay how losing weight will improve your overall health.

A research or formal expository essay also may demand that you avoid the use of "I" in writing. If you are forbidden the use of "I" by an instructor, respect that condition. Some disciplines encourage the use of "I" because it grants ownership of the material to the author; others discourage it because it introduces a personal bias. When you use "I," you effectively become a "character" with a role to play in your writing. Instructors will inform you if that is an appropriate stance for a particular assignment.

Do, however, try to avoid awkward impersonal constructions and self-conscious references. Never refer to yourself as "the writer" or "the author."

On the other hand, if "I" is acceptable, *use* it. Your relationship to your reader in a formal essay is meant to be a professional one, but that does not mean that personality has no place, simply that you must know its place and respect the polite distance imposed between you and the reader.

Example ✗ It is the opinion of this writer that . . . (too stuffy)
✗ In my opinion . . . (too weakly subjective)

✓ This paper contends that . . .
✓ I will show that . . .

Tones to Emulate

Modulate Your Writing Style

A modulated voice is controlled. Despite the moods of the writer, it shows restraint, politeness, and judgment. Your tones in private conversation may be more varied; in the essay, however (except in the freer personal essay), your tone should be cool, professional, unruffled, and firm. This is not to say that you should be detached from your topic. An essay, even a fairly objective research essay, takes a stand, advocates strenuously for something, and carries with it a message of personal conviction.

Imitate the Best

Read newspaper editorials and newsmagazines, as well as your fellow students' essays. Textbooks and critical material may also serve as examples, though you must choose with discretion. And listen: the tone of classroom lectures is often a good indication of what is expected in a paper.

Construct Your Audience Carefully

To some extent, you need to construct a vision of the audience you intend your paper to reach and the reaction you expect that audience to have. Admittedly, the primary audience of an assignment is the professor, but an excellent paper does not just take aim at the revealed preferences of the professor, so you should try not to think of him or her as the sole reader. That will mean that you are writing to multiple readers and that you are seeking a wide audience, perhaps in print or online, that may comment or respond to your research. Research essays, from a professional perspective, are aimed at like-minded members of your field. The research materials advance thinking in the field and are meant to be built on, not just to display your knowledge or to get a grade. A good researcher tries to construct a profile of his or her likely audience: are the readers your age group, are they predominantly male or female, are they likely to be accepting of or hostile toward the ideas that you are supporting? Knowing whom you are talking to will help you formulate how you will proceed. Writer and reader negotiate their relationship, and you need to think about the terms of the relationship as you begin to write.

Keep Your Purpose Firmly in Mind

All written documents have a purpose. You need to make sure that the tone works effectively to help you achieve that purpose. Consistency is important. In a formal document, such as a cover letter for a job application, your writing needs to be formal and professional (as well as clear, accurate, and polite) in order to introduce yourself and convince the hiring committee to grant you an interview. Be wary of any discordant note—a slang word, an exaggerated claim, an insincere attitude, or anything that might jar the reader who is considering your suitability. The written document is often your representative; it needs to speak cogently for you.

CHAPTER 2 EXERCISES

1. Find an essay in a learned journal and analyze its tone. Find an essay on a related subject and do the same with an article in a popular magazine or a newspaper. Describe the tone of both pieces. How do the works differ in terms of audience and purpose? Compare them in terms of vocabulary, use of personal pronouns, use of specialized language, complexity of sentence structure, and assumptions about the reader's familiarity with and interest in the subject under discussion. How is the tone, whether formal or informal, created in each case?

2. Write four paragraphs, each with roughly the same story written for different ears. The story is how you returned home late after a party. Write the first paragraph to your best friend, in whom you confide everything. The second is to your brother, who does not like the people who gave the party. The third is to your mother, who has always discouraged you from going out on weeknights, and the fourth is to your roommate, who was awakened when you returned in the middle of the night.

3. On the Internet, find an interview with a well-known writer or a public figure whose written work you know or are currently studying. Compare and contrast the tone of the interview with your impressions of the written work. How does the tone of the interview differ from the written work? How is it similar? A good source for information and interviews with Canadian writers is located at Athabasca University <http://www.athabascau.ca/writers/>.

4. Explain to a friend, as persuasively as you can, why you should get a particular grade in the course you are taking. Next write a paragraph explaining why you should get that grade to your instructor. Note the differences in tone.

5. Write a cover letter for a job in the field you would like to work in after graduation. Use a specific advertisement from a newspaper or an Internet source, and highlight the skills in your résumé that fit the demands of the position. Trade your letter with another student. Each of you should analyze whether the letters address all the relevant demands of the job and justify your résumés. Would your letters persuade that particular audience to hire each of you? Why or why not? What improvements could be made?

Choosing Words: Avoiding Jargon, Slang, and Stereotypes

> Words are all that we have.
> —SAMUEL BECKETT

In this chapter:

- How and why to avoid slang
- How and why to avoid jargon
- How and why to avoid biased language
- How to use a dictionary and a thesaurus

Word choice is perhaps the most accurate index of the status of a writer. The words you choose depend in part on the role you mean to play in relation to the reader.

Word choice is not only important to tone, but it is also crucial to clarity. The words you use should be weighed carefully; you need to be fully conscious of all the nuances of meaning that they may conjure. We often use words in a number of quite different ways; if we substitute one for another too blithely, we may find ourselves rather embarrassed. Take, for example, the simple adjective "dirty." If you were to look it up in a thesaurus, you would find a list of words, including, perhaps, "soiled," "unclean," "polluted," "filthy," "foul," "lewd," and "obscene." In this example, it is obviously not adequate to substitute "lewd" for "dirty" in the context of someone's dirty hands. Similarly, a word like "dissipated" means "scattered" when it refers to clouds. If, however, you describe a person's behaviour as "dissipated," you are suggesting that he or she is drunk and disorderly. Exact meaning is absolutely demanded if word choice is to be clear.

An added complication these days arises from a journalistic tendency to use a great deal of jargon, often around new technology. Acronyms, abbreviations created by using the initial letters of a number of words, may also be a culprit. Hence, readers may find themselves bombarded with CPUs, PCs, IBMs, and BBSs, not to mention a host of neologisms that may be unfamiliar.

Good writing demands more than clarity, however. It demands attention to the delicate relationship it has with a reader. It must strive not to say more than it intends, or to create unpleasant, unsuitable, or ludicrous associations in the reader's mind. When you choose your words, stay aware not only of their denotations, but also of their connotations. It is now, for example, important to use language that is deliberately inclusive. While standard grammar once sanctioned the use of "his" or of generic words like "men" to mean "human beings," contemporary readers are more likely to take issue with such an exclusive approach to the sexes. This is another area that demands close attention if you are to form a good relationship with your reader.

Diction: Fit, Form, and Function

Choose language that satisfies the criteria of fit, form, and function for the assignment in question. What follows are some pointers on how to choose (and how to revise) the language of your essays.

Be Consistently Formal or Informal

Choosing formal or informal language is rather like observing a dress code. Paying attention to the conventions of a dress code does not mean that you must wear a uniform inhibiting all expression of personality. It means, simply, that you must conform to certain standards—happily, in this case, quite flexible standards. Word choice depends to a large extent on context, just as choice of clothing is dependent on the occasion.

Keep these guidelines in mind:

1. Fit—Does your writing suit its purpose and audience?
2. Form—Does it conform to convention?
3. Function—Does your writing make your message clear?

If the idea of conforming for the sake of conforming disturbs you, remember what the consequences of not conforming may be: perhaps being misunderstood, ignored, or considered offensive. To avoid any of these perils in your use of language, and in your word choice particularly, keep these hints in mind.

Write to Communicate—Not to Impress or Provoke

When you write an essay, you should address your reader as an equal; the information you impart and the viewpoint you defend are offered as reasonable choices for readers as clear-thinking as you are. Treating your reader as an equal means that you will neither seek to impress nor browbeat, and that you will choose subject matter and language accordingly. Don't worry that your professor is an expert in the field; the research essay assignment is meant as a training ground. The essential thing is that you show your ability to use the language of the discipline and that you make a clear point about your findings. Focus on being clear and you will avoid any embarrassment.

To make a point clearly for a reader, you need to show what you know and express a willingness to share it. If your words do not allow you to share your results because they are too technical or too vague or carelessly chosen, you will have alienated your readers. Remember that, in the formal essay, the emphasis is less upon you and the reader personally than it is upon the subject at hand; your relationship is entirely professional. But in the informal essay, your personality and that of your reader play more pronounced roles: you expect that the reader will enjoy your company.

Make Yourself Comfortable in the Language of Your Subject

Determining your status, and thus the proper diction for an essay, is sometimes a great challenge. After all, you may not feel much like the equal of the professor giving a course in which you feel shaky or ill prepared. Obviously, the more conversant you become with the terminology of a discipline, the easier it will be to feel like an equal and to write a stimulating, learned discussion.

Just as important, however, is the confidence with which you can play the role of an equal. Think of your paper not as just another assignment written by a student to an instructor, but as an opportunity to speak the language of the discipline to someone who understands it.

Choose Your Words Stylishly

The "rules" that govern diction cannot be listed here, simply because word choice depends upon context. A formal essay demands formal language, just as a formal occasion demands evening dress. Likewise, informal writing allows you more freedom in self-expression and a more casual approach.

Avoid Overdressed Language

1. DO NOT USE TOO MANY TECHNICAL OR SPECIALIZED TERMS OR ACRONYMS.

Too many terms may actually prevent your reader from seeing your underlying meaning. Technical subjects clearly demand some technical terminology, but while it is partly your task to demonstrate your ability to use terms with skill and ease, you must not use them to confuse your reader or to avoid the issues. Acronyms like HTML (for "hypertext mark-up language") may be meaningful to you, but if you intend to use such shortened forms throughout your essay, you should identify them at the outset in order to avoid confusion. The best form is to use the term in its entirety first:

> Computer disks that are readable and writable (CD-RWs) are available to consumers   **Example**
> who wish to make high-quality recordings in their own homes.

2. AVOID NEOLOGISMS USED OUT OF CONTEXT.

Words, like everything else, have a history. A word like "lifestyle," of modern derivation, is inappropriate when used to describe the feudal way of life, for example.

3. AVOID THE CURRENT TENDENCY TO MAKE VERBS OUT OF NOUNS.

"Impact" until recently was accepted as a noun and not a verb; now, its usage as a verb is standard. Note that trends in language should be examined carefully especially before they become part of your own academic language. A similar problem occurs with words ending in "ize" and "ization." Many are now acceptable, but some are questionable recent coinages, often unnecessary and vague. "Prioritize," for example, should be replaced with "establish priorities."

4. AVOID PRETENTIOUS WORDS AND CONSTRUCTIONS.

Often these pretentious constructions appear as groups of nouns, attached in such a way that the reader cannot visualize the object described. The tendency to use such abstract and depersonalized language comes partly from our desire to appear sophisticated, but the effect is rather like wearing designer labels on the outside of our clothes. Such a high-sounding style may intimidate or amuse, but it does not really communicate.

Example   ✗ In your new position, you will need to interface with the marketing department.

Replace "interface" with "meet with" to ensure clarity.

Example   ✗ Because our organization is not unmindful of client needs, we are endeavouring to develop a host of new product lines.

Replace "not unmindful" with "aware" and make the sentence more direct by avoiding needless words and lengthy verbs.

Example   Because we are aware of our clients' needs, we are developing new product lines.

Example   ✗ We can use a plethora of strategies to diagnose the illness.

The word "plethora" is unnecessarily complex. Replace it with "many."

5. AVOID "FLASHY" WORDS.
Sometimes a student will fervently consult a thesaurus, seeking some clever ways of varying vocabulary. Although this is a commendable practice, never forget that no two words mean exactly the same thing or have precisely the same impact. When you find a synonym, check it in the dictionary to make sure that it means what you think it does. Make sure your words know their place.

A longer word is not necessarily a stronger word. A word selected simply "for show" may be as out of place as a diamond tiara worn with a soccer uniform. Context is the first consideration in these matters. Don't use a word just because it sounds elevated.

Example   ✗ At any time of year, upon entering this voluminous structure, one cannot help but notice the low roar of conversation as the voices of the museum's patrons reverberate from one concrete wall to the other.

How can a museum be "voluminous"? A glance at a dictionary will show that the word means "extensive" or "copious" and is most often used to refer to language. Although the writer may mean that the structure was large, the connotation is not correct. Replace this word with something more suitable—like "huge" or "imposing."

Avoid Sloppy Language

1. CONSULT A DICTIONARY TO FIND THE PROPER USAGE OF A WORD.
When you look up a word in the dictionary, you will find information vital to its usage. Usually, one of the first things you will see in a listing is an abbreviation that denotes what part of speech the word is. For example, if you look up the word

"impact," you will find it listed as a noun. If you are in doubt about what any of the abbreviations used in your dictionary mean, check them in the list of abbreviations, usually provided at the beginning of the dictionary. Also pay special attention to samples of idiomatic usage that may be given; such samples may offer you more help in how to use a word more accurately than an abstract knowledge of its meaning alone. Dictionaries give current information about how to use a word in standard English; they are reliable sources in determining whether a word's usage is archaic, dialect, colloquial, or slang.

2. AVOID SLANG.

There are, admittedly, times when slang fits the mood. You may, for instance, wish to draw attention to the common language for a particular term, or report some dialogue. Beware of enclosing slang in quotation marks ("swell"); it may seem forced and unnatural. Unless you are sure that slang will add colour and character to your writing, avoid it. Careless slang is sloppy and perhaps more revealing than you wish.

Try to be conscious of your use of slang. It is easy to pick up words and phrases that seem to be in vogue and to use them unthinkingly. A word or phrase that comes too easily will not help you do any original thinking; the reader may just glide over the usage without reflection as well. Worse still, the reader may not know the particular usage you have in mind.

> ✗ I avoid reading psychology books because I think the subject is flaky.   **Example**
> ✓ I avoid reading psychology books because I do not respect the subject.
> ✗ The idea of euthanasia weirds him out.
> ✓ The idea of euthanasia repels him.
> ✗ I was really clueless on that last exam.
> ✓ I did not know the material on that last exam.

3. AVOID COLLOQUIAL CONSTRUCTIONS.

Colloquial constructions may include slang, but they also include language that is chatty, takes too much for granted, or is not completely clear. A carefully selected colloquial word or phrase may add unexpected life to a formal paper, but the overuse of language generally confined to speech may lead the reader to dismiss the value and importance of what you are saying.

Because you have no chance to reinforce your words with body language (a raised eyebrow, a smile, a frown), your reader will need the most precise, specific language you can possibly find. You need all the power and clarity of the words at your command.

> ✗ Voters were initially enthused with Jean Chrétien's plans to increase employment   **Example**
>   among Canadians.

Replace "enthused with" with "enthusiastic about."

4. AVOID SAYING THE OBVIOUS, ESPECIALLY IN A HACKNEYED WAY.

What you have to say may not be entirely new, but your approach to the subject should be fresh, and your way of expressing yourself should give the reader a new angle of perception.

Avoid language deadened by overuse, whether it be jargon or cliché. Use language that enlightens, that sparks thought, that provokes discussion, that wakes up your reader. Saying the same old thing in the same old way may be the easy way out, but it will not have the same impact that a thoughtful or inventive use of words may have.

The cliché does, however, have its place. For instance, in the paragraph above, the phrase "the easy way out" is a cliché. In the midst of some fairly abstract prose, its presence can startle just because it is a different kind of language than what precedes it. Use clichés sparingly, and don't use them thoughtlessly; otherwise, they may have all the impact of a joke too often repeated.

Example   ✗ Those who are employed in the service industry often feel they are working for peanuts.

Replace "working for peanuts" with fresher, more thoughtful phrasing, perhaps "not paid enough to eat properly."

5. BE ESPECIALLY CAREFUL TO AVOID BIAS IN YOUR LANGUAGE.

Unintended bias occurs when people are not scrupulously careful about their language. To avoid bias, you should be sure to use inclusive language. For example, in a letter you should use the salutation "Dear Sir or Madam" rather than "Dear Sir" if you are unsure of the recipient's identity, thus avoiding accusations of sexism. You should be cautious about assuming things; make sure that you respect the terms that individuals or groups use to identify themselves rather than assigning labels to them. This tactic usually ensures that you will be using a specific term rather than a generalized or even a stereotypical one. For instance, the word "Korean" is more specific than "Asian" and may be more accurate. Be wary of "pseudogeneric" words such as "mankind" or "chairman" that seem to be inclusive but are not. "Humankind" and "chair" are preferred in these cases. Make sure that the language you choose treats everyone equally. An expression like "the man and his wife" does not accord equal treatment; substitute either "the man and the woman" or "the husband and wife." Why, after all, should one of the individuals be identified only in relation to the other? Finally, it is always a good idea to use a term that puts people first. Do not say "the disabled," but "people with disabilities," or, if the characteristic is irrelevant, don't mention it at all.

6. AVOID CONTRACTIONS IN FORMAL ESSAYS.

Contractions such as "don't," "can't," or "shouldn't" are not generally acceptable in formal writing. While they are acceptable in spoken language and in the reporting of dialogue, make a special effort not to use them when you are writing an essay meant for the classroom.

7. AVOID THE EASY CHOICE.

Describing someone as "nice" may not do that person's character justice. Describing a room as "dirty" is similarly not usefully descriptive. Use your words to create a visual image for your reader. "Generous" is more specific than "nice" and may be a more accurate word for what you mean. "Dirty" does not tell the reader much: replace it with "filthy," and the reader gets the picture.

8. AVOID TRENDY ABBREVIATIONS IN FORMAL LANGUAGE.

Abbreviations used in text messages work well in informal situations, but they are distracting as well as confusing in a formal context. Text messages work well among friends who know each other and are also familiar with the language of text messaging but are not appropriate for formal writing even in an online discussion, where grades are sometimes given for style as well as content. Clarity is the key to word choice, and it is assuming too much to use abbreviations that leave readers wondering about your meaning.

What Works?

Diction is the most nebulous area of the English language and the hardest about which to give specific advice for improvement. But some things will certainly help. First, aim to increase your vocabulary by making a note of words that you come across in your reading. If these words are specific to a discipline, all the more reason to note them and make an effort to use them in your writing. Many introductory courses at the college and university level exist in large part to help familiarize students with a particular academic vocabulary. Those words are the tools of the trade. Next, focus on ferreting out meaning by examining context and etymology of the words you find. Language makes the most sense in context, so notice where and how a word is used. Similarly, try to work out the meaning of a word by unpacking its etymology. Dictionaries provide information not only about the exact meaning or denotation of a word, but also about its origins, and its uses in various contexts. Now that dictionaries are online as well as paper, they are easier than ever to access!

Look at this example, taken from a job letter:

✗ I would do an excellent job as the program coordinator in charge of marketing because I am very communicable.   **Example**

Obviously what the student meant was this:

✓ I would do an excellent job as the program coordinator in charge of marketing because I am very communicative.   **Example**

To make sure you use the word that has the best fit for the occasion, ask your friends to read your materials before you submit them. That way, you can avoid embarrassing mistakes. When it comes to word choice (and indeed many aspects of writing), everyone needs an editor.

CHAPTER 3 EXERCISES

1. Make a point of learning new vocabulary. Read widely and take notes as you go along. Try to establish the newness of new words by context. Look up new words that you find in your reading, say them aloud a few times, add them to a list of new words, and make a point to use them in your conversation and in your writing. Treat the learning of new words like a game. And remember that crossword puzzles and games like Scrabble can help increase your vocabulary.

2. Examine a "cluster" of euphemisms. Start by looking up the word "euphemism" in the dictionary if the term is not familiar to you. Proceed with a word that describes something unpleasant like "death" or "failure" or a less than attractive adjective like "aged" or "unintelligent" and make a list of euphemisms to express the concept.

3. Make a list of common expressions we use to describe drinking too much. The list might include such phrases as "getting loaded." Try to analyze the origins and the functions of these expressions. Do the same thing with words and expressions used to describe sleeping.

4. List slang expressions that are dated, such as "groovy" or "the cat's pyjamas." Can you list some contemporary expressions that are similar?

5. Look for clichés or stock phrases in newspapers or magazines. Many words seem automatically and unthinkingly to go together, such as "illegal alien." Make a list of phrases you find and explain why they are ineffective.

6. Read over essays you have written, and note any slang you find. Though slang can be colourful, its context is significant. Rephrase the sentences, substituting fresh language.

7. A. Identify problems in the following sentences and suggest alternative wording. (Turn to p. 278 to check your answers.)
    1. Diana Krall and Avril Lavigne are well-known Canadian songbirds.
    2. The perpetrator of the crime was an illegal alien.
    3. A victim of polio, Lou used a scooter.
    4. The handicapped need your help.
    5. The girl who works on the switchboard must be well-spoken.
    6. Call the firemen if you smell smoke.
    7. Margaret Atwood is a celebrated Canadian poetess.
    8. Man cannot live by bread alone.
    9. Whenever he went to the variety store, he felt that he was gypped.
   10. Lin Song was an Oriental student.

   B. Identify problems in the following sentences and suggest alternative wording.
    1. Indians often choose to live on the reservation.
    2. A victim of West Nile virus, Bette is paralyzed and confined to a wheelchair.
    3. There were many men in the office, along with the girls at the reception desk.
    4. The aged and the infirm use this transportation system.
    5. A man and his wife came in this morning to rent an apartment.
    6. AIDS victims take special medications.
    7. The disabled can apply for supplemental income.
    8. Dodi was committed to a school for wayward teens.
    9. Men accompanied the ladies to the celebration.
   10. May I speak to the master of the house?

Part Two

DESIGNING THE ESSAY

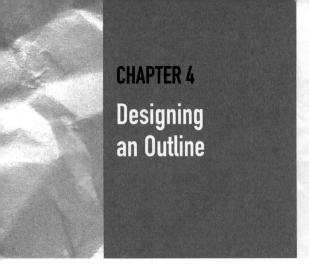

CHAPTER 4

Designing an Outline

The discipline of the writer is to learn to be still and listen to what the subject has to tell him.
—RACHEL CARSON

In this chapter:

- How to sort through your notes
- How to connect your points
- How to create a unified structure for your essay

Once you have decided upon your topic, determined your thesis statement, and considered your audience and purpose, you need an outline. It is important that you write things down as you go along, even if what you write is not neat or organized. As you sit down to try to establish an outline, you will have notes gathered from thinking about the subject, from tentative research, and from class discussion. Some of these ideas may fit into your essay outline; others may be sacrificed as merely stages in your early thinking about the subject.

Never attempt to write an essay without some kind of outline—whether it be a formal, detailed itinerary or a hastily jotted map showing your destination, your direction, and the stops you wish to make along the way.

When preparing an outline, remember that it is only a sketch of your paper. The final design of the essay may be quite different from what you originally intended. A sketch does not nccd to bc pcrfcct. Thc outline is meant to help you write the paper, not to restrict your line of thought. Keep the outline flexible so that you can tinker with it as you go along. It is simply a tentative blueprint, a description of the contents of your paper, rather than a prescription of its requirements.

Make a Table of Contents

Think of the outline as your own flexible table of contents. It is, after all, your note to yourself, your reminder of what details you wish to include, and what points you want to make. Like a table of contents, the outline labels what the reader may expect to find contained in the work itself.

Take a look at the table of contents of this book to see what information you can glean from it. Not only does it tell you what is included in the book, but it also tells you what the major and minor divisions of the work are. For instance, you will find the chapter entitled "Devising a Thesis" under the part heading "Developing the Essay."

In other words, the table of contents gives the reader a sense of the book's dimensions. You see, for example, that the book you are holding in your hand has seven major parts, each of which is divided into a number of chapters. Thus, it gives you a sense not only of the work's overall shape, but also of the size of each component, and, at the same time, of the orderly arrangement of its position within the work. What follows is not a set of rules for composing outlines, but a series of suggestions about what they may contain.

To make your outline as useful and as organized as a table of contents, keep the following steps in mind:

Sort Through Your Ideas

1. THINK ABOUT THE LOGIC OF YOUR SUBJECT MATTER.

You may find the best way to proceed is to use descriptive or explanatory language, to describe or explain why something is the case in your paper. Your outline may show why human rights education should be part of the school curriculum, for example. Or, you may use sequential logic; that is, you may show the readers how something works by taking them through a process. You may show readers how to compare two learning theories; for example, Skinner's behaviourism and Maslow's hierarchy of needs. Alternatively, you might use your outline as a springboard to a discussion that moves chronologically. With this kind of outline, you could explore developments in multimedia and their impact on information technology. You might also organize an essay according to an evolutionary development that explores change. This kind of essay might discuss the shift in thinking from the traditional novel, written by authors such as Kipling or Galsworthy, and the stream of consciousness novel written by authors such as Woolf or Joyce. An outline might also be explicitly deductive (moving from general to specific), such as an argument that posits that the economy is headed for a crash, and citing details that demonstrate its decline. More commonly, an essay outline might be explicitly inductive in its direction, arguing that the characteristics of a play mark it as a romance rather than as a comedy.

2. MAKE SURE YOU HAVE ESTABLISHED YOUR PIVOTAL POINTS: THE THESIS STATEMENT AND PURPOSE.

Use your thesis statement (subject to revision) and your selected purpose as the launching points for your outline. All the ideas, arguments, facts, and figures you have gathered will emanate from these points. Many of the essays you write will be argumentative; that is, they will make a claim, usually somewhat controversial, and provide evidence to convince the reader that this position is reasonable. Argumentative essays of this type defend a position. Other essays that you write may have a simpler purpose: they may just intend to explain a point or teach the reader something valuable without defending a particular position. Both kinds of essay, the expository and the argumentative or persuasive, will have a thesis statement, that is, a pivotal point that the essay makes. Here are some examples of typical thesis statements for each type of essay:

Expository Essay

Making a soufflé is simple if you understand some basic culinary chemistry.

Rheumatoid arthritis is manageable with medications, self-care, and an understanding of the condition.

This paper will show what a wiki is and how it might be used to great benefit by students.

Argumentative Essay

Royal weddings should not be televised as public events since they encroach on privacy and celebrate an outmoded tradition.

Genetically modified food needs to be explicitly labelled to protect the public.

Online education is inferior to classroom teaching.

3. GATHER YOUR NOTES.

With your tentative thesis statement on paper in front of you, gather your tentative remarks, your research, and your questions about the topic. One good way to take notes is to list separate ideas on index cards (remembering to include sources, if any). This way, you can shuffle or discard material easily.

Keeping your purpose in mind, organize the material you have selected, discarding any information not strictly related to it. If you are discussing kinds of stage props, for instance, don't include material on their development in the history of the theatre.

4. CLASSIFY YOUR MATERIAL.

Decide how many steps your exposition or argument contains. Then classify your notes accordingly. If, for example, you mean to consider three reasons that border relations have deteriorated between Americans and Canadians, decide in which of the three discussions to include a statistic about people detained at the border.

5. ORDER YOUR MATERIAL IN A LOGICAL WAY.

This process demands that you decide exactly when you mention a particular point you want to make. Here you must decide what your opening point, your follow-up, and your last word should be. Keep in mind the tried-and-true notion that a strong point is best placed at the beginning or end of an essay. Keep in mind, too, that some of your organizational decisions depend on the pattern of development you selected at the outset. If you know, for instance, that your reader will need to understand your definition of national security to get the most out of your essay, put it where it will be most accessible. Or, if you are explaining a process, make sure the reader is able to follow it step by step.

6. RANK YOUR POINTS ACCORDING TO THEIR IMPORTANCE.

Sorting your ideas according to rank means deciding whether an item has a major role or a minor role to play. The ranking itself will give you an excellent idea of what you have to say and of how developed your thought is. Where you have much to add or to explain, the idea is vital and may serve as a significant part of your evidence; where your idea is almost all you have to say on the subject, you may relegate the point to a minor status. Focus on the areas of your outline that support your point and for which you can build adequate support.

Rank your ideas by assigning them numbers or letters, beginning perhaps with capital Roman numerals for major sections, moving to capital letters for important supporting sections, through to Arabic numbers for less important support material, and to lowercase letters for the minor details. The points you are making are primary in rank; the support you gather for them is secondary.

Border relations between Canada and the United States have deteriorated because of differences in immigration policy and in attitudes towards security and armed conflict.   **Example**

A. Americans became extremely cautious after the terrorist attacks of September 11, 2001. (REASON #1)

   1. The United States felt that Canada was too lenient in its immigration policies.
      a. People were allowed to enter Canada from a number of destinations from which the United States would not accept immigrants.
      b. Canadian policies toward refugees and toward deportation are notably less strict than American ones.

   2. The United States felt that Canada was too lenient in its policing of the world's longest undefended border and demanded that Canadians produce passports for visits to the U.S.
      a. Americans felt that in Canada people were simply "waved through" without investigation, even after September 11.
      b. Airports in Canada tended to be loose on security measures, according to American standards after September 11.

B. Canada believed that America was blaming it and other countries for the events of September 11, without sufficient evidence to back up its claims. (REASON #2)

   1. Canadians did not approve of the war against Iraq, launched by America partly as a response to perceived terrorist threat.
      a. The Canadian government did not support the war in Iraq under the Chrétien government, and Harper's support of it subsequently has met with controversy and considerable dissension.
      b. Surveys show that the Canadian people largely do not support the war either, despite our official involvement.

The form of notation does not matter particularly, but it should permit you to see at a glance the relative scope of the point you are making. A carefully ranked outline will show you the ideas within ideas.

7. INVENT A TITLE.

Although you still have not arrived at a finished product, the point you make in your essay should be clear enough to you that a title should pose no problem. Just bear in mind that a title should give the reader specific information about the subject you are writing about. Don't entitle your paper "Alice Munro"; instead, call it "Alice Munro's *View from Castle Rock* as a Study in Memoir." Do not underline your title; reserve underlining for the titles of published works. A title should be catchy and not too lengthy, but don't sacrifice clarity for flourish. To be clear, a title should not be a complete sentence, though it should repeat and reinforce keywords used in the thesis statement. To make your exact direction doubly clear, you should consider using a "subtitle" after a colon. For example, you might say "Alice Munro's *View from Castle* Rock as a Study in Memoir: How the Personal Becomes Fictional."

Tailor the Outline

As you outline, you may well notice some rags and tatters among your papers, bits of research material that seemed valuable at the time you took the notes, though they now seem unrelated to the development of your thought. If you cannot use these scraps in the final fabric of your paper, do not hesitate to toss them out. Remember that one of the main functions of the outline is to show you how well the material you have gathered actually fits the viewpoint you have chosen. Each point of the outline ought to represent an area that you can fill with developed thoughts, facts, and evidence. If you find that all you have to say on a particular point can be fleshed out in one sentence, then you must find a way to incorporate that small point into another place in your outline, or perhaps you may have to eliminate it altogether. What isn't useful or appropriate for your thesis statement should be left behind.

The outline below shows a short essay developed by examples, definition, classification, and even comparison/contrast. Basically, the essay consists of three or more points that demonstrate the thesis, plus supporting evidence. These patterns of development will be discussed in the next chapter.

Note that each section has a small thesis statement (or topic sentence) of its own. These are best written as sentences in the outline to ensure clarity. Note also that the subdivisions allow you to see at a glance what items have the most support (and conversely, what might be in need of greater support or development).

The example below provides one of the commonest structures for the essay—the funnel. In this structure, the essay develops from a general point that is narrowed down in the thesis statement. Not every essay, however, will move from the general to the specific. Some may follow a pattern dictated by the internal structure of the particular evidence that you uncover in your research. Also, while this essay uses a familiar three-part structure, an essay is easily expanded or contracted depending on the breadth and depth of information you include.

Outline for an Expository Essay   **Example**
  TOPIC: Headaches

  PATTERN OF DEVELOPMENT: Classification

  I. INTRODUCTION: Everyone suffers a headache at one time or another, though the pain can vary in degree. Some headaches respond to acetaminophen; other headaches are excruciating, perhaps chronic or debilitating.

  THESIS STATEMENT: There are suitable treatments available for headaches, provided one can diagnose them properly.

  PREVIEW: There are four types of headache: the tension headache, the cluster headache, the sinus headache, and the migraine.

  II. BODY
    A. A tension headache
      a. Cause: muscle contraction
      b. Symptoms: dull, steady ache; tightness around the scalp or neck
      c. Triggers: stress, anxiety, repressed emotion
      d. Treatment: acetaminophen

    B. A cluster headache
      a. Cause: unknown
      b. Symptoms: burning, piercing pain, often behind one eye; occurs periodically for days, weeks, or months; less than an hour in duration
      c. Triggers: smoking, alcohol consumption, histamines, or nitroglycerine
      d. Treatment: medication, such as ergotamines, inhaled or held under the tongue

    C. A sinus headache
      a. Cause: any disturbances blocking the passage of fluid from the sinuses
      b. Symptoms: gnawing pain, rise in temperature
      c. Triggers: same as cause
      d. Treatment: nasal decongestants and antibiotics

    D. A migraine
      a. Cause: not known
      b. Symptoms: nausea, dizziness, cold hands, tremor, sensitivity to light and sound; sometimes a day or longer in duration
      c. Triggers: irregular eating and sleeping; ingestion of cheese, chocolate, red wine, or caffeine
      d. Treatment: no cure, but some medications prevent or abort headaches; lifestyle changes are recommended

  III. CONCLUSION: Relief from headaches is possible for most people if they learn to seek the safest and most effective treatment available.

Example Outline for a Persuasive Essay

TOPIC: Computer Games

I. INTRODUCTION: If you believe the media, computer games are a threat to produc-tivity and a dangerous contributor to physical inactivity. If we believe the newspapers, we can only conclude that playing computer games will lead inevitably to weight gain, lack of productivity, and addiction. Despite these accusations, there are some ben-efits to computer games.

THESIS STATEMENT: Computer games are not necessarily bad for us, though admit-tedly some may be better than others.

PREVIEW: Computer games have benefits: they sharpen our thinking, they pro-vide relaxation, they can be an outlet for negative emotions, and they, incidentally, improve our computer skills.

II. BODY
   A. Cognitive development
      a. method of learning new skills
      b. improvement in reflexes
      c. improvement in problem solving
   B. Relaxation
      a. opportunity to play alone or with others
      b. pleasure of winning
      c. opportunity to escape everyday problems temporarily
   C. Emotional outlet
      a. harmless outlet for aggression
      b. broad range of virtual experiences
   D. Improvement in computer skills
      a. knowledge of computer functions
      b. speed and coordination

III. CONCLUSION: Computer games, though associated with many harmful effects, are not all bad and can help players learn, relax, express themselves, and develop skills at the computer.

CHAPTER 4 EXERCISES

1. For Exercise 2 below, spend fifteen minutes brainstorming one of the topics to develop possible sub-topics to be used in your outlines.

2. Develop outlines, complete with thesis statements, for any of the following topics:
   a. genetically modified food
   b. building muscles
   c. the Internet and privacy
   d. the school registration process
   e. your favourite local gathering place
   f. the importance of nutrition
   g. the cost of higher education
   h. self-employment vs. the corporate position

    i. the environmentally conscious consumer
    j. isolation and the Internet
    k. Canada's immigration policies

3. Read a classmate's essay and sketch an outline of its structure. Is each section clearly delineated? Is adequate support given for each point that your classmate raises? Is the movement of the paper logical and easy to follow? What advice would you give on how to make the essay's structure clearer?

4. Read an article related to your field of study. Make an outline of it, complete with thesis statement, arguments, and support.

CHAPTER 5
Shaping the Essay

The wastepaper basket is the writer's best friend.
—ISAAC BASHEVIS SINGER

In this chapter:

- How to start writing your first draft
- How to sift through your evidence
- How to structure your paper to fit reader expectations

As you develop your outline from its bare structure to its fully dressed form, remember that the shape of the essay is in your hands. Though there are guidelines you can follow, the essay is not a form to be filled in. You create the form itself, by selecting what is included and what is left out. That said, there are conventions, based on the expectations of readers about what an essay should provide.

The Conventional Shape of the Essay

In order to control your material, you must strive to achieve unity within your essay. An essay's unity is the wholeness of the vision, the focus that holds the disparate parts together. Without such wholeness, your essay will seem incomplete or rambling.

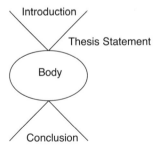

To do justice to your assembled arguments and support, the shape of your essay should meet certain of its readers' expectations. To make a good first impression on the reader, your essay should include these basic elements, as the diagram shows:

1. an *introduction*, moving from general topic to specific thesis, perhaps including a preview of its content (the introduction starts broadly but ends narrowly as it culminates in the thesis statement)
2. a *body*, developing in turn each of the main points used to support your thesis statement
3. a *conclusion*, reinforcing and/or summarizing what has been the focus of the essay and suggesting further implications (the conclusion opens out broadly to suggest how the research may have an impact on future studies or fit into the wider subject area)

Observing these conventional forms will ensure that your essay is clear, pointed, and emphatic from beginning to end.

A good essay possesses a sharp, comprehensive introduction and conclusion, with an expansive body that develops and supports the thesis.

The First Draft

To make the first draft of your essay easier to write, keep the following advice in mind:

Write While You Think, Not After

To move from outline to essay, you need to develop your thoughts. This development does not involve long delays and cautious planning. Writing is not the expression of thought; it is thought itself. To avoid getting tangled up in a web of confusion, or worse, procrastination, write as you think, rather than after you have thought. Putting pen to paper, even in an unpolished way, will help you overcome the terror of the blank page and will enable you to examine your thoughts more objectively later on.

That many students now use a computer to write their papers from start to finish is a great boon, or it can be. The initial fear of the blank page is less daunting when you use a computer, if only because you can change everything so easily. The computer screen indeed seems to demand less commitment from a writer than paper and pen. Use that quality to good effect. The ease with which you can make revisions should mean that you experiment more often and write more drafts in your efforts to achieve clarity.

Think of the advantages a computer screen can provide as you write your first draft. First, you can add, delete, move, or change text with surprisingly little effort. Next, you can save multiple versions of your draft, in different stages of your thinking, so your good ideas won't get away. You can leave formatting decisions like spacing, margins, font, and titles for afterwards. And, best of all, you are not at all restricted to beginning at the beginning and continuing on till the end. You can start wherever you feel comfortable, assured that sooner or later you will fill in the gaps essential to creating a brilliant introduction or a strong opening argument.

Worry as You Write

This may sound like odd advice in a book meant to help you compose an essay, but the worrying stage, uncomfortable though it may be, is usually productive. Worrying is thinking. Keep the essay in the back of your mind as you do other things; carry a small notebook and make a record of passing ideas.

Plan to Rewrite Later

Don't demand perfection of your prose the first time out. Writing demands rewriting, not only to correct, but to beautify as well. The need for revision does not mean that your first draft is a failure. Writers revise not only to correct errors, but also to find the smoothest, the most succinct, the most elegant way to say something. Writing without revision is like getting dressed without looking in a mirror.

Revision involves a conscious decision to take several passes at the essay. Word processors make this process manageable. Do not make the mistake of thinking that the first draft will suffice, even though the first draft that spews from your printer may look quite respectable, unlike the pen and paper version. Take the opportunity that the computer provides to revise your paper, with an eye to making it the best it can be. Revision is a snap when even large chunks of text can be easily moved, changed, added, or deleted. Don't let the computer's convenience make you a lazy reviser.

Allow Yourself Freedom to Experiment

Say something. The essay is your chance to say what you want to say (within the limits of decorum!) the way you want to say it. All that is demanded in an essay assignment is that you think independently (perhaps with a little help from source material) and write in your own words (perhaps with the occasional quoted expert). Don't allow the fear of criticism to paralyze you at the outset. In your first draft especially, write to suit yourself. Drafting a paper means setting revision aside for a later date. The priority when you draft is to get words down on paper that express your point of view.

Allow Yourself Space to Write and to Make Mistakes

Although the preferred method of composing these days is sitting directly in front of the screen, you don't have to do things that way. Some of the strategies incorporated into the computer are the same things many of us have done regularly on paper. You can, if you like, cut and paste on paper, if you have glue and scissors handy, and if the physical layout of the paper helps you think more clearly. Either way, give yourself the chance to see the complete sequence of ideas.

At the very least, make an effort to take frequent breaks from the computer screen. It is easier to look at a draft with fresh eyes; for that reason, don't hesitate to print out a small section, read it over, make some changes on paper, and then revise later on the screen. Such things will keep your mind more awake to subtle nuances of phrasing and make you more able to question minute points.

Double or triple space. Leave wide margins so you can add written emendations as you re-read your draft or provide more details for support or documentation. Leave one side of the page blank. Use pencil if you like, or use coloured markers so you can see immediately what you add or delete.

Develop Your Own Methods of Quick Notation

As you write, include references immediately after their occurrence in the text. Generally, use the author's last name and a page number in parentheses just after the quotation or the reference in your paper. If you use the documentation style suggested by the MLA (see Chapter 23), this notation may be all you need. If you are using APA, the author's last name and the date may be sufficient, though you would need a page number if you quote something verbatim. Notes, of course, can be amended later to conform with demands of documentation.

If You Are Using a Computer

If you compose your essay on a computer, take advantage of any of its special features that will enable you to write more quickly and efficiently. Here are some guidelines:

1. Experiment. Use the speed of the computer to allow yourself a look at various possibilities in wording and in structure.
2. Write more critically than when you write on paper. Take advantage of the freedom from drudgery offered by the word processor to move paragraphs and to revise wording. When you write a sentence, stop and query its relevance to the rest of the paper. Ask "So what?" of every sentence you write. You need to be able to defend its logic and its connection to your thesis statement.
3. Be wary of proofreading from the screen. Although you may feel confident with what you see on the screen, double-check your proofreading. Check the screen first and then make a hard copy and check it.
4. Don't expect the machine to do everything for you. Even though the mechanical aspects of the essay should be simpler on a computer, don't fool yourself that careful writing or rigorous revision can be eliminated.
5. Use the time you save by writing on a computer to think your topic through more carefully, to do more intensive research, and to ferret out every small error. Remember, of course, that if you have an Internet connection and access to the World Wide Web then you may do some part of your research there. While you do need to develop some skills to discriminate among reputable and disreputable websites, your research can often benefit from a careful search of this quick, broad, and current source of information. Bear in mind, however, that many Internet sites are unregulated, so don't believe everything you read there.
6. Don't approach your paper in a strictly linear fashion. Take advantage of the computer's ability to work on any section of your essay that you feel ready to tackle. If the introduction is giving you problems, skip over it for a while. Move on instead to some part of the paper over which you have more control. The writing process is recursive, rather than linear; if technology permits, you can make your composition mirror the creative process.

7. Simplify your thinking about the revision process. When you come to revise your paper, there are only four operations available to you: you can add, delete, move, or change materials. The computer makes all these aspects of revision much easier than with pen and paper.

8. Since it is unusual for a writer to produce his or her best work in one single draft, you would be wise to save several drafts of your paper, shifting back and forth between them as you decide how best to express your ideas.

9. Take advantage of features that are often part of word-processing software packages, such as the spell checker, grammar checker, and the thesaurus. These functions are intended to help you overcome your own inadequacies as a writer and to speed up the entire process. Don't rely too heavily on them, since they can miss many small errors. The grammar checker, in particular, needs to be used with vigilance. It can provide suggestions and warnings; you need to know enough grammar to override suggestions when they do not fit your needs.

10. Let the speed of a computer afford you the time to revise more carefully and rethink more deeply.

Taking Notes and Assembling Evidence

Remember the Purpose of Your Research

Make sure you take adequate notes from your classes and from your research. Writing your paper from a hazy memory of the texts in question is not a good idea. To avoid notes that read like a shopping list, try to listen or read for structural cues. Remember that what you need to work with is not the exact words themselves (in fact, using them could lead to charges of plagiarism if unacknowledged). More important than the words you copy are the concepts that you understand from your listening or reading. To ensure that you have a grasp of the concepts, allow yourself time to reflect on your notes and to come to grips with the structure of the ideas and your own comprehension of it. To this end, make notes of concepts and terms that strike you as useful, but make sure you place them in a context, and make sure that you can explain them to others in your own words. Then your notes will be an invaluable guide for study or for assembling an essay.

Your research is intended to help you find support for the claims you make in your paper. Because an essay presents an argument, you want to confine your search to those things that will help you defend yourself. Your evidence will explain why you think what you think and why your reader should be inclined to do so as well. Because the research is not meant to give you information on everything about the subject in question, and because what you are writing is an essay, not a report, you must keep this purpose firmly in mind.

The purpose of your research is especially important when you use the Internet to help you gather information. Most instructors believe that the Internet is a good current supplement to library information, but not sufficient as a source of information in itself. When you use the Web as a source, it is vital to consider what you will be using the information for, because that will help determine which of the many sources you will cite. The Internet is a body of information, both expert and amateur, both objective and subjective, with authors of all ages and with all kinds of reasons for being there. It is up to you to determine which sources belong in your paper.

Determine What Counts as Evidence

In any essay, there are really only four kinds of support that you could gather from your research materials: examples, statistics, authorities, and reasons. Seldom would you use all four kinds of evidence in any one short paper. When you assemble your research material, working outline in hand, you want to be able to isolate relevant parts of others' work to strengthen your own. Keep your priorities straight. What is important here is that you select research material relevant to your particular focus on the subject. Examples and reasons are more likely than the others to be drawn from your experience and from your own thinking, though this is not always the case; they are the most common and closest to home, and may be either real or hypothetical. Examples are usually the best way to make an abstract point concrete. Reasons, by contrast, represent your thoughts and questions about key terms and your critical evaluations of the arguments of others. Statistics and the citing of authorities are useful methods of garnering support for your position. In both of these cases, however, you must be careful how you use the material in question and don't make the mistake of assuming that it speaks for itself; otherwise, your meaning will be obscured, and you will lose control over the paper itself. When you cite someone else's words, you must show the reader what you intend him or her to see in the passage; the meaning is not self-evident. Similarly, the meaning of a statistic must be related to your overall position in the paper; it is your responsibility to draw conclusions about what these findings mean for your claims.

The Internet makes the question of what sources to include even more complex since everyone, from scholars to children, is part of that vast conversation. With care, you can find the best sources for your purposes and use them properly. What makes this task challenging is that everything is there in a fluid, unregulated state. Before, reference librarians and teachers imposed some order on the information you were likely to turn up. Now, you have access to more materials, and it falls on you to figure out how to use them wisely. It is best to think of the Internet not as a source of information, but as a means by which you can examine an issue from a variety of different points of view in order to arrive at your own take on the question in front of you.

Make Outlines of Relevant Arguments in the Research

Strengthening your own case is often easier if you have made brief outlines or paraphrases of the arguments you encountered as you went along. It is often a wise idea to summarize your findings from a particular chapter or journal article in your own words, so that you can make the transition from notes to essay more smoothly. A summary of a journal article might consist of one page that outlined its thesis, its main points, an assessment of its support, and some general comments of your own in response to it. This method will record your engagement with your research materials better than any mere transcription of quoted materials might do.

Take the Opposition into Account

The best approach to take with materials that argue against your position is to approach them head on, assuming, of course, that you have decided your position is reasonable and defensible. Once you make up your mind to argue on a particular side of a question, your best line of defence is to read opposing views carefully and use materials from them to show flaws in their thinking and your own counter-arguments. If you take this advice, your argument will be more complete and more encompassing in its perspective.

Bear in mind that the Internet, if your instructor sees it as a possible avenue of research, will provide something close to field research. In other words, your online searches will probably uncover a multitude of differing opinions and perspectives. In general, you should search for sources that bear the marks of authority, usually because of the reputation of their authors. You should also beware of inordinate bias and problems with accuracy in materials found online.

Avoid "Tunnel Vision"

The success of your essay depends not only on your ability to make your case, but also on the maturity of your critical approach—your fairness and sensitivity to flaws in methodology (yours and others'). Don't let emotions prevent you from assessing the evidence thoroughly. To defend your position, you need to be well aware of opposing views. You may, for example, feel strongly that Canada should provide aid to developing countries, yet when writing an essay on the subject of development aid, you will have to assess the claims that such aid leads to economic dependency. Objectivity is essential. When in doubt about sources, particularly those on the Internet, ask a teacher or a reference librarian what you should be reading and how you can make sure that you have arrived at a balanced approach to your subject.

Interpret Your Findings

You cannot expect the citation of a statistic or the inclusion of a quotation to make your point. You must *interpret* the meaning of such evidence. A survey that indicates that 75 percent of the student population approves of aid to developing countries does not speak for itself. In order to interpret such findings, you need to know how many people were actually surveyed, whether or not the survey involved a fair random sampling, and whether the questions that made up the survey were clear and unbiased in their wording. Only when you have taken these factors into account can you use the figure to claim, for example, that the student population is, to a large extent, willing to support developing countries.

Avoid "Blind Spots"

An essay demands that you take a position with regard to the evidence you uncover. That position must, however, be based on a careful reading of the facts as well as a spirited defence of your position about them. To ensure that you do not willfully (or otherwise) misread your evidence, try to formulate both the case for and the case against your position. Include in your essay not only a defence of your thesis, but also arguments that have led you to reject contrary interpretations. For example, if you are arguing that aid to developing countries is a humanitarian obligation, you must consider the charge that the resulting private foreign investment is exploitative. You may find that you must concede some points. Such qualification makes your argument all the more persuasive in its evaluation of the data.

Realize that the shape of your essay is in your hands. Do not make the mistake of thinking that you can "cover" all the material that you find. Your job is to make editorial decisions as you go along, searching out and reading materials. Aim at currency, but don't forget the value of credibility and accuracy. The ease of research these days sometimes lulls writers into accepting as true all the "facts" that they can so easily discover. Be discerning in your use of sources.

Aim at a Better, Not an Ultimate, Theory

When you use evidence to defend your thesis, be realistic in your goals. Your research and your thought have led you to understand the data in a certain way. Your task is to show that your reading of the material exhibits common sense and attention to recent data. Your theory about the meaning of the evidence should help to explain something. You may find, for instance, that economic dependency only partly explains the continuing problems in developing countries and that internal, national factors play a part as well. Your theory won't be perfect—just the most reliable interpretation of the facts you have found.

Maintaining Unity in the Essay

An essay is a unit: a discussion centred on one basic point. Remember that your essay should focus on your thesis statement. An essay meant to grapple with the Canadian presence in Afghanistan should not devote space to previous lack of Canadian involvement in Vietnam, except perhaps by way of comparison. An essay treating the issue of free will in *Paradise Lost* should find no place for a discussion of epic conventions. Your essay should reach widely and show a broad acquaintance with your topic, but make sure that you show the relevance to the thesis statement of every point you raise. You need to make sure that you stay on topic, that you maintain a consistent attitude toward the topic and that you organize your work so that your reader does not lose sight of your main point.

To keep your essay unified:

1. Keep your purpose and basic pattern of argument firmly in mind.
2. Avoid digressions, however interesting, if you cannot connect them to the thesis statement.
3. Avoid padding for the sake of word length. Instead, develop your ideas by referring to Chapter 6 on patterns of development, and relating them to your proposed thesis statement.
4. Redesign your thesis statement (within the limits of the assignment, of course) if you find your initial focus unappealing or too limited in scope. Remember that

a thesis statement should avoid suspense. Its purpose is not to look at all sides of the question and then decide. Your thesis statement and the arguments you make in defence of it must not waffle.

5. Use the repetitive rhetorical structure of the conventional essay as well as consistent wording to make the connections between your points clear. Keep terminology consistent throughout, and use the three-part structure of the essay to reinforce the points that you are making.

Above all, remember the principle of unity: Everything in an essay should relate directly to the main focus of the paper that you express in the thesis statement.

Look at this sample draft of a paragraph to understand the concept of unity:

The most frustrating job I ever had was working at the local coffee shop—naming no names, lest those who frequent the chain may be offended. I found that we often ran out of something that customers really wanted long before my shift was over. It seems that we could never meet the demand for dutchies or chocolate chip muffins, no matter how hard we tried, and the customers might take it out on us. Worse still, I had trouble making the correct change. Perhaps it was coordination or lack of skill in arithmetic, but I often riled customers who discovered my mistakes in giving them change. I found dealing with the public difficult, usually because they wanted everything immediately and were often disrespectful of each other when waiting in the queue. Working with the public in the coffee shop, admittedly, was not as challenging as when I worked selling toys in a department store. There I had to deal with screaming children and adamant parents as well as dealing with cleaning up constant disarray in the weeks before Christmas. Upon reflection, I wonder if this latter job was not actually a good deal more frustrating than my job at the coffee shop.

In this short example, the student clearly gets off topic in the final three sentences and loses track of the central focus of the piece. It is a good idea to re-read your work with an eye to maintaining its unity by asking, "So what?" after every sentence. The point is that you need to be able to establish why everything is there and how it relates to your thesis statement. When you write a draft, you may re-think your thesis, but if you end by changing your opinion, you should make significant changes to your thesis statement. You need to make sure the reader follows your argument.

CHAPTER 5 EXERCISES

1. Consider what arguments you might make to support the thesis statements below, keeping unity as your guiding principle:
   a. Canadian literature should take priority over American or British literature in introductory English classes
   b. portable music devices are diminishing our sense of community
   c. stem cell research should be legal
   d. humanities or arts courses ought to be required for every student regardless of program
   e. assisted suicide ought to be legal for those terminally ill patients who choose to end their lives

    f. a mandatory retirement age is healthy for the economy

    g. the *Young Offenders Act* should be revoked

    h. mortgages should be tax-deductible in Canada

    i. courses that teach life skills should be mandatory

    j. schools should operate year-round

    k. young people are discriminated against because of their age

    l. marijuana should be legalized

    m. separate schools should not be publicly funded

    n. the Internet will make copyright a thing of the past

2. Read over an essay for a classmate, and note every time the writer digresses from the main focus of the essay and every time you find "padding."

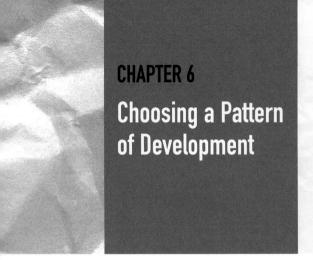

CHAPTER 6

Choosing a Pattern of Development

Everything has been thought of before, but the problem is to think of it again.
—GOETHE

In this chapter:

- How to develop your argument using these rhetorical patterns: Definition/Description, Example, Classification, Process, Comparison/Contrast, Cause and Effect, Narration

After you have established your thesis statement and made your outline, you need to choose the pattern or patterns of development that will do them justice. The pattern of development gives structure to your thoughts.

Essays can be expository or persuasive; that is, they can explain something or make a case for something, and sometimes they do a bit of both. Essays typically present evidence and reasons that an idea is valid or that a course of action is the best one to take. Essays thus can be quite complex: not only do they present reasons for accepting a particular line of reasoning, but they also attempt to counter possible opposing arguments, anticipate objections that might be raised, and analyze the assumptions on which any reasoning is based. To be persuasive, an essay must win a reader over by engaging emotions and by presenting reasons and support that are trustworthy and reliable.

Audience analysis is a major factor in writing a persuasive argument. You need to use authorities, statistics, examples, and reasons that will convince your readers and command their respect. Argument is the process by which you lay out the good reasons for making your case—the reasons that any well-informed reader would also accept as compelling.

Look at the following outline. An argument is stated and a number of kinds of support are used to defend its position and win over its readers:

Example   THESIS: Dieting is not a good way to maintain one's health.

Reason 1:   Most diets are unbalanced to begin with, encouraging dieters to skimp on starch, or to avoid entire food groups, like fats, unwisely.

Your support for Reason 1 might include examples of low carbohydrate diets (like that espoused by Dr. Atkins) or fat-free diets (like that advocated by Susan Powter).

Reason 2: Diets are too often considered the key to avoid being overweight when, in fact, poverty may be the real culprit.

For Reason 2, you might cite the words of an authority, such as an economist who can show that eating fast food and living a stressful life without adequate nutrition or health care education may lead to being overweight.

Reason 3: Most diets fail because dieters are not willing or able to change their eating habits permanently. Their habits are often a product of socioeconomic necessity.

To support Reason 3, you might cite the statistic that 85 percent of all diets fail since the dieters in question regain most of their excess weight within a year.

Reason 4: Diets can lead to problems because they encourage obsession with appearance rather than with feeling strong and healthy.

You might support your last claim, Reason 4, with the reason that dieting is based too often on a cultural obsession with appearance that has nothing to do with health and, in fact, may be detrimental to it.

This argument does not prove conclusively that diets do not work to maintain health, but it does muster a number of powerful reasons that they do not work to maintain health. Arguments in general do not prove anything beyond a shadow of a doubt; they do, however, marshal forth facts and reasons that together work to persuade a reader. Your job, when constructing a good argument, is to assemble pertinent facts and reasons with an eye to making your audience see things your way. In a strong expository or persuasive essay, the facts you choose and how you assemble them will benefit from an understanding of some basic patterns of development.

Usually an essay will demand several patterns in support of its thesis, as the sample outline in the preceding chapter demonstrates. In order to support your thesis with a similar variety of arguments, you must look for methods by which to direct your thought. The following tactics may serve as structural guidelines or blueprints for your thought:

Definition/Description (asks "What is it?")

Example (asks "What would an individual instance look like?")

Classification (asks "How can the term be divided into parts or seen as part of a larger whole?")

Process (asks "How does this work?")

Comparison/Contrast (asks "How does this measure up against something similar or different that is still related to it in a meaningful way?")

Cause and Effect (asks "What might have led to this?" and "What might this lead to?")

Narration (asks "What story can illustrate how this works?")

These patterns are some of the directions that an argument or an exposition might take, though none can be entirely separated from one another. Usually, a writer will use several patterns to develop one essay. Refer, for example, to the outline in Chapter 4. It uses many different kinds of argument, including definition, classification, comparison/contrast, and example.

A paragraph that defines "dreams," for example, may contrast a simple dictionary definition with a more elaborate definition offered by a psychologist. Examples of dreams may be given to show something about their essential nature, perhaps demonstrating the creativity of the unconscious mind.

The patterns listed below should offer you some inspiration when you get stuck in the process of outlining your thoughts. Refer to this section when you need help in amplifying an argument.

Definition/Description

Definition suggests the use of a dictionary to define a term explicitly. This tactic ensures that there is a general consensus between writer and readers as to the term's meaning in the context of the essay.

Although dictionary definitions are important, don't rely too heavily on them. Belabouring a definition already familiar to your readers may alienate them: it may sound condescending. Furthermore, a critical reader will be concerned more with what you *make* of a definition than with its content per se. If you do cite a dictionary definition, make sure that you use it to make a point.

What comprises a useful definition? First, it must supply the reader with characteristics that describe something. Occasionally, it may describe by way of comparison/contrast, by showing what the thing is not. And, it may give some enlightening history of the term, showing how it came to have the meaning it has. It may then show what something does, in order to describe more concretely what it is. Lastly, it may give an example, meant to epitomize the nature of the thing described.

Example   What, exactly, is a dream? Webster's says nothing more than that it is a "hallucination in sleep."[1] This rather bland attempt at definition masks the essential problem. The truth is that we do not really know what dreams are, though there has always been a great deal of speculation about their nature. Some modern psychologists, such as Carl Jung, maintain that dreams are unconscious subjective re-creations of reality: "the dream is the theater where the dreamer is at once scene, actor, prompter, stage manager, author, audience, and critic."[2] But, even among modern psychologists, there is still considerable disagreement about the source of dreams.

This definition introduces the subject and provides two possible definitions of what dreams are.

Example

Because readers usually find it easier to understand what they can picture, examples are often the best means of amplifying an argument. Whether you use an extended example, meant to illustrate your general point in a series of specific ways, or whether you use a variety of small examples to achieve the same end, examples lend support to your argument.

> One of the most famous recorded dreams is Kekulé's account of his discovery of the nature of benzene. In 1865, Kekulé, a chemist, fell asleep and dreamt of a snake with its tail in its mouth.[3] His intuition about the structure of benzene—that its molecules were not open structures but rings—was one of the cornerstones of modern scientific thinking. This episode illustrates that some dreams have a creative component capable of communicating, in a flash, something that the conscious mind has been seeking in vain. Some dreams apparently can bring about a breakthrough in understanding.

Example

This example supports the idea that dreams are sometimes creative.

Classification

In order to explain something more precisely, a writer often has recourse to methods of classification, by which he or she can make necessary distinctions within a subject area. Classifying different parts of a subject involves making decisions about what belongs where. A large subject may be divided into smaller or more manageable sections to make important distinctions clear. In order for classification to work convincingly, the reader must be assured that the categories are tidy, include everything essential, and do not substantially overlap.

> Although dreams have been a subject of much study throughout history, there is still no consensus about what dreams mean. Some philosophers, like Bertrand Russell, contend that dreams cannot be differentiated from reality, that, in fact, we do not know which is real, the waking state or the dreaming state.[4] Others maintain, even in certain modern cultures, that dreams have divinatory qualities that tell us something about what might happen. Modern psychologists argue that dreams are proof of unconscious activity in the mind, and their studies of dreams seek to understand the springs of behaviour.

Example

This classification lists some of the different interpretations of what dreams mean.

Process

It is often necessary in the course of an essay to explain how to do something or how something works. When describing a process, think of yourself as a teacher. It is part of your job to supply your readers with all the information they require to understand, without confusion, a given process. At the same time, you must be careful to assess their level of understanding accurately, if you are to avoid writing that is boring or condescending. It is also part of your job to present the material in a logical, step-by-step manner, so that the reader is spared needless cross-referencing and rereading. Check your description of the process to see if its steps can be easily followed.

Example   The Freudian view of the process of dreaming, recorded in *The Interpretation of Dreams* in 1899, suggests that dreams are stimulated by bodily reactions, experiences during daylight hours, and infantile memories. When people dream, according to Freud, they give way to primitive impulses, to repressed wishes, often displaced or represented in symbolic terms. When they awaken, dreamers revise their dreams by rationalizing and elaborating upon their reports of them. To understand these subconscious processes, Freud suggested that the content of dreams be analyzed through free association that would allow the dreamer to become aware of the hidden meanings and symbols of the dream.[5]

This paragraph outlines the steps in Freud's interpretation of the process of dreaming.

Comparison/Contrast

Comparisons are an essential part of expository writing. No pattern of development is more common on examination questions, for instance, than comparison/contrast.

A comparison typically includes both similarities and differences. When you contrast, however, you focus exclusively on the differences between things.

When comparing, keep the overall structure in mind. You may first present one thing and then the other (organizing material in blocks), or you may alternate between the two sides of the comparison (point-by-point comparison). Alternating between the two is best if the material to be covered is complex or lengthy. Beyond these typical categories, one might also organize according to similarities and differences.

Example   From earliest times, there has been sharp disagreement about the sources of dreams. One school of thought sees dreams as a natural phenomenon; the other sees them as something supernatural. Even the basic division between Freud and Jung on the nature of dreams can be seen this way. Freud holds that dreams are explainable in terms of what he calls "day residue" and of external stimuli;[6] that is, they are borrowed from the images of daily life accompanied by bodily disturbances. Together these elements produce a dream that reveals much about the dreamer's repressed desires and feelings. Jung's account of the source of dreams is more spiritual and less a part of natural human functions. He argues that a "dream is the small hidden door in the deepest and most intimate sanctum of the soul,"[7] and his studies of individuals' dreams attempt to relate the dreamer to the larger patterns of human consciousness throughout history.

This paragraph illustrates the main differences between Jung and Freud on the subject of dreams.

Look at the following table. Point-by-point comparisons usually succeed better, especially if the topic is complex, because you do the comparison more overtly in that argument structure. You make three points about apples and oranges, and then you organize your argument around your points, rather than just doing one side of the comparison (the apples) and following with the other side (the oranges). After all, the point of a comparison/contrast essay is for you to compare and contrast. Don't make the reader do it.

<table>
<tr><td align="center">BLOCK COMPARISON</td><td align="center">POINT-BY-POINT COMPARISON</td></tr>
<tr><td align="center">(for simple short topics only)</td><td align="center">(usually the better choice since the reader doesn't have to do all the work alone)</td></tr>
<tr><td align="center">APPLES</td><td align="center">POINT 1</td></tr>
<tr><td align="center">Point 1</td><td align="center">Apples vs. Oranges</td></tr>
<tr><td align="center">Point 2</td><td align="center">POINT 2</td></tr>
<tr><td align="center">Point 3</td><td align="center">Apples vs. Oranges</td></tr>
<tr><td align="center">ORANGES</td><td align="center">POINT 3</td></tr>
<tr><td align="center">Point 1</td><td align="center">Apples vs. Oranges</td></tr>
<tr><td align="center">Point 2</td><td align="center"></td></tr>
<tr><td align="center">Point 3</td><td align="center"></td></tr>
</table>

SIMILARITIES AND DIFFERENCES

<table>
<tr><td align="center">APPLES ARE LIKE ORANGES BECAUSE . . .</td><td align="center">APPLES ARE DIFFERENT FROM ORANGES BECAUSE . . .</td></tr>
<tr><td align="center">Point 1</td><td align="center">Point 1</td></tr>
<tr><td align="center">Point 2</td><td align="center">Point 2</td></tr>
<tr><td align="center">Point 3</td><td align="center">Point 3</td></tr>
</table>

Cause and Effect

This pattern traces the relationship between the cause of an event or a condition and its results. When seeking to develop an argument by tracing causes and their effects, keep in mind two potential dangers. First, beware of trusting the idea of causality too much. Simply because one thing follows another chronologically does not mean that the second event was caused by the first.

Second, do not limit effects to one cause alone. Usually more than one determinant brings about an event or a trend. Don't wear blinders in your zeal to establish connections.

> Recent studies show that there is a physiological correlation between sleep patterns and the frequency of dreams. In the 1950s, researchers found a link between bursts of rapid eye movement (sometimes called REM sleep), increased electrical activity in the brain, and frequency of reported dreams. If a dreamer is awakened during a period of REM sleep, there is a much greater chance that he or she will report and remember a dream. These studies show that dreams usually, though not always, occur in conjunction with certain patterns of activity in the dreamer's brain.[8]

Example

This paragraph points out a relationship between sleep patterns and dreams. It also illustrates one of the problems in establishing an argument; note that while the author of the paragraph does mention a correlation between two things, there is no claim of a definite cause-and-effect relation between them. Often, there can be no positive declaration of cause and effect. Be cautious in your claims.

Narration

Telling a story, like telling a good joke, is hard to do. You narrate, or tell a story, in a piece of expository writing in order to bring your argument to life.

To be effective, the narrative you use in an essay should contain carefully selected, telling details—enough to be vivid, not so many that it is boring. The narrative must be well timed: it should draw your reader into the writing or graphically illustrate a point you are making. It should hold the reader's attention: do not expand the story endlessly with "and then . . . and then . . . and then."

Use narration sparingly in essay writing. Most commonly, you will find it used to relate case studies, brief anecdotes, and extended examples. Do not engage in narration when writing a literary essay; there your object is to analyze the writing, not to re-tell the plot or to summarize the action in any way. Literary essays assume that readers have read the book, but seek further clarification of its meaning.

Example
The Bible contains many stories of dreams used as prophecies. Perhaps the most famous is the story of the dreams of the Pharaoh of Egypt. He dreamed of seven fat cattle, followed by seven lean cattle, which devoured the first. Then he dreamed of seven good stalks of corn, which were destroyed by seven lean stalks of corn. These dreams Joseph interpreted as prophecies about the fate of Egypt. First, it would experience seven years of plenty, then seven years of famine. In response to Joseph's interpretation, the Pharoah stored enough food from the seven good years to protect the country from starvation during the famine that followed.[9] Such treatment of dreams as prophecy are part of many religions and illustrate the captivating power of the dream on the human imagination.

This paragraph retells a familiar biblical story to make a point about the imaginative appeal of dreams.

The superscript numerals used throughout the sample paragraphs indicate places where a writer would have to acknowledge sources. In this case, traditional note numbers have been used. For more information on the subject of citation of sources, see Chapters 22 and 23.

Tips on Choosing the Right Pattern

Your choice of pattern may depend to some extent on your subject. In English, for example, one of the most common patterns is *comparison/contrast*. In political science and sociology, you may find yourself most often choosing *definition* or *classification*. History makes most use of the *cause-and-effect* pattern. The most common pattern in all writing is *example*. Choose your pattern wisely; keep its relevance to the overall thesis statement always in mind.

CHAPTER 6 EXERCISES

1. Develop one of the following thesis statements by using at least two appropriate patterns of development:
   a. Mandatory retirement is a breach of human rights.
   b. Stem cell research is a danger to humanity.
   c. Fashion houses have a moral obligation to showcase normal body types.
   d. The threat of terrorism in North America has led to racism.
   e. Affirmative action is necessary to address past social injustices.
   f. A licence to have children would be a good idea.
   g. Popular forms of culture may lead to violence and must be censored accordingly.
   h. Genetically altered foods, or so-called "frankenfoods," should be monitored carefully.
   i. Tuition for colleges and universities needs to be drastically reduced to allow greater access for lower socioeconomic groups.
   j. The Internet has led to a severe reduction in users' level of physical activity.

2. Develop a thesis statement for one of the following topics:
   a. Canada's relationship to American popular culture
   b. the advantages or disadvantages of chain stores
   c. the Internet vs. face-to-face relationships
   d. the symptoms of depression
   e. advertising and its relation to personal debt
   f. the legalization of "soft" drugs
   g. the *Young Offenders Act* and its repercussions
   h. live vs. "canned" entertainment
   i. the value of reading fiction
   j. the importance of the vote

3. Analyze the patterns of development in a paper written by a classmate. What are the most common patterns? What patterns could be used more effectively?

4. Analyze the patterns of development you find in a chapter in a textbook. List any techniques you find that you could emulate in your own work.

5. Write a set of instructions for how to make or how to fix something. The instructions should guide the reader clearly through the process involved to create the final product. Use the basic structure of a recipe as a guideline for your set of instructions, remembering to tell the reader what materials are needed and what methods are to be followed in a logical, step-by-step order.

6. Listen carefully to a speech delivered by a politician or a media celebrity, or study the text of a speech (sometimes these are available online). How do the techniques of an argument delivered orally differ from those used in essays?

7. Write two definitions of a word you commonly use. Design the first definition so it explains the word to a group of your peers; next, rewrite the definition so it is suitable for a grade-one class. What techniques did you use to accomplish the second task?

8. Write an essay that compares two places you have lived. Obviously, you first need to decide what the point of the comparison is. For example, you might compare Edmonton and Winnipeg in order to show that one is more pleasant than the other, or to show that one of the places is more interesting than the other. Make sure that the comparison is not simply perfunctory; you are comparing the two places to make some point to the reader.

9. Compare the methods of characterization in two short stories you have studied. Use point-by-point comparison. Alternatively, analyze the patterns of development you find in one of the essays you have read in your course.

10. Compare the persuasive techniques in two argumentative essays that you have studied. Use block comparison.

Part Three

PUTTING THE ESSAY TOGETHER

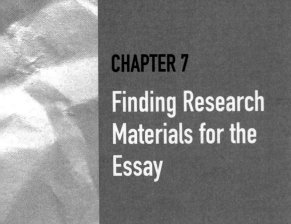

CHAPTER 7

Finding Research Materials for the Essay

If a man will begin with certainties, he will end in doubts; but if he will be content to begin with doubts, he will end in certainties.
—FRANCIS BACON

In this chapter:
- How to use the library
- How to take good research notes
- How to evaluate sources

Finding and Using Library Resources

While the Internet is a very useful resource, libraries are indispensable for the exploration of your research topic. Make sure you know where these items are in your educational institution's library:

1. the circulation and reference desks
2. reference books
3. periodicals and their indexes
4. the card catalogue and computer card catalogue
5. CD-ROMs, microform, and online databases
6. sources available through library terminals
7. government documents

If you don't know where all of these items are in your library, take a tour, or make an appointment with a reference librarian and find out.

The good news is that libraries these days have excellent online resources too, if you are a registered student. Have a look at the library's website to see what research guides have been established. Many libraries list by subject heading (e.g., Canadian Literature) followed by the major encyclopedias, bibliographies, and online databases available in that subject area, including any important works of reference (both online and printed). To get a sense of the potential direction of your own research, it is often a good idea to scan these headings to determine significant topics and subtopics.

Start with the general and move to the specific even when you are browsing through a subject area. General information sources like *The Canadian Encyclopedia*, for example, can give you a good overview of the area you would like to pursue further. Looking up keywords in subject encyclopedias may also help you get a feel for the scope of your topic.

Follow these broad categories in your search for increasingly specific materials:

1. reference works
2. periodicals
3. books from the library's collection
4. library sources beyond books and periodicals
5. information beyond your own library

1. Reference works can be found online or in the physical library and are often labelled REF. These include dictionaries, almanacs, yearbooks, atlases, encyclopedias, directories, and books of quotations. There may also be specialized references in your field of study, for example, works like *Literary History of Canada*.

   If you are well acquainted with your library, reference works like encyclopedias and bibliographies will be easy to find.

2. Periodicals are publications issued regularly, weekly, monthly, semiannually, or annually on a variety of subjects. Magazines are periodicals with a general audience, while many periodicals are very specialized. These are often excellent sources for current information since they publish more quickly and regularly than books. These days, many periodicals are available only online, though usually you will need a mixture of print and online sources to make sure that you have done a thorough research job. Online periodicals may not include early references, so print is needed to supplement them. Many online periodicals in databases go back only to the 1990s, so if you need something less current, print periodicals can easily be accessed in your library's holdings.

   Here are some examples of works that will help you locate periodicals, many of which can be found online:

   The Reader's Guide to Periodical Literature. New York: Wilson, 1900 to date. (Also available on CD-ROM and online.)

   Magazine Index

   Academic Index

   Business Periodicals Index

   Humanities Index (scholarly articles from 1974 to date)

   Social Sciences Abstracts (scholarly articles from 1974 to date)

   PsychINFO

   ERIC: educational materials from the Educational Resources Information Center

   Historical Abstracts: abstracts of periodicals in history

   MLA International Bibliography: index of books and articles published about modern languages, linguistics, and literature

   Philosopher's Index: a guide to books and periodicals in philosophy

Note that many journal and newspaper articles can be located in electronic indexes such as *CBCA Current Events* and *Canadian Newsstand,* or through services like Factiva, usually organized by subject matter.

You can usually find periodicals by title on your library's website, but if you need help, ask a reference librarian.

3. Books

These will be important sources for your research essay and can be accessed through the online catalogue by subject, title, author, or keywords.

4. Other Library Sources

These may include Special Collections (unpublished manuscripts or rare books), Vertical Files (clippings, government pamphlets, or materials from special-interest groups), Media such as CDs, DVDs, films, and multimedia. Often you must use this information in the library since it cannot usually be borrowed.

5. Sources Beyond the Library

These include Interlibrary loan, which may allow you to borrow a book that is not in your library, as long as you allow enough time for it to arrive from its place of origin. Government documents may also be accessed online. The main directory for the federal government is < http:// www.gc.ca/depts./major/depind_e. html >. You may also find a pathfinder document on your library website to point the way to various federal and international government sources. You can also access federal government information by dialing 1-800-OCANADA, to find specific information. If you need statistics to support your research, begin by visiting Statistics Canada at < http://www.statcan.ca >.

Don't forget that primary sources may include your own interviews, surveys, or experiments. It may even include first-hand materials based on a visit to a museum or attendance at a play. This kind of information may be an invaluable source of unique information on a research question that you are pursuing.

Keeping Track of Sources

1. Record everything you need to find a source again, including page numbers.
2. Note what you found useful and why.
3. Keep track of your reading, quoting, and paraphrasing.
4. Put sources in alphabetical order for easy entry into a bibliography.

Doing Research on the Internet

The sheer convenience of the World Wide Web makes it a desirable research tool. It is often more up-to-date than printed sources, and is able to combine many different media. It also has a broad range, including popular items as well as scholarly ones. There are, of course, disadvantages to the Internet as well. For one thing, materials are fluid there; they may change without warning or disappear altogether, or they may look different on different browsers. Because they allow anyone to publish, without the intervention of gatekeepers such as publishers, they are more democratic and broader in their range. Everyone from expert to amateur may be on the Web, so be aware that many resources are not in any way subject to peer review to set standards for the work that is produced. This, of course, means that it is up to you to decide how you evaluate the materials that you encounter on the Web. Be wary of depending too heavily on resources that lack credibility: Wikipedia, for example, while a good place to get some general information quickly, is not necessarily written by experts, and the information is often unsubstantiated because it may involve collaborative work on a controversial subject. Do not rely on it as a major source for your essays.

You must, of course, also take your instructor's preferences into account. If he or she does not want you to use the Web for a particular assignment, respect that request. Most instructors, however, are open to the Internet as a possible resource, provided that you keep good track of what you found and where you found it, and that you apply certain standards to your use of source material. Don't neglect online library resources. The library pays subscription fees for a number of authoritative, up-to-the-minute resources that can answer your questions more reliably than a mere cursory personal search on the Internet. Remember, too, that the Internet is best for very current, popular topics, but less likely to provide definitive information for more traditional areas. And unless you know a good deal about your subject before you engage in an Internet search, you could be easily misled.

Evaluating Web Resources

Here are some questions you might ask of a website you are considering as a source for your research:

1. Who is the author? How well known is he or she?
2. Does the website or the author have a professional or academic connection?
3. Is the website sponsored by an academic institution?
4. Is the website objective, or does it have obvious bias?
5. Is the website well designed?
6. Is the website updated?
7. Have articles on the website been peer reviewed?

CONDUCTING WEB SEARCHES. Many search engines are available on the Internet. Yahoo! and Google are among the best because they are directories organized in a hierarchical index by human beings who provide descriptions and reviews of the listed websites. Other search engines, like AltaVista, may produce more hits because they attempt to catalogue every known website. To narrow down a search on AltaVista, however, it is possible to choose a particular domain—say, for example, only websites that end in ".edu" to focus especially on educational sites.

Advanced Web searches demand more than simple keywords if you need to keep the search focused. If you use three keywords, such as "apples oranges bananas," you will get all the websites that have any one of those words in them. If you type the word AND between them, the engine will select only those websites that contain all three words. If you type the word NOT between "apples" and "oranges," you will get websites with the word "apples," but not those that contain the word "oranges." Note that AND or NOT will narrow a search and OR will broaden it. If you want a search engine to look for three or four words exactly as they appear together, you should put them in quotation marks or in parentheses, as in "deep dish apple pie" or (deep dish apple pie). Remember that an asterisk (*) works like a wild card so you can use it to stand in for letters at the end of a word. For example, a word like Canad* will bring up resources with different endings, such as Canada and Canadian. When you conduct a name search, on the other hand, most search engines assume that two capitalized words together (Winston Churchill) will appear in that order and are, in fact, a name. You may need to experiment, however. Every search engine has its own approach to advanced searches.

KEEPING TRACK OF WEB SOURCES. You need to collect the following information, if it is recorded on the website: the author's name, the title of the page, the title of the larger work that the Web page comes from, the publication date of the page, the URL or Web address, and the date that you accessed it.

You can, of course, bookmark relevant files—or save bookmarked files to a USB key if you are working at a public computer—but that may not save all the relevant information if the page happens to undergo changes or be removed from the Web altogether. You can also copy and paste the relevant information to your word-processing program, to be printed later. Another option is to save the entire page to a USB key for safekeeping, something that guarantees that you will find it again, should you need to.

It's not a bad idea to keep a written log of what sources you consulted on the Web. One safeguard against the charge of plagiarism is a written record of your thinking at every stage, from brainstorming through to first and second drafts. Many instructors ask to see this record as a verification of your participation in the writing process.

STAYING HONEST. Remember that, even though you can easily copy and paste someone else's words from the Internet directly into your paper, you must acknowledge them. It is a good idea to use a different font for words that you have pasted into your paper, so that you are always clear about which words you are borrowing and which words are your own. Remember that if it is easy for you to find material on the Web, it is also relatively easy for an instructor to find out if the words are really yours. Programs like "Turn It In," now a common standard, make detecting plagiarism simple. Indeed, some instructors encourage students to check their own papers with this program before they submit them. Even ordinary search engines can be quite useful for detecting plagiarism, so be careful to acknowledge any sources that you use.

For Materials to be Published on the Web

If you will be publishing your work on the Web, be prepared to ask permission if you feel you need to use materials from a source that constitute more than what is considered "fair use." A small citation is usually considered acceptable fair use, but if you want to quote something in its entirety—say, a song—it may well require copyright permission. You don't need to request permission for excerpts in papers submitted to an instructor.

A Review of the Research Process

Read widely at first to locate the best sources. Then read deeply in order to get at the heart of the matter. Explore the topic with your tentative thesis in mind, revising it as you go along. A good researcher moves from the general to the specific.

1. Find general information in an encyclopedia, dictionary, or other reference book, either in print or online. Remember, though, that these general sources only scratch the surface.

2. Find information in the library computer system or card catalogue. Look under the subject heading or use the names of authors or titles that you have found in any of the encyclopedias you consulted.

3. Consult periodical indexes for further information. Often periodicals, particularly those online, will give you more current material than is available in books. *The Canadian Periodical Index (CPI)* lists all articles published in Canadian journals for a given year.

4. Examine your sources with your specific topic in mind. Check the table of contents and the index of the books you find to search for suitable material.

5. Note bibliographical information for any of the sources you consult. Small note cards (7.6 cm × 12.7 cm) (3" × 5") are useful. Record the library call numbers for your sources.

6. Follow the rules of documentation that apply to your discipline at this stage, and you will save time and trouble toward the end. Check to see which style of documentation your instructor prefers (whether APA, MLA, University of Chicago, or other style) and make your notes accordingly.

SAMPLE BIBLIOGRAPHY CARD

<u>Modern Language Association of America.</u>
<u>MLA Handbook for Writers of Research Papers.</u>
7th ed. New York: The Modern Language Association
of America, 2009.

LB 2369.G53 2009

CHAPTER 8

Paraphrasing Sources and Integrating Quotations

It is the little writer rather than the great writer who seems never to quote, and the reason is that he is never really doing anything else.
—HAVELOCK ELLIS

In this chapter:

- How and when to use paraphrase
- How and when to use quotations
- How to avoid plagiarism

Not all essays will demand that you use sources other than your own imagination and general knowledge of the world. Many essays, however, will include, as part of the requirements, a knowledge of background sources, all of which must be acknowledged to avoid charges of plagiarism. Plagiarism is a serious charge. If a student deliberately plagiarizes someone else's work and passes it off as his or her own, there are often strict consequences, which may include expulsion from the class, the program of study, or even the institution in question. You must acknowledge where you found facts, ideas, and exact wording to avoid the charge that you are plagiarizing. Whether intentional or not, plagiarism seriously affects the credibility of your work and undermines your abilities as a researcher. If the reader might at any point ask, "How do you know that?", the essay is likely remiss in acknowledging sources. It is the writer's duty to give credit where credit is due and to assist readers to find and check the sources used. Not to do so is to violate the reader's trust and also to defeat the purpose of the research essay in the first place.

Source material, while often a significant part of the essay, does not speak for itself. Remember that the function of paraphrased and quoted matter is to provide support for your arguments. You are responsible for the use you make of the source material. Not only must you be accurate in your representation of it, but you also must be prepared to use it thoughtfully to support your viewpoint.

When you find an idea or a quotation in another source, you are obliged to inform your reader of its origins, even if it is an idea that you already had yourself. Except for the classroom, which is usually considered common domain, the sources of your ideas must be listed in your papers. If you are in doubt about whether or not to include a source for some particular information, put yourself in the reader's place. Would he or she ask, "How do you know this is true?" If so, you need to mention the source.

Quotations and paraphrase are used as support in rather different ways. Quotations are most often used in an essay dealing with literature or a book review, where the main trustworthy source of information is the text of a work itself.

Paraphrase, on the other hand, is used when the exact words are not as important, but the facts they present are; hence, paraphrase is the most common method of using source material in the social sciences. If you find that you must refer to a theory or to an explanation of the meaning of some data, the best plan is to paraphrase. Remember, as you take notes, to paraphrase rather than to quote, taking special care with statistics and their implications.

When you paraphrase some part of a book or article for inclusion as support in your essay, try to get at its meaning. Try to rephrase the thought as if you were teaching the material to someone. Make notes with this principle in mind, taking care to "boil down" the facts and reduce them to their simplest terms, without distorting them. Focus on the thesis statement, topic sentences, and key words, and don't let yourself get bogged down in details. Think the words through rather than just copying them.

Both quotations and paraphrase are used to support your arguments. When you select material from sources, consider the use you intend to make of it. None of the sources will speak for itself; you must demonstrate how a source relates to the case you are building. For this reason, you should usually introduce source material and comment on its function in your paper, rather than assuming the reader will make the necessary connections.

Borrow Only What You Need

Borrow words, phrases, and sentences only if they add something essential that you do not already possess. Among these essentials are **credibility, power,** and **eloquence.**

The quotations that follow are taken from George Orwell's famous essay, "Politics and the English Language," which addresses the importance of simplicity and clarity in communication.

Credibility

Quote to improve credibility by citing a respected and recognized authority. Or use the quotation as a target for attack, to illustrate that the source itself is doubtful and the object of your critical scrutiny. Orwell uses the following words of Harold Laski to demonstrate one of the faults of modern prose: a tendency to use too many negatives.

> "I am not, indeed, sure whether it is not true to say that the Milton who once seemed not unlike a seventeenth-century Shelley had not become, out of an experience ever more bitter in each year, more alien [*sic*] to the founder of that Jesuit sect which nothing could induce him to tolerate."   **Example**

Orwell uses this passage to point out some facts about his writing: "Professor Laski . . . uses five negatives in fifty-three words. One of these is superfluous, making nonsense of the whole passage, and in addition there is the slip—alien for akin—making further nonsense, and several avoidable pieces of clumsiness which increase the general vagueness."* Without using a direct quotation as the target of his attack, Orwell would not be able to make his point so clearly.

Power

Quote to demonstrate the power you have at your fingertips, but only to the extent that you will use the quotation. A carefully integrated quotation will show the reader that you have become comfortably familiar with the sources you have used. Your work will then illustrate your power to cut through trivial details to find the point that demands attention.

Example   Orwell next quotes Professor Lancelot Hogben and then analyzes his words in detail. Here is the original quotation: "Above all, we cannot play ducks and drakes with a native battery of idioms which prescribes such egregious collocations of vocables as the basic *put up with* for *tolerate* or *put at a loss* for *bewilder*."

Orwell is scornful of the language used in this passage. He writes, "Professor Hogben . . . plays ducks and drakes with a battery which is able to write prescriptions, and, while disapproving of the everyday phrase *put up with*, is unwilling to look *egregious* up in the dictionary and see what it means."[†]

Eloquence

Quote rather than paraphrase when no rewording could ever hope to recapture the obvious eloquence of the original writer. Bear in mind that these instances are rare. Orwell uses the following verse from *Ecclesiastes* to demonstrate the stark power of language that cannot be easily modified or paraphrased:

Example   "I returned and saw under the sun, that the race is not to the swift, nor the battle to the strong, neither yet bread to the wise, nor yet riches to men of understanding, nor yet favour to men of skill; but time and chance happeneth to them all."

Orwell's use of this quotation demonstrates the simplicity and concreteness of the language of the Bible in contrast to modern abstract language.

Begging, Borrowing, and Stealing

In order to avoid accusations of theft, a writer, when quoting, must acknowledge a debt to a source. Don't interpret this to mean that you must quote whenever you borrow. When you paraphrase or when you make reference to an idea, you will also admit your indebtedness. Quote only when it is rhetorically the best tactic: that is, when it adds credibility, power, or eloquence.

---

* † *Politics and the English Language*, by George Orwell (Copyright © George Orwell, 1946). Reprinted by permission of Bill Hamilton as the Literary Executor of the Estate of the Late Sonia Brownell Orwell and Secker & Warburg Ltd.

Excerpts from "Politics and the English Language" by George Orwell, copyright 1946 by Sonia Brownell Orwell and renewed 1974 by Sonia Orwell, reprinted from his volume SHOOTING AN ELEPHANT AND OTHER ESSAYS by permission of Harcourt, Inc.

Technically, you have not stolen an idea as long as you document its original occurrence. Failure to acknowledge a source is illegitimate borrowing, or plagiarism.

Legitimate borrowing takes place when a writer makes sparing use of some source material by fitting it carefully in the body of his or her essay, and quoting it without altering it or distorting it in a way that would upset the author.

Avoid borrowing quotations in such a way that the original meaning is changed or even contradicted. The classic example of this shifty tactic is the movie review cited in an advertisement. It may read, for example, "stunning . . . amazing . . . not to be believed," when what the reviewer really said was, "A work stunning in its ignorance, amazing in its clumsy handling of the script, and not to be believed when its advertising describes it as the movie of the year."

The Fit, Function, and Form of Quotations

The quoted material must fit. It must relate directly to the point under discussion, and it must say something significant. Although quoting often seems like a form of pedantic name-dropping, that is not its rightful purpose.

The function of the quotation is usually to illustrate a point that you have already made in your own words. Bringing in an authority on the subject does not, after all, prove anything; it simply shows your awareness of the position of the experts, whether they are on your side or against you.

The form of the quotation is often the most difficult part of essay writing for the novice. Wherever possible, weave borrowed material unobtrusively into the body of your paper, rather than simply tacking it on.

Tacking Quotations On

While it may be a relief to stop writing and turn over the responsibility for illustrating your thesis to an authority, proceed with caution. Stopping in the midst of a sentence to introduce someone else (usually with a grand and unnecessary flourish) will diminish your own authority as a writer.

When you quote, you must remain on the scene, controlling the situation, rather than giving the floor to someone else. Remember, at all times, that the essay is *your* work. When you quote, do not withdraw completely as if another speaker has been hired to do the job for you.

If you have been in the habit of employing long quotations from your source material, try this experiment with one of your past essays. Read the material through quickly. Do you find yourself skimming over the quoted material, or worse, skipping it altogether? Imagine what effect this kind of reading will have on an essay that depends heavily on outside to make its case. Readers are interested in what you have to say; the quotations are support, not the main structure of the essay.

Weaving In Quotations

Wherever possible, make quoted material part of your own sentence structure. This tactic is more difficult, but it is worth the extra effort. First, it will ensure that your reader cannot so easily skip those sections of the paper. Second, it will probably force you to cut quoted material down to the bare essentials, to look at it more closely, and to think of its direct relation to your own thought. Note that documentation issues are not considered here for the moment, though if you were using quotations in APA, you would need author, date, and page number. In MLA, you would need author and page number only.

Example   Orwell uses a quotation here to show how tired many common expressions are.

> *By this morning's post I have received a pamphlet dealing with conditions in Germany. The author tells me that he 'felt impelled' to write it. I open it at random, and here is almost the first sentence that I see: '[The Allies] have an opportunity not only of achieving a radical transformation of Germany's social and political structure in such a way as to avoid a nationalistic reaction in Germany itself, but at the same time of laying the foundations of a co-operative and unified Europe.' You see, he 'feels impelled' to write—feels, presumably, that he has something new to say—and yet his words, like cavalry horses answering the bugle, group themselves automatically into the familiar dreary pattern. This invasion of one's mind by ready-made phrases (lay the foundations, achieve a radical transformation) can only be prevented if one is constantly on guard against them, and every such phrase anaesthetizes a portion of one's brain.**

To make this technique work to its fullest advantage, there are some rules to keep in mind.

1. Use an ellipsis (. . .) to indicate words that have been left out. But never use ellipses in a way that misrepresents the original. Ellipses are permissible only when you are making cosmetic changes (such as omitting a connective structure that would not make sense out of context). Keep in mind that you do *not* need ellipses at the start of a quotation, even if you did not include the beginning of a sentence in what you quoted, and remember that four dots are used when the omitted words come between two sentences. In other cases, only three dots are necessary.

Here is the original:

Example   Political language—and with variations this is true of all political parties, from Conservatives to Anarchists—is designed to make lies sound truthful and murder respectable, and to give an appearance of solidity to pure wind.†

Your version might read this way instead:

> "Political language . . . is designed to make lies sound truthful and murder respectable. . . . "

---

2. Use square brackets to indicate words that you have added. Usually, you will need these square brackets only to indicate small cosmetic changes (such as changing a pronoun to a noun or changing a verb tense to make it consistent with the rest of the verbs in your sentence). Occasionally, you may need square brackets to add a word or two to clarify the context of the quotation.

Here is the original:

Words of this kind are often used in a consciously dishonest way.* **Example**

For the sake of precision, you might alter Orwell's paragraph by adding some words to make your meaning clear without the need of quoting the whole passage.
Yours would look like this:

"Words [with no agreed-upon definition] are often used in a consciously dishonest way."

It is important here to note that Orwell's original meaning has not been tampered with.

3. When you use a complete sentence to introduce a quotation, follow it with a colon. Otherwise, use a comma or whatever punctuation you would use if the quotation marks were not there.

Orwell argues that euphemism is partly responsible for horrendous political action and should be carefully avoided:

Consider for instance some comfortable English professor defending Russian totalitarianism. He cannot say outright, 'I believe in killing off your opponents when you can get good results by doing so.' Probably, therefore, he will say something like this: 'While freely conceding that the Soviet régime exhibits certain features which the humanitarian may be inclined to deplore, we must, I think, agree that a certain curtailment of the right to political opposition is an unavoidable concomitant of transitional periods, and that the rigors which the Russian people have been called upon to undergo have been amply justified in the sphere of concrete achievement.†

4. Make the terminal punctuation of the quoted material serve your purposes, rather than those of the original. In other words, if the quotation appears at the end of your sentence, close it with punctuation that suits your own sentence, even if other punctuation was used originally. This advice applies only if it is clear that you are quoting selectively and hence do not need to indicate missing words by ellipsis.

---

* † *Politics and the English Language*, by George Orwell (Copyright © George Orwell, 1946). Reprinted by permission of Bill Hamilton as the Literary Executor of the Estate of the Late Sonia Brownell Orwell and Secker & Warburg Ltd.

Excerpts from "Politics and the English Language" by George Orwell, copyright 1946 by Sonia Brownell Orwell and renewed 1974 by Sonia Orwell, reprinted from his volume SHOOTING AN ELEPHANT AND OTHER ESSAYS by permission of Harcourt, Inc.

Orwell's cure for overuse of negatives is memorizing the sentence "A not unblack dog was chasing a not unsmall rabbit across a not ungreen field," a remedy which is likely to cure even the worst offenders.

5. Quote exactly. Do *not* distort a quotation, accidentally or deliberately. The first offence is carelessness, the second fraud. If you detect an error of spelling or grammar in the original, you may tell your reader that it is not your mistake by following it immediately with the word [*sic*] (italicize or underline, and set in square brackets as shown). This notation will tell the reader that the fault is not yours.

Example   Orwell does this in the passage that quotes Harold Laski, also used above:

> *"I am not, indeed, sure whether it is not true to say that the Milton who once seemed not unlike a seventeenth-century Shelley had not become, out of an experience ever more bitter in each year, more alien [sic] to the founder of that Jesuit sect which nothing could induce him to tolerate."**

6. Use single quotation marks for a quotation within a quotation.

Orwell does this in one of the preceding examples, repeated here for ease of reference:

> By this morning's post I have received a pamphlet dealing with conditions in Germany. The author tells me that he 'felt impelled' to write it. I open it at random, and here is almost the first sentence that I see: '[The Allies] have an opportunity not only of achieving a radical transformation of Germany's social and political structure in such a way as to avoid a nationalistic reaction in Germany itself, but at the same time of laying the foundations of a co-operative and unified Europe.' You see, he 'feels impelled' to write—feels, presumably, that he has something new to say—and yet his words, like cavalry horses answering the bugle, group themselves automatically into the familiar dreary pattern. This invasion of one's mind by ready-made phrases (lay the foundations, achieve a radical transformation) can only be prevented if one is constantly on guard against them, and every such phrase anaesthetizes a portion of one's brain.†

Note, however, that in an essay, a quotation of this length would appear without the outer marks and would be indented as a block quotation. See Chapter 22 for more details on layout.

7. When writing an academic essay, indent passages of prose that are longer than four lines and passages of poetry longer than two lines. When you indent, quotation marks are no longer necessary.

---

*† *Politics and the English Language*, by George Orwell (Copyright © George Orwell, 1946). Reprinted by permission of Bill Hamilton as the Literary Executor of the Estate of the Late Sonia Brownell Orwell and Secker & Warburg Ltd.

Excerpts from "Politics and the English Language" by George Orwell, copyright 1946 by Sonia Brownell Orwell and renewed 1974 by Sonia Orwell, reprinted from his volume SHOOTING AN ELEPHANT AND OTHER ESSAYS by permission of Harcourt, Inc.

Orwell writes "Politics and the English Language" as a call to action to eliminate inaccurate and misleading language. He concedes that the movement is
ambitious:

> *One cannot change this all in a moment, but one can at least change one's own*
> *habits, and from time to time one can even, if one jeers loudly enough, send*
> *some worn-out and useless phrase—some jackboot, Achilles' heel, hotbed,*
> *melting pot, acid test, veritable inferno, or other lump of verbal refuse—into the*
> *dust-bin where it belongs.**

8. When you have gone to the trouble to obtain a source, use it. Explain it, remark on
   its significance, analyze it, do something to show what it contributes to the whole
   paper. Don't assume its importance is self-evident.

You might elaborate on the last quotation, for example, by saying something
like this:

Orwell clearly believes that language influences thought as much as thought influences language or perhaps more; hence, it is vital that we take responsibility for our
habits of language and make our best efforts to say what we mean without subter-
fuge or vagueness.

9. Use quotations sparingly. The essay is meant primarily to present your views on
   a given subject. That said, quotations are a vital part of any literature essay where
   they are primary sources that carry a great deal of authority. In other disciplines,
   they need to be used less because exact words are not as important as your
   words, most of the time.
10. Make sure you use quotations to make a point. Do so by "unpacking" them for
    the reader; that is, taking them apart in such a way as to make the progression
    of your thought and your reason for quoting them in the first place clear to your
    reader.

Orwell is a master of this technique to ensure clarity. To illustrate meaningless
words, he uses the following hypothetical example:

> *"When one critic writes, 'The outstanding feature of Mr. X's work is its living*
> *quality,' while another writes, 'The immediately striking thing about Mr. X's work*
> *is its peculiar deadness,' the reader accepts this as a simple difference of*
> *opinion."†*

---

*† *Politics and the English Language*, by George Orwell (Copyright © George Orwell, 1946). Reprinted by
permission of Bill Hamilton as the Literary Executor of the Estate of the Late Sonia Brownell Orwell and
Secker & Warburg Ltd.

Excerpts from "Politics and the English Language" by George Orwell, copyright 1946 by Sonia Brownell
Orwell and renewed 1974 by Sonia Orwell, reprinted from his volume SHOOTING AN ELEPHANT AND
OTHER ESSAYS by permission of Harcourt, Inc.

To make it clear what he means, Orwell elaborates:

> *"If words like black and white were involved, instead of the jargon words dead and living, he would see at once that language was being used in an improper way."**

Being able to make the point you want in your own words makes the value of the quotation and your meaningful use of it clear to your reader.

Avoid "Accidental" Plagiarism

Academic integrity demands a knowledge of how to use sources honestly and accurately. Charges of plagiarism may still be incurred even if the incidence was not deliberate. It is your responsibility to make sure that sources are properly accounted for. There are a number of ways problems may arise. Make sure that you do not inadvertently use materials in these ways.

List your sources even in your rough notes.

> Chronic illness related to arthritis, cardiovascular disease, cancer, diabetes, and lung diseases is by far the leading cause of mortality, accounting for 60% of all deaths worldwide.

If no source is named here, the reader is bound to ask, "How do you know?" Granted, this is a paraphrase, but even those must be acknowledged accurately to avoid charges of plagiarism.

> Chronic illness related to arthritis, cardiovascular disease, cancer, diabetes, and lung diseases is by far the leading cause of mortality, accounting for 60% of all deaths worldwide (World Health Organization, 2006).

Change the wording of your sources as completely as you can, by mastering the art of paraphrase. Use quotation marks around phrases that are cited exactly as they appear in the source.

> Bevis and Watson (1989) argue the development of nursing curriculum not only influences the type and quality of graduates but also influences the way nurses view their work.

This use of paraphrase suggests that exact words were not used, but a glance at the source reveals that the words are actually exactly repeated from it. Here is what the reference should look like:

> The development of nursing curriculum "not only influences the type and quality of graduates but also influences the way nurses view their work" (Bevis & Watson, 1989, p. 110).

---

* *Politics and the English Language*, by George Orwell (Copyright © George Orwell, 1946). Reprinted by permission of Bill Hamilton as the Literary Executor of the Estate of the Late Sonia Brownell Orwell and Secker & Warburg Ltd.

Excerpts from "Politics and the English Language" by George Orwell, copyright 1946 by Sonia Brownell Orwell and renewed 1974 by Sonia Orwell, reprinted from his volume SHOOTING AN ELEPHANT AND OTHER ESSAYS by permission of Harcourt, Inc.

Indeed, given that the materials used could be easily paraphrased, it is better to avoid the quotation altogether and write this instead:

> The development of nursing curriculum has an impact on the kind of graduates produced, their abilities, and their perspective on nursing as a profession (Bevis & Watson, 1989).

Take care to treat your sources with respect.

CHAPTER 8 EXERCISES

1. Look at the example below and explain how the writer uses the sources to support her argument:

   Attempts to accept "mosaic" concepts of different cultures often lead to failure, it seems, if only because some aspects of the immigrant culture are not truly accepted; others are condemned immediately as not compatible with North American notions of equality and democracy. Take, for example, the treatment of women in many minority cultures. Many argue that the goals of multiculturalism and feminism are doomed to clash. Susan Muller Okin, for instance, argues that "many culturally based customs aim to control women and neuter them, especially sexually and reproductively, servile in men's desires and interest" (1999). Okin then proceeds to cite a number of practices considered abhorrent in North American culture, and certainly counter to women's rights. These include clitoridectomy, polygamy, the forced marriage of girl children to men selected by their families, and the forced marriage of women to their rapists, practices that continue today in many parts of the world. Unlike some cultural practices, these unenlightened practices nullify human rights. Still, it is often the pattern of governments not to intervene in some of these customs, in the name of multiculturalism.

2. Use the following quotations in paragraphs that you devise. In each case, quote only a few words, not a complete sentence. Make sure to weave the quotation neatly into your sentence structure:
   a. "The voyage of discovery is not in seeing new landscapes but in having new eyes."—*Marcel Proust*
   b. "The unexamined life is not worth living."—*Socrates*
   c. "I object to violence because when it appears to do good, the good is only temporary; the evil it does is permanent."—*Mahatma Gandhi*
   d. "All successful newspapers are ceaselessly querulous and bellicose. They never defend anyone or anything if they can help it; if the job is forced on them, they tackle it by denouncing someone or something else."—*H.L. Mencken*
   e. "Children don't read to find their identity, to free themselves from guilt, to quench the thirst for rebellion or to get rid of alienation. They have no use for psychology. . . . They still believe in God, the family, angels, devils, witches, goblins, logic, clarity, punctuation, and other such obsolete stuff. . . . When a book is boring, they yawn openly. They don't expect their writer to redeem humanity, but leave to adults such childish illusions."—*Isaac Bashevis Singer*
   f. "Politics is the skilled use of blunt objects."—*Lester Pearson*
   g. "A little sincerity is a dangerous thing, and a great deal of it is absolutely fatal."—*Oscar Wilde*

    h. "Human beings have an inalienable right to invent themselves; when that right is pre-empted it is called brain-washing."—*Germaine Greer*

3. Find quotations that you can use as part of paragraphs on each of the following topics:
    a. identity
    b. guilt
    c. marriage
    d. responsibility
    e. creativity
    f. Canada
    g. death
    h. sex

CHAPTER 9
The Research Essay

I write in order to attain that feeling of tension relieved and function achieved which a cow enjoys on giving milk.
—H. L. MENCKEN

In this chapter:

- How to develop your research topic
- How to make an outline of your materials
- How to write a rough draft from your research

A research paper is a formal essay based on your exploration of other people's ideas, rather than simply an analysis of your own thoughts. Although both the expository essay and the argumentative or persuasive essay may use source material to some extent, the research essay is unique. Its purpose is to formulate a thesis based on a survey and assessment of source material.

The following steps are essential to the development of a research paper:

1. Mapping out the area of exploration
2. Drawing up an outline
3. Recording source material
4. Writing and documenting your essay
5. Maintaining control

The Role of the Research Paper

A research paper must be modified to suit its readers and its special aims.

AUDIENCE: an informed, curious reader whom you address on a professional level

PURPOSE: to demonstrate your skill in exploring, evaluating, and recording source material in a manner that shows how you have synthesized it

Mapping Out the Area of Exploration

Before you begin to explore the library, you must find a subject area that is appropriate for investigation. A good research topic will have the following characteristics:

1. SCOPE.

Your subject should be neither too broad nor too narrow in its focus.

> sleep—too broad
>
> why we sleep—not enough research material available
>
> what we now know about sleep and sleep disorders—more focused

2. SUPPORT.

Your subject must be treated in written sources that are available to you. For example, a recent subject may not be a good choice because there may not yet be enough written about it. Also, remember that your sources must be treated objectively, so that the final paper reflects what is known about a subject, rather than just what you believe to be true about a subject. For example, your discussion of sleep must attempt to integrate the reader's questions about sleep with what advances the research has made.

You can also find support for your arguments by conducting a search of Internet resources. Remember, though, that the Internet is best used as a supplement to your use of written sources. Over-reliance on the Internet may lead to a bibliography that is current but that does not take into account the history of your subject matter. Also, the Internet, as an unregulated source of information, does not always provide you with the landmark studies in a particular field. Don't assume that everything you need to know is online.

3. SIGNIFICANCE.

Find something that you want to explore and that needs exploration. It would not, for instance, be enough to announce that you were going to show what new under-standing scientists have reached in the study of brain chemicals affecting sleep. You must explain how these chemicals operate.

Drawing up an Outline

An outline for a research essay takes its direction from your preparatory reading. Follow the instructions in Chapter 4 on how to design an outline with these precautions in mind:

1. Your outline must be flexible enough to accommodate all the information pertinent to your thesis statement.
2. Your outline must be fair and must reflect an objective approach to the material.
3. Your outline must be firmly established in your mind so that you do not attempt to include more material than can be adequately handled within the limits of the assignment.
4. Your outline is designed to be used. In the case of a research essay, the outline dictates the direction of your note-taking. It should help you stay on track in your explorations and help you limit yourself to what is possible.

Recording Source Material

Like an explorer, you must accurately record the steps of your journey. You need a system. Here are some suggestions to simplify the task:

1. Take notes on large index cards (10.2 cm × 15.2 cm [4" × 6"] should do) or keep track electronically.
2. Identify the source on each card as briefly as possible. Usually, a last name and a page number will do.
3. Quote or paraphrase as the occasion demands (remember that too much quotation is dull). In addition, paraphrasing as you read will help you make sense of the material.
4. Limit yourself generally to one note per card to make sorting easier. This tactic will keep you from unconsciously relying too heavily on any one source. If you keep track electronically, keep track of your reliance on any one source as you copy and paste items into your essay (or paraphrase them, acknowledging as you go, of course).
5. Sort through your material at intervals to decide where it will fit into your working outline. If it won't fit, revise the outline or throw the irrelevant information out—no matter how attractive it is.
6. Copy accurately. If a printed passage is very lengthy, photocopy it to ensure precision, but be aware of copyright laws. For an electronic source, make sure the material you paste in cannot be confused with your own words or thoughts. There are severe penalties of plagiarism, intended or accidental.

WHY BOTHER? Note-taking is such a painful chore that it is tempting not to do it. Don't succumb to the temptation. Note-taking is an essential part of research. It will help you determine the value of your sources. Ask these questions as you take notes:

1. Are the sources reliable?
2. Are they recent?
3. Are the sources themselves respected and well reviewed by others?
4. What are your own reactions to the sources?

This last point shows the need to record your own reactions to source material as you proceed. Add these ideas to your note cards to help you develop ideas later. You can differentiate them from source material by adding your initials.

Remember, the object of research is not to record facts, but to evaluate and synthesize your findings about an unsettled matter according to the viewpoint or thesis of your paper.

Writing and Documenting Your Essay

Prepare an outline, complete with intended patterns of argument, as suggested in Chapters 4 and 6 of this text. Then, write the first draft of your essay's introduction, body, and conclusion. This time, however, you must make sure to acknowledge your debt to any source as you write. One good way to do so is to include an abbreviated version of the source in parentheses immediately following the quoted matter in your essay.

Example   Ward Churchill, for example, writes about the disservice done to Native Americans who are obliged to tolerate the trivialization of their heritage, when confronted by names of sports teams like the "Braves," the "Chiefs," or the "Indians." He dismisses the view that these names and symbolic representations are just harmless and argues instead that they are offensive to the people in question. Just as we would not tolerate "nicknames" used in a trivial way for other groups, so we should not accept sports' appropriation of these names to mere games. The names are important, and they demonstrate a level of injustice that cuts deep in North American culture. As Churchill claims, indigenous groups "have the right to expect—indeed, to demand— . . . that such practices finally be brought to a halt" (1993, p. 43).

This example shows abbreviation in the APA style of documentation. It is also an example of the benefits of good preliminary note-taking.

For more information on documentation in MLA, APA, and traditional footnote style, see Chapter 23.

Maintaining Control

The special challenge of the research paper is to handle your source material in a controlled way. To control your research paper, remember these guidelines:

1. KEEP IT LIMITED.
Qualify the aim of your essay and stay within the limits of the thesis and the assignment.

2. KEEP IT CONCISE.
Avoid pretentious diction. (See Chapter 3 for more information.)

3. KEEP IT FORMAL.
This suggestion may even mean that you should not use the pronoun "I," in order to maintain objectivity (although it is often acceptable to do so). Ask your instructor for specific advice on this point.

4. KEEP IT CLEAN.
Small errors reduce the essay's credibility as an accurate record of research.

5. MAKE IT YOURS.
Don't lose yourself in assembled bits of research. Assimilate the material. Learn from it. What you include and how you use it determine your success as a researcher. Passing off information as your own constitutes plagiarism. Whether intentional or not, it is a serious academic offence to be avoided at all costs.

6. AVOID PLAGIARISM.

- Distinguish between a paraphrase and an exact quotation as you make notes, to avoid using instances of exact wording without acknowledging the source.
- Make sure to list sources and to present materials in differing fonts as you copy and paste from the Internet.

- Be sure to acknowledge someone else's wording.
- Be sure to acknowledge someone else's thinking.
- Be sure to acknowledge the source of any facts that are not unarguably public knowledge.
- Keep separate your ideas, your notes on others' ideas, and exact words and phrases that you borrow.
- Don't hand in the same work in two different courses. Doing this may result in failing the assignment or the entire course.
- Check with your instructor when in doubt.

Sample Research Essay—APA Style

The following is a sample research essay whose format conforms to the new APA guidelines. Study it carefully, noting the format and the method of documentation.

Use abbreviated title as page header throughout essay.

Running head: SH*T HAPPENS

1

Number all pages in the top right corner of the page.

Sh*t Happens

Daniel Rosenfield

Technology and Society, Arts and Science 3B03

Professor K. Garay

Courtesy of Daniel Rosenfield

2.5 cm

Sh*t Happens

The title of the paper should be typed at the top of this page, below the page header, centred, and double-spaced.

Despite the invention of a plethora of technologies over the past 2500 years, few have stood out as much as modern sanitation techniques as having the most significant influence for the largest number of people. Modern sanitation techniques have allowed human beings to live in large groups together, without succumbing to the threats of disease and death that accompany improperly disposed human excrements. Throughout this paper, the terms "sanitation techniques/technologies" refer to items such as toilets, pipes, sewer systems, and other systems that facilitate proper sanitation.[1] The history of sanitation and human cleanliness is not all progress; rather, sanitation technologies have also created many social divides, fostering the formation of social barriers and inequalities. Various case studies will show the benefits and drawbacks of various sanitation technologies, from Roman aqueducts to modern piping. Concluding illustrations will reveal that the challenges of the past are still present today, especially in underdeveloped nations where a lack of proper sanitation is severely impeding development.

The first forms of organized sanitation were created by the Romans, who possessed a very sophisticated system of aqueducts and bathhouses (Stephens, 1967). Roman designers had the foresight to try to minimize unsanitary conditions in both public areas and private homes, as hygiene was taken very seriously. As Roman architect Vitruvius (1999) explains in his chapter on city planning:

Indent long quotations 1.3 cm or five spaces.

> In the case of the walls these will be the main points: First, the choice of the most healthy site. Now this will be high and free from clouds and frost, with an aspect neither hot nor cold but temperate. In this way a marshy neighborhood will be avoided. For when the morning breezes blow towards the town at sunrise, as they bring with them mists from the marshes and, mingled with the mist, the poisonous breath of the creatures of the marshes [i.e., microorganisms], to be wafted into the bodies of the inhabitants, they will make the site unhealthy (p. 25).

2.5 cm

Courtesy of Daniel Rosenfield

SH*T HAPPENS   3

Despite not having advanced scientific knowledge, Vitruvius was still aware of the problems that stagnant water could cause, and thus advocated that cities not be built in "marshy" areas. He was worried about "creatures of the marshes," what we know today as disease-causing microorganisms (McDaniel, 1997).

Roman sanitation was made possible through the advent of aqueducts, which provided Roman cities with a near constant supply of clean water. Frontinus, the Water Commissioner for the Romans, recognized that clean water would be necessary for health when he said "my office . . . concerns not only the usefulness of such a system [aqueducts], but also the very health and safety of Rome" (McDaniel, 1997, par 5). With a constant supply of water, latrines were made viable, and were commonplace in bath complexes and the homes of the wealthy (Small, 1974).

Since most of the water was directed to locations dictated by the rich, the majority of Romans did not have access to bathing facilities. Thus, while the Patricians (elite and upper class Romans) were clean and lived in sanitary environments, these same conditions did not trickle down to the Plebeians (general Roman population). Although little research has been done on the hygienic conditions of the general population, records suggest that the life span of the average Roman was approximately 20–35 years, thus indicating that despite an emphasis on sanitary techniques, there were no tangible health benefits in terms of life expectancy (Langner, 1998; Parsche, 1991).[2] Nevertheless, experts agree that living conditions for privileged Romans were much higher than the conditions experienced by those without access to proper sanitation (McLaughlin, 1971; Small, 1974).

According to historical records, the Romans were the first civilization to create an organized infrastructure for bringing fresh water to cities. This infrastructure, coupled with their emphasis on cleanliness, undoubtedly facilitated the advancement of their civilization since they did not have to occupy themselves with fighting off many diseases and/or repercussions that resulted from filth, including vermin, rats, and cholera. According to McLaughlin (1971), "the Romans were clean mainly because

SH*T HAPPENS   4

they set great value on public and collective life: if a man is going to spend most

of his time talking, debating, working . . . he can do this with more grace and less

distraction if the smell and appearance of his face and body do not offend his neigh-

bors" (p. 10). In essence, since the Romans were concerned with almost Epicurean

values, surrounding the here and now, proper sanitation was a necessity. This is in

direct contrast to the early Christians, who were much more focused on the afterlife,

and thus placed sanitation and cleanliness as a distant priority.[3]

   With the decline of Roman civilization and the rise of Christianity, many of

Rome's advances, especially in the field of sanitation, were lost. According to

McLaughlin (1971), "cleanliness and urbanity go together. The Romans were clean

mainly because they set great value on public and collective life. . . . this same

urbanity and interest in social life was anathema to the rising cult of the Christians,

who were firmly convinced that the things of this world were vanities" (p. 11). For

example, St. Benedict pronounced "to those that are well, and especially to the

young, bathing shall seldom be permitted" (McLaughlin, 1971, p. 11). St. Jerome

criticized many of his followers for keeping too clean, and a fourth century pilgrim

to Jerusalem "boasted that she had not washed her face for eighteen years so as

not to disturb the holy water used at her baptism" (McLaughlin, 1971, p. 12). Thus

in earlier Christianity, filth became not only culturally acceptable, but nearly a reli-

gious doctrine. In early Orthodox Judaism however, strict regulations existed around

bathing and cleanliness, and thus "the orthodox Jews who followed these hygienic

laws [stipulated in religious texts] managed to survive plague periods and other epi-

demics" better than the general population (McLaughlin, 1971, p. 6).

   With the fall of the Roman Empire, medieval cities reverted to local wells or

other nearby surface water supplies, and most Roman aqueducts were neglected

and fell into states of disrepair (Small, 1974, p. 104). This occurred for a variety of

reasons, but primarily because there was no organized central authority in medieval

Europe, something characteristic of the Roman Empire. As a result, "there was little

Use the abbre-
viation "p." for
page and "pp."
for pages.

Courtesy of Daniel Rosenfield

SH*T HAPPENS   5

or no co-ordinated activity directed toward the planning of new urban water supplies"

(Forbes, 1950, p. 97). Paris, which became Europe's largest city after the fall of

Rome, built its own aqueducts in the 12th century; however, "the quantities of water

available were far from sufficient to meet the city's requirements" (Small, 1974, p.

105). Throughout the entire middle ages, up until the 16th century, no attempts to

increase the water supply to Paris were made. Estimates suggest that "in 1450,

the public water supply of Paris was equivalent to only one quart per capita per day"

(Small, 1974, p. 105). This lack of water was commonplace across Europe, and

resulted in very poor sanitary conditions for the majority of urban Europeans.

    Medieval London had "at least 13 public latrines and they were all constructed

over streams and rivers" (Hansen, 2004, p. 8). In large groupings of housing, there

was often inadequate sanitation; for example, in 1479, public constables deter-

mined that "57 households within Tower Street, containing 85 people, had only

three privies" (Hansen, 2004, p. 8). Since citizens had nowhere to dispose of their

excrements, dumping of such waste onto city streets was commonplace. Despite a

proclamation from the King in 1347 stating that dumping garbage or human waste in

city streets was prohibited, by the late 14th century, these practices became socially

acceptable once more (Eveleigh, 2002). Ignoring royal decrees regarding sanitation

was somewhat common at the time, as the King attempted to make numerous sani-

tation laws, but they were seldomly obeyed. Medieval society did not place a high

value on sanitation, as laws (and the degree to which they are followed) typically tend

to mimic social values.

    Social stratification was somewhat eliminated during this period, because the

rich and poor dumped their wastes in similar locations: local rivers and streams.

The net result was that the majority of medieval citizens were drinking, cooking, and

cleaning themselves with sewage filled water, and thus outbreaks of cholera and

E.coli were rampant (Stephens, 1967).[4] In addition, the filth that accumulated in the

streets gave rise to another enemy of the medieval citizens—rats. The rats brought

Note that APA uses author/date style.

No page numbers are needed with paraphrase.

Courtesy of Daniel Rosenfield

SH*T HAPPENS   6

the plague, and outbreaks of the plague killed millions of people. The plague has

been referred to as 'the great equalizer,' since both rich and poor people suffered

greatly from its effects (Carmichael, 2003). Since the majority of Europe was preoccu-

pied with coping with the effects of the plague, any existing organized forms of sani-

tation were neglected even further. It is ironic that had medieval Europeans placed

a higher emphasis on cleanliness and sanitation in the first place, the plague would

never have been an issue. However, due to their neglect of adequate sanitation, the

filthy cycle perpetuated itself; the city became sick because it was filthy, and once it

was sick, it became filthier.

Throughout the Enlightenment and Renaissance there were many advancements

in sanitation technology, but true change did not begin until the Industrial Revolution.[5]

Due to the rapidity of industrialization, few cities were prepared for the massive num-

bers of people soon to inhabit them. For example, from 1831 to 1851, London's

population went from 1.5 million to 2.5 million (Small, 1974). As many as 30 people

lived in a single residence, and "one well pump and one privy often served 20 houses

in some areas" (Stephen, 1967, p. 25). This resulted in cholera, typhoid and yellow

fever epidemics which consequently led to high urban mortality rates. In addition, the

overcrowding of European cities encouraged emigration to the United States, and this

resulted in overpopulation in many American cities. Unlike the past, however, govern-

ments began to react and enforce laws to curb the spread of disease and finally

address the root cause of the squalor that plagued cities: the lack of proper sanitation.

In 1795, the first Board of Health was established in Manchester. By the

1830s, a public health and medical service was set up to "cope with the cholera

epidemic of 1831" (Small, 1974, p. 192). Many individual contributions were critical

in bringing sanitation reform to the forefront of public attention, but the work of Sir

Edwin Chadwick was of particular importance. He submitted a report to the House of

Commons in 1842 investigating the sanitary conditions in England, and the results of

his survey led to the creation of the world's first Public Health Act in 1848. Chadwick,

Courtesy of Daniel Rosenfield

the sole author of the report, demonstrated that living conditions were the lowest and mortality rates the highest in poor, working class areas of England (Sram, 1998).[6] The report "went on to describe the unsanitary conditions, and specifically mentioned the lack of potable water supply, the grossly overcrowded living quarters of the factory workers and the poor, the inadequate and defective drains and the unsatisfactory privy and latrine facilities" that were present throughout England (Small, 1974, p. 193). Chadwick's report was a watershed because it was the first government commission to tangibly identify and describe the root of the health problems that had plagued Europe for centuries. In addition, the 1848 Public Health Act incorporated nearly all of his suggestions. This Act, combined with the implementation of proper sewage systems and adequate water supplies in urban settings allowed cities to flourish. The 1848 Public Health Act laid the foundation for many future acts designed to protect the general health of city dwellers. These acts codified, and thus legitimized, proper sanitation, providing the impetus for urban growth. However, despite industrialization and public health acts, conditions for the poor were not alleviated in all cities, or for all people.

Philadelphia offers a counterexample to much of the progress experienced during the Industrial Revolution, as by 1870, Philadelphia had been nicknamed 'Filthydelphia,' due to its deplorable sanitary conditions (Alewitz, 1989). On the exterior, Philadelphia was a prosperous city, building many new roads, schools and industries. However, this image, purported by the rich, masked the truth that industrialization was exacerbating social and economic disparities throughout the city. Even after successful public health endeavours in England were reported to Philadelphia legislators and officials, "politicians refused to cede some of their power to separate and independent public works and health agencies" and thus no public health laws were enacted (Alewitz, 1989, p. 2).

Philadelphia offers a particularly poignant example of how human interests can come between technology and its proliferation. By the late nineteenth century, all

SH*T HAPPENS   8

the technologies were in existence so that nearly a million Philadelphians could live in sanitary conditions, but it was not until the mid-twentieth century that these technologies made their way to the city's poor working class (Alewitz, 1989). One of the primary reasons was politics; many legislators were only concerned with the health of their constituents, or financial interests of big business.[7] Improving sanitation was expensive, and thus many policy makers would only advocate it if it were absolutely necessary. In essence, there was ample public money to finance a profitable industry like transportation; however, funds were scarce for building 'unprofitable' infrastructure, like sewers and piping for the city's poorer areas. This situation is most aptly summed up by Sam Alewitz (1989) who said,

> The most disconcerting aspect of this intolerable situation was not only the lack of needed sanitary services or the lack of activity by the municipal authorities in behalf of sanitary reform; the most frightening was the lack of support and moral indignation of the physicians, engineers, educators, clergy and businessmen, those to whom the people looked for leadership who allowed these unhealthy conditions to exist, relatively unchallenged (p. 4).

Thus, it was not only legislators who were at fault, but nearly every group in the upper classes. However, when sickness and disease began jeopardizing the livelihoods of the wealthy by endangering the working class, legislation finally caught up to the English laws, and social divides (at least along sanitary lines) were minimized.[8] In 1870, the first American board of health was established in Massachusetts (Eveleigh, 2002). This board (and subsequent public health acts), combined with an increase in the understanding of bacterial infections through the research of scientists like Louis Pasteur, solidified the link between sewage, drinking water and disease (Eveleigh, 2002). Thus, policy makers could no longer hide behind a shield of 'ignorance' regarding the negative consequences of unsanitary conditions, and social policies finally began to mimic the new understanding.

SH*T HAPPENS   9

In England, comprehensive sanitary legislation was enacted throughout the nation by the end of the 19th century.[9] Subsequently, by the early 1900s, incidents of cholera, typhoid and yellow fever caused by the contamination of sewage and drinking water were significantly reduced. This resulted in an increase in living conditions for the majority of English citizens, and a dramatically lower infant mortality rate (Lewis, 2002). Today, most cities in industrialized nations have addressed sanitation issues; however, the same cannot be said for cities in the developing world.

Most industrialized cities do not have to worry about the effects of poor sanitation, and outbreaks of E.coli or other sewage related diseases are rare. Although a full examination of how a lack of proper sanitation has affected development is beyond the scope of this paper, around the world, many major urban centers (and nations as a whole) experience the crippling effects due to a lack of proper sanitation infrastructure. Examining sanitation on a global scale, close to 100% of Americans have access to a sewer connection; in Europe, this number is roughly 92%. This is in contrast with approximately 13% of Africans (WHO, 2000). The parallel between cities in developing countries and medieval cities can easily be drawn; the respective development of contemporary cities can only go so far before the health effects brought on by poor sanitation either decimate the population or contribute to disorder in the city. The cycle of filth discussed earlier is prevalent today in these regions, and unfortunately it is difficult to break. Even 'developed' countries are not immune from the effects of unsanitary conditions, as seen most recently in the wake of hurricane Katrina. The people of New Orleans were left without drinking water and adequate sanitation, and immediately, the media was drawing parallels between New Orleans and the third world (Lobe, 2005). As such, more efforts need to be invested into creating appropriate sanitation and water delivery infrastructures in developing countries.

In the past 2500 years, humanity has made tremendous progress in terms of sanitary technologies. The Romans were one of the first cultures to recognize the need for cleanliness; however, early Christianity did not share this value, and throughout the Dark Ages, society regressed. Once people began moving into cities and living in close proximity to one another during the industrial period, the need for proper sanitation techniques became apparent. Despite a significant lag time between urbanization and the first public health acts, legislators eventually realized that providing adequate sanitation was a necessity for all constituents, even the poor, and this was an important step towards leveling social inequalities. However, even today these inequalities continue to exist, as most commonly seen in developing countries. Human progress seems to be linked to the progress of sanitation technologies, and thus hopefully the day will arrive when the technologies developed countries take for granted (toilets, sewer systems and running water) will be commonplace across the globe. Until then, unsanitary conditions will undoubtedly be responsible for retarding the growth of many nations.

Courtesy of Daniel Rosenfield

SH*T HAPPENS   11

References

Note that references may be listed like paragraphs for ease in word processing. Each entry appears as a hanging indent.

Alewitz, S. (1989). *Filthy dirty: A social history of unsanitary Philadelphia in the late nineteenth century*. New York: Garland Publishing.

Carmichael, A. (2003). Plague and more plagues: The black death transformed. *Early Scientific Medicine, 8*(3), 253–66.

Note that all page numbers need to be included in a reference to an article in a periodical.

Eveleigh, D. (2002). *Bogs, baths and basins: The story of domestic sanitation*. London: Sutton Publishing.

Forbes, R. J. (1950). *Man the maker, A history of technology and engineering*. New York: Wolff Book Manufacturing.

Note differences in capitalization of books and periodicals.

Hansen, R. (2004). *Water-related infrastructure in medieval London*. Waterhistory.org. Retrieved from http://www.waterhistory.org/histories/london/london.pdf.

Langner, G. (1998). Estimation of infant mortality and life expectancy in the time of the Roman Empire: A methodological examination. *Historical Social Research, 23*(1–2), 299–326.

Lewis, M. E. (2002). Impact of industrialization: Comparative study of child health in four sites from medieval and postmedieval England (A.D. 850–1859). *American Journal of Physical Anthropology, 119*(3), 211–23.

Lobe, J. (2005). *Katrina exposes the "Third World" at home*. Inter Press Service News Agency. Retrieved from http://www.ipsnews.org/columns.asp?idnews530125.

McDaniel, A. (1997). *Antiqua medicina: Aspects in ancient medicine*. University of Virginia Health System. Retrieved from http://www.healthsystem.virginia.edu/internet/library/historical/artifacts/antiqua/stextb.html.

McLaughlin, T. (1971). *Coprophilia*. London: Cox & Wyman Limited.

Parsche, F., & Zimmermann, P. (1991). Results of computer-assisted studies of population structure and burial practices of adults of the late Roman burial ground in the Minshat Abu Omar (east Nile delta). *American Journal of Physical Anthropology, 49*(1–2), 65–83.

SH*T HAPPENS   12

Small, F. (1974). *The influent and the effluent: The history of urban water supply and sanitation*. Saskatoon: Modern Press.

Sram, I., & Ashton, J. (1998). Millennium report to Sir Edwin Chadwick. *British Medical Journal, 317*(7158), 592–96.

Stephens, J. H. (1967). *Water and waste*. New York: St. Martin's Press.

Vitruvius, M. P. (1999). *Ten books on architecture*. Ingrid D. Rowland & Thomas Noble Howe, (Eds.). (Ingrid D. Rowland, Trans.) Cambridge: Cambridge University Press.

World Health Organization. (2000). *Global water supply and sanitation assessment* 2000 Report. Retrieved from http://www.who.int/docstore/water_sanitation_health/ Globassessment/Global2.htm.

Note that the authors' first names are reduced to initials.

The best source for up-to-the-minute information on Web citation is APA on the Web: <http://www.apa.org>.

Courtesy of Daniel Rosenfield

Endnotes

[1] To narrow the scope of the paper somewhat, I will also only refer to sanitation technologies developed in Western society.

[2] It has also been suspected that due to the heavy use of lead in their plumbing, many Romans experienced lead poisoning, shortening their life spans dramatically. It is ironic that the same technologies that helped advance their culture may be somewhat responsible for its demise.

[3] Not all Romans were clean, in fact, clean living conditions were experienced primarily by the rich. Roughly 90% of the Roman population lived in 'slums', areas highly conducive to typhoid and cholera. However, the important difference is that these Romans did not choose to live this way because of religious or cultural beliefs, but rather due to poverty.

[4] I will not delve into the health effects of E.coli, typhoid and cholera, but they typically entail violent diarrhea and rapid dehydration, resulting in death, if untreated. Further symptoms can be found searching an encyclopedia.

[5] I do not mean to gloss over an important period of history (enlightenment and renaissance), but during these periods, only minor sanitary advancements were made, and are outside the scope of this paper. They include, but are not limited to, advancing medical (and scientific) knowledge, and an increasing awareness that unsanitary conditions cause disease.

[6] Sir Chadwick was the sole author because "other commissioners thought the contents of the report were too radical and controversial" (Small, 1974, 193).

[7] I am reminded of the actions of Robert Moses, as described in *The Artifacts of Politics*. Moses' political goals were advanced via technology, and this parallel can be drawn in Philadelphia, as many legislators wanted to protect the rich, by not giving the poor adequate sanitation, the same way Moses prevented the poor from coming to wealthier areas by designing low bridges.

SH*T HAPPENS   14

[8] Legislators finally acted to remedy sewage related disease in 1888/89, when close to 800 people died of typhoid, and Philadelphia had the highest typhoid prevalence and mortality rate in the nation. This was hurting Philadelphia's image on a national scale, and thus many have argued that legislators acted to improve their image, not to improve the lives of their poorer constituents (Small, 1974). Sanitation legislation was enacted at a wide variety of times in each individual city throughout the industrial revolution. I by no means wish to present America as lagging behind the English; however, most American cities enacted sanitary legislation later than their English counterpart.

Part Four

DRAFTING THE ESSAY

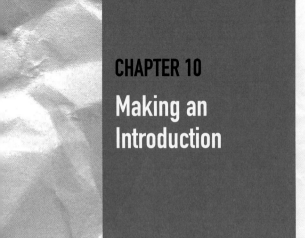

CHAPTER 10
Making an Introduction

The last thing we decide in writing a book is what to put first.
—BLAISE PASCAL

In this chapter:

- How to introduce your essay effectively
- How to engage your reader
- How to develop the background to the subject of your essay

Introductions are often the most challenging part of the essay to write, and students sometimes write the final version of the introduction only after they have completed everything else. There are a number of strategies you can use to introduce an essay that may help you overcome insecurity about where to start. Here are a few things you might try:

Ice-Breaking: Tactics for Opening the Essay

If you are at a loss for words when writing your introduction, try one of the strategies in the following list. Suppose, for example, that your essay topic is "health hazards in the environment caused by humans."

1. TAKE THE STRAIGHT AND NARROW PATH.
State your thesis bluntly and without preamble. Follow it with a brief statement of the steps in your argument.

Example It is our fundamental human right to live in a healthy environment. For this to happen, we must protect the environment from health hazards caused by humans.

2. TRY SHOCK TREATMENT.
Give your reader a striking, perhaps shocking, example, statistic, or statement to get him or her interested in reading further.

Example One-year-old Diane Fowler woke up in the middle of the night in the midst of a convulsion. Her temperature was dangerously high. She was rushed to the Hospital for Sick Children in Toronto, where she was diagnosed as suffering from lead poisoning.

Soon after, five more members of Diane's family were diagnosed as having lead poisoning. Within two years, a large group of citizens, all living near a Toronto-based lead plant, were found to have elevated levels of lead in their blood.

3. ENGAGE YOUR READER.

Remind the reader that the subject under discussion matters to him or her by showing its general importance, before you settle down to your specific line of argument.

While some people think that environmental health hazards affect only those who work in risky occupations or who live in certain neighbourhoods, it is clear that the problem is more widespread than that. Everyone's life is endangered. Lead, for example, is in the water we drink, the air we breathe, and the food we eat. For Canadians, the likelihood of exposure to serious environmental hazard is now 100 percent, and even low-level exposure to substances like lead can cause serious health problems.

Example

4. OPEN WITH A QUOTATION.

> *Someone said: 'The dead writers are remote from us because we* know *so much more than they did.' Precisely, and they are that which we know."*
>
> —T.S. Eliot, "Tradition and the Individual Talent"

As Eliot makes clear, the study of the literature of past cultures should never be considered too remote to be relevant; it is, in fact, the foundation on which we stand as readers in the present day. Students of literature need to study the works of the past as well as contemporary material in order to arrive at a knowledge of literature as a discipline.

This approach will be appropriate in a literary essay, especially if you quote from the primary source or from a critic who says something pithy that relates to your essay. Be careful with this tactic, however. Instructors will balk if you use quotations capriciously without showing their relevance to your paper.

5. DEFINE KEY TERMS.

The introduction is an excellent place to establish the terms significant to the paper. Defining your terms at the outset is hence a good way to begin. Don't take this path, however, if you have nothing inventive or imaginative to say. The reader will hope for more than a mere dictionary definition. Use your imagination to avoid banality.

6. SUMMARIZE OPPOSING ARGUMENTS BEFORE SETTLING DOWN TO YOUR THESIS.

This approach does some of the critical groundwork of the essay by establishing what the essay is up against. Showing why the essay is on a provocative subject is key to making it interesting to readers.

A good introduction captures the reader's attention, provides necessary background, and gives some indication of where the rest of the essay is headed.

Here is an example of how this might look:

When Canadian novelist Yann Martel won the Man Booker Prize in October 2002, he thanked his readers for "having met his imagination halfway" ("Joyful"). Indeed, reading a magic-realist fable like *Life of Pi* involves something akin to a leap of faith

Example

for readers, in several ways: first, the story tests the credulity of readers by asking them to embrace a surreal parable; second, the story helps readers have faith in the god of their choice; and third, the story reminds readers that reality is a story we choose, and it is our responsibility, along with the writer, to pick the better story between the two options provided for us.

This introductory paragraph pins down the subject matter of the essay in its first sentence, and in the second sentence demonstrates how the essay will explore that magic realism in a three-part structure that illustrates the relationship between writer and reader.

Beyond simple strategies, you need to consider what is essential to an introduction. Think of your essay, for a moment, as if it were a person. Since an essay will establish some kind of relationship with its readers, the analogy is not altogether far-fetched. Here is some advice on how to proceed after you say "hello."

Strike Up a Conversation

Obviously, writing a formal essay is more complicated than starting a conversation. But the analogy should provide you with a place to start. How should you begin a conversation? You need to make an impression. One way is to startle your listener by presenting an exciting piece of information, as a preview of coming attractions. Or, as a recommendation of the value of the work you have done, you can report the words of a well-known, respected authority in relation to your topic. Another method is to pick a fight, by stating the claims, or defining the terms, of the accepted position and then challenging them. Remember that your first task is to convince your audience to pay heed to what you are saying. What all of these tactics have in common is their ability to provoke a response.

Introductions must take readers by the hand and invite them in. You do not want the introduction, or indeed, the essay, to seem perfunctory. Generally, you should use the introduction to explain the purpose of your paper, its scope, and the point that it intends to make in the thesis. Note, however, that some introductions do not lead to a thesis, but are more open in their assessment of a problem. There is a move towards inquiry that may demand an introduction without a specific thesis statement as its culmination, but your instructor will let you know if that is what is required in your case. Whether open or leading to a thesis statement, an introduction gains the attention of the reader. It may be true that professors are a "captive" audience, but readers should not feel captive; they should be captivated instead. Your introduction should seduce your reader into reading further.

Write with Control

Perhaps the most common pitfall among essay writers in establishing the basis of their arguments is long-windedness. Remember that an introduction should be no longer than about one-fifth of the entire essay's length (the best introductions are short and comprehensive—don't go on). If you find that your introduction demands more space than that, you have not narrowed your topic down to a manageable size, or you should be writing a book instead! Never promise in the introduction more than you can deliver in the paper. The first few lines are the best place to limit the scope of your discussion and state the qualifications of your theories. Maintain control of your material, and have some consideration (if not some pity) for your poor beleaguered reader.

Avoid writing introductions that are too broad in scope. You can't do everything in 1500 words, nor should you try. Here are some examples of the kind of thing to avoid:

> ✗ The advent of the electronic book, as heralded by Stephen King's decision to publish some recent work online rather than via a traditional publisher in book form, indicates that the book, as we know it, is dying. Printed books are becoming a thing of the past, and more and more people are turning to the Internet as the most convenient source of information available.

Example

In this opening paragraph, the author sets out to establish that all books have become redundant now that the Internet is here. This approach does not, however, take into account that roughly 20 percent of North American homes currently have access to the Internet, nor does it consider how much the Internet relies on the form of the book for its own formatting of information. No one essay could take on this entire subject. It would be better to concede that the electronic book is making inroads in our reading habits, rather than to overstate the case.

> ✗ Censorship of any kind is reprehensible. American schools that ban Mark Twain's *Huckleberry Finn* because of its allegedly "racist" language and Canadian schools that ban Margaret Laurence's *The Diviners* are acting against our right to read whatever we want.

Example

This introduction oversimplifies the case that might be made. While it is true that the censorship of some books in schools seems ludicrous, it is difficult out of hand to argue that all censorship is inappropriate. Much will depend on age groups that are reading or accessing materials. Much, too, will depend on the accuracy and the purpose of the materials being circulated. Would hate literature, for example, be acceptable in a world without censorship?

Write with Conviction

To avoid accusations of boredom, make sure that the introduction shows *how* what you have written matters—to you and to anyone concerned with the subject. Convincing readers that a topic is important is not simply a matter of telling them so; you have to show them, by the tone of your writing, that you are deeply engaged with the topic. Write with conviction, with the feeling that what you are saying will make a difference. Don't negate its value by suggesting that the essay's position is only your opinion. Approach the essay as if it were one side of a lively conversation. Because there is some distance between writer and reader, this interchange is not as immediate as that of conversation; remember, however, that there is a reader "at the other end of the line." Imagine your reader's responses as you introduce your material, just as you imagine your friend's face as he or she answers the telephone.

Be Conversant with Your Subject

Your introduction is meant to foster an existing knowledge and interest on the part of the reader. Don't tell the reader what he or she already knows. In the case of a literary essay, for example, there is no need to provide a plot summary. Any reader of such an essay should have that material well in hand. In other disciplines, this advice means avoiding the mere recital of material discussed in class, or the careful delineation of a definition that is neither contentious nor germane to what will follow. Write to communicate.

To avoid sounding pretentious, you must use your own voice and your sense of what is appropriate to the occasion. In the introduction, you must lead the reader into your way of thinking. The introduction must make you and your reader comfortable. To get comfortable with a topic that, three weeks ago, may have been completely unfamiliar to you is part of the task of essay writing. Only when you can *talk* knowledgeably about the subject of your paper are you ready to write about it.

Communicate with Your Reader

If carefully designed, your introduction should tell the reader some essential things about you and your work: that you sincerely wish to communicate; that you are conversant with your subject and have convictions about it; that you are confident, in control, and considerate of your reader. All these words beginning with "con" or "com" suggest the necessity of forming a relationship *with* someone or something. An introduction with these attributes demands attention and commands respect.

CHAPTER 10 EXERCISES

1. Go to a scholarly journal in your own field or to a newspaper or magazine article, and find examples of paragraphs that introduce an essay. Explain how these introductory paragraphs work and evaluate their success in acquainting the reader with what is to come.

2. Write introductory paragraphs, complete with thesis statements, on the following topics:
   a. a goal you would like to accomplish
   b. a movie that made a lasting impression on you
   c. a constant preoccupation
   d. the influence of other people's advice on your life
   e. your relation to your relatives

3. Analyze the opening paragraph of one of your classmates' essays. What introductory techniques are used there? Try making suggestions to rewrite the opening to make it stronger.

4. Locate an introductory paragraph in this or any other textbook. Analyze how an introductory passage has used particular techniques to introduce its subject.

5. Read the following student paragraphs, all of which served as introductions to essays. Analyze the techniques by which they arouse the reader's interest.

   a. Some say that television cannot teach me anything about real life, and that is the reason why I am currently engaged in a staring competition with my set. So far the tube has won best three out of five, but as Dr. Schuller says, "If it's going to be, it's up to me." That TV has to blink sometime. So, while I wait for sweet victory against the naysayers of educational TV, I will set my mind to learning and become a couch potato.

   b. A person whose soul has already been separated from his or her body is still able to experience feelings such as regret, fear, and isolation. This is the belief of over 33% of the world's population—the Muslims. Therefore, Muslims are very gentle with their dead, and the washing and shrouding of the body are done very methodically, leaving no room for error. Because Islam lays significant importance on the existence of the afterlife, its followers are often flabbergasted by the degree of vanity in the burial practices of the West. Since the Islamic code emphasizes simplicity, burial practices are straightforward, with no unnecessary expenses.

   c. Leslie Marmon Silko has found a way to transfer oral Native American stories onto the page. She does this by keeping in her stories many of the conventions of Native American storytelling, especially the unconventional and non-Western form of her work. In her works "Yellow Woman," "Cottonwood Part One: Story of Sun House," and "Cottonwood Part Two: Buffalo Story," Silko maintains the idea that stories are tools for the community. Though she is often not considered among mainstream writers of literature, her use of the oral tradition in her work has led to her popularity as an author who is widely respected by critics and by her own community.

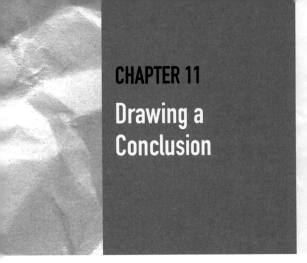

CHAPTER 11

Drawing a Conclusion

Every exit is an entry somewhere else.
—TOM STOPPARD

In this chapter:

- How to sum up your argument
- How to leave your reader satisfied with your argument

Your concluding paragraph is not only your last word on the subject, but also an opportunity for you to reinforce and synthesize the points in your argument. Listed below are four techniques by which you may reinforce your argument in order to end your paper strongly and convincingly. The essay that builds toward a powerful conclusion will not fade out, but will reverberate in the reader's mind. As the diagram of the shape of the essay suggested in Chapter 5, the conclusion moves from the specific case examined back to the general and encourages readers to consider the implications of what has been shown in the paper.

Retrace Your Line of Thought

Retracing does not mean repeating. Since both you and the reader know where you have been, all you need to provide in your conclusion is a reminder of the steps of the journey. You need only mention key words that have gathered meaning as the argument has proceeded in order for the astute reader (the one for whom you have been writing all along) to "catch your drift." Echo for effect, rather than for reiteration.

To remind the reader of the inherent structure of your essay, make certain to restate the thesis statement in a conclusive manner, and in different words from those that you used in the opening. Doing so will enable you to check to see if the essay has really lived up to your expectations of it. Keep in mind that the essay is meant to be a lively, though formal, conversation. A subtle reminder of the point you have made will aid the readers; a word-for-word repetition will annoy them.

Example   One thing is clear: after reading the facts and the statistics related to the increase in diabetes across Canada, among all age groups, one sees the need for greater funding for this disease. As this paper has pointed out, diabetes may well be the third largest killer after heart disease and all types of cancer combined. Such facts show the vital importance of increasing funding for research into the treatment of diabetes.

Refocus Your Argument

Just as a film director may end a scene by changing the camera focus to wide angle or by softening it, so too can the essay take a broader and less stringent view of its subject in its closing.

Widen the focus as you conclude by showing the importance of your topic beyond the immediate concerns of your paper. Beware, however, of writing an overblown conclusion such as "Milton is the world's greatest poet." Instead, include a suggestion for change or perhaps a solution to the problem you have so carefully outlined in the core of the essay. Look at this example, which praises an author, but does so in a way that reinforces the point of the essay that came before:

> In some respects, Martel's *Life of Pi* is the quintessence of Canadian fiction, especially if one sees Canada, as Martel clearly does, as a mosaic rather than as a melting pot, the image typically used of America. As Martel comments, "Canada is very open to other voices. . . . the world is in Canada. It's a country with two official languages but no official culture. So people from all over the world are welcome to come and tell their own stories" ("Ask"). His study of the boy at sea in a lifeboat demonstrates that all creatures from all cultures, everywhere, are in the same boat and must use their imaginations to transcend the ordinary and to tell their own stories of life, with luck, as imaginatively and courageously as Martel's does.

Example

Encourage Response

While the body of your essay requires you to provide answers and to be clear and definite in your thinking and wording, there is *some* room in the conclusion for you to mention tentative ideas, to pose questions, or to offer challenges to the reader. You shouldn't open the floodgates too widely, but it is a good tactic to provoke a response in your reader, provided it is relevant to the topic in question. Beware, though, of starting something you cannot finish, or of introducing a topic that sounds suspiciously like what your essay should have been about.

> Human rights issues demand that we consider others as much as we consider ourselves. Rights are not an individual question: what happens to each one of us has an impact on us all. As Eleanor Holmes Norton writes, "The only way to make sure people you agree with can speak is to support the rights of people you don't agree with." Human rights are fundamentally communal rights, rather than individual matters, even though the issue often rises in relation to specialized individual needs.

Example

Make Your Words Resound

By the time you reach your conclusion, you should feel that no important argument for your thesis statement has been neglected. This attitude of confidence will allow you to end your paper with a bang rather than a whimper (to invoke, or rather invert, the words of T.S. Eliot). Make sure that the tone conveys a sense of finality, a sense that you have done all that can be expected within the precise bounds of your thesis statement. The conclusion should not, of course, make grand claims that your essay cannot substantiate.

Note that the concluding paragraph of an essay reverses the structure of the opening paragraph, where the writer typically moves from the general to the specific. In the conclusion, the paragraph most often moves from the specific points the essay has been making to some generality, often taking a broader view of the subject and opening up other questions for the reader to ponder.

Example   Alice Munro's *The View from Castle Rock* thus continues the exploration of home and of belonging that is so much a part of her work. Finally drawing material from her own personal life and from her own family tree, Munro manages to create for us a profound sense of place, a territorial sense of home that makes us acutely conscious of Huron County and its environs as "Alice Munro country."

Drawing to a Close: Tactics for Ending the Essay

When you come to the end of your essay, consider one of the following ways of formulating a conclusion. Suppose, for instance, that your paper is about the dangers of pollution:

1. DECIDE THAT ENOUGH IS ENOUGH.
If you find you have nothing pressing to add, say nothing. Make sure, however, that your argument ends on a strong note. Don't stop writing just because you are tired.

Example   There is nothing that we do, nothing that we eat or breathe, that does not relate to the state of our planet, and therefore to environmentalism.

2. TAKE THE WIDER VIEW.
Examine some of the broader implications of your thesis and the questions it may have raised.

Example   There are many actions we can make to help preserve the environment. Although some of these solutions may involve giving up a few comforts, we can no longer blame others and do nothing ourselves. The poverty, pollution, and poisoning were caused by all of us and can be eliminated only with everyone's co-operation.

3. REINFORCE YOUR CLAIM.
Remind the reader gently of your line of thought and reiterate your thesis in a slightly different form.

Example   We are all affected by pollution, but just as we are part of the problem, so we can be part of the solution. Remember these guidelines: reduce, reuse, recycle, and rebel. Reduce the use of electricity and fuel. Reuse things, rather than automatically disposing of them. Recycle refillable containers made of glass, paper, and metal. And rebel by encouraging the government to back tougher legislation to protect our environment.

CHAPTER 11 EXERCISES

1. Read and discuss the following conclusions:
   a. Malcolm Gladwell in *Blink* ultimately shows the reader that decision making is often a matter of snap judgment, but the arresting point is that snap judgment does not have a negative impact of the quality of thinking. The only flaw in Gladwell's *Blink* may be the author's own tendency to provide glib anecdote rather than detailed research. But then, that may be part of his point.
   b. In *Guns, Germs, and Steel,* Jared Diamond does more than simply argue that the environment is responsible for historical outcomes. Diamond's use of geographical isolation as one of the key factors in Western dominance does, however, put to rest racist notions of European superiority.
   c. The strongly anti-Petrarchan tradition in Shakespeare's time might seem unduly hard on Petrarch. But at this point it would be wise to remember that it is the conventions that Shakespeare, Donne, and others were mimicking, not Petrarch, nor his poems. Though by the end of the sixteenth century, the Petrarchan worship had decreased somewhat from the time when Ascham commented that "men have in more reverence the *Triumphs* of Petrarch, then the Genesis of Moses" (834), Petrarch was still read and widely admired. It is ever thus in a world where imitation is considered "the sincerest form of flattery," but the imitators are weak, unwise, and unskilled. And in our far-removed modern world of often graphic realism, it is much easier to believe in the real than the ideal, and to laugh in agreement over Shakespeare's startling lines: "Men have died from time to time, and worms have eaten them, but not for love" (*As You Like It*, 4.1.101–02).
   d. In *Frankenstein* the conceptualization of nature with regard to landscape, society, human experience, and behaviour seems, on first analysis, Romantic. That is, for the most part, the novel evokes a pantheistic natural world that elevates emotion and individualism as sources of virtue. However, I would like to posit that the novel contains arguments for restraint and qualification of this concept along lines compatible with Enlightenment thinking. In Mary Shelley's concept of nature, some accommodation of both rationality and natural law is seen as essential to avoid catastrophe. Enlightenment notions of nature remain important reference points, creating a fundamental tension in Shelley's work.
   e. In conclusion, robots have already made a heavy impact on society. Their precision and accuracy has allowed them to create better quality products. Their fast production rates have them a viable choice for businesses to increase their profit, and they are free from almost all human limitations. Since technology is constantly being upgraded, robotics will keep bringing more and more benefits to the society and alleviate more and more problems. Even today, it has become something of a standard for huge businesses to use robots in order to keep up with the competition. The production rate of robots is rising, and it is only a matter of time before it will be completely common to see a robot doing the same job as you. If they can produce better than you, faster than you, and are not affected by your limitations, there is absolutely no reason why a business would want you instead of a robot. This is why the usage of robotics will increase in the future, and will impact society even more than it has today.
   f. Men's recreational leagues should not include women. It is important to separate the sexes in such leagues in order to maintain a fair level of competition and to ensure a relaxed atmosphere.

2. Read the following outlines, and then write a concluding paragraph suitable for each.

a. Thesis statement: Physical exercise has many health benefits.

It helps with weight control.

It increases the strength of your bones and muscles.

It raises your endorphin levels and thus improves your mood.

b. Thesis statement: Credit cards are dangerous to the financial well-being of many consumers.

Consumers are encouraged to buy more than they can afford.

Consumers run up enormous debts at huge interest rates.

Credit card companies increase credit levels to facilitate even greater levels of debt.

c. Thesis statement: Stricter rules are needed to keep impaired drivers off the road.

Many accidents are caused by elderly drivers.

People with bad driving records are currently treated too leniently in the courts and thus tend to be repeat offenders.

The rate of mortality due to traffic accidents has increased every year in Canada for the past ten years.

CHAPTER 12
Writing Paragraphs

We think in generalities, but we live in detail.
—ALFRED NORTH WHITEHEAD

In this chapter:

- How to write strong topic sentences
- How to add support for your topic sentences
- How to keep your paragraphs unified
- How to use transitions logically

Paragraphs are the logical building blocks of an essay. Though an essay may not be, strictly speaking, a work of art, it is a construction based on logic that also offers opportunities for the stylistic arrangement of your material. What follows are some suggestions on how to develop your paragraphs and how to check to see that paragraphing in the final paper is unified and coherent.

A paragraph must be about one thing. This principle of unity should be so clear that you could compose a heading for each paragraph if the assignment demanded it (and some may).

Logical connections within each paragraph must also be clear. Leaps in logic or unstated assumptions are flaws in your argument that will affect the coherence of the final paper and lose your reader's good will.

Each paragraph is a small step in your total argument, meant to lead the reader onward through your thought process. Hence, each small part must contribute to the whole pattern. Remember that each small section of your argument, each paragraph, is in fact a miniature model of the essay structure itself.

The length of paragraphs depends to a large extent on the reader's comfort. It is important to write paragraphs that suit the layout of the page. Too many paragraph breaks lead to choppiness; too few make the reader long for a respite from the flow of words. Let the "look" of the paragraph on the page be a guide.

Each paragraph, like the larger essay, should contain the following elements:

1. a topic sentence that reveals the controlling idea of the paragraph
2. support related to the topic sentence
3. unity of focus
4. a smooth transition to the next paragraph

The controlling idea is key: without it, readers get lost. Consider this example:

Example   ✗ Working out requires discipline. Going to the gym on a snowy morning when your bones ache is always a challenge. Including sports like tennis or golf demand discipline, even if you enjoy them. Team sports, though they provide social activity, also are better when you have the discipline to practise. Success in any kind of sport is dependent on discipline.

Here it is clear that the best expression of the topic is in the final sentence of the paragraph. If it came first, it would provide a clear guideline for the reader of what was to follow. Often, in a first draft, the topic does not emerge clearly until the end of the thinking process. Make sure that you edit with an eye to giving the reader guidance as to your meaning and your ultimate direction in each paragraph.

The Topic Sentence

A typical paragraph in an essay begins with a topic sentence, a general "umbrella" statement that explains what the rest of the paragraph is about. Anything that does not relate to this controlling idea should be left out. Sometimes, writers feel that it is unprofessional to make the topic sentence too obvious, but, despite their fears, a clear topic sentence is an asset. Because the essay is, by its nature, rather repetitive in structure, you may be simply repeating, in different words, a point that you previewed in your thesis statement. For instance, your thesis statement may be that triage is an essential, if difficult, part of a good health-care system because it enables medical teams to decide which patients must be attended to first. In your first paragraph, you have defined the term "triage." In the second paragraph, you might begin by stating that one of the criteria for setting priorities for care is the patient's chance of survival. Your next paragraph might begin with a topic sentence that mentions the next criterion: the patient's ability to wait. Each of these criteria would be developed in turn.

A topic sentence need not necessarily begin your paragraphs, but for less experienced writers, and in essay writing generally, it usually does.

Remember that a topic sentence expresses a specific opinion. Look at the following examples:

Example   ✗ Harper won a majority government after many years of minority rule.

This topic sentence states a mere fact; it does not provide any lead into a deeper discussion. Instead try this:

Example   Harper's majority government may be helpful to domestic growth, but it does not bode well for international affairs.

This topic sentence advances an opinion, which the rest of the paragraph must support.

Example   ✗ Mental health treatment in Canada needs more attention.

This sentence may express an opinion, but its focus is too broad to be manageable. Instead try this:

> Canadian prisons need to be supported by compassionate mental health treatment centres.   **Example**

> ✗ Canadians typically scorn Americans.   **Example**

Try instead:

> Canadians need to learn how to develop a sense of identity that is not just based on anti-American sentiment.   **Example**

The Support

Your support may take several forms:

1. examples
2. statistics
3. connected reasons/definitions
4. authorities

Approach the undeveloped arguments in your outline with these four categories in mind. The sources of support will depend on the nature of the assignment: a formal research essay may require all four; a less formal paper will rely chiefly on reasons and examples for its strength.

Developing Support for Your Paragraphs

Remember, as you weave your outline into paragraphs, that each discrete unit must ultimately contribute something to the illustration of the essay's thesis statement. The paragraphs argue in its defence or show its validity.

Some of the following methods are formal adaptations of techniques of argument you may have used before. The list is by no means complete; try to think of other equally effective strategies.

Present the Facts of the Case

These facts may include statistics to prove your point. Don't take for granted that your readers know what you know about the subject.

> Frozen dinners, according to their manufacturers, are steadily increasing in popu-   **Example**
> larity, perhaps because of the widespread use of microwave ovens and because of
> the pace of modern society. Indeed, according to one producer of these goods, more
> than 80% of households buy these products on a regular basis. One wonders, how-
> ever, how anyone can bear to eat them.

The use of this statistic "grounds" the paragraph. The fact is all the more powerful because the writer uses it to show astonishment at frozen food's popularity, rather than to support it. Remember that you can use sources, such as quotations and statistics, to argue against something as well as in favour of it.

Show and Tell

To keep the line of thought going, remember that it is always best to argue by example, rather than by precept. Don't just tell your readers about something. Show them, wherever possible, how your idea works by giving an example.

Example   Lumped in one plastic partition of the frozen dinner is a white, viscous mound with a substance faintly resembling butter sliding greasily down its pasty sides. Its likeness on the box wrapper indicates the presence of potatoes in that location, but the taste is reminiscent of the last stamp you licked. The texture is perennially similar across all brands of frozen dinners—that of wet plaster. Incredibly, manufacturers of frozen dinners get even their potatoes to taste like wet plaster, an unfortunate consistency, if you will excuse the pun.

These examples are especially effective because they are so descriptive. Concrete, precise words are much more evocative than abstract generalities.

Establish Connections

Find something in the point you are making that relates to your own experience or to that of your readers. If the essay is formal rather than informal in tone, adapt this advice to show your readers why the subject is important to them.

Example   Hope springs eternal as the harried consumer tries different brands of frozen dinners. The diabolically clever chemists must do freelance work for all the major manufacturers, because Brand A's "Chicken Marengo" tastes disconcertingly like Brand X's "He-Man Beef Platter." We may wonder how they do it. A better question may be "Why do we let them?" The answer is probably that fast food, despite its drawbacks, is ubiquitous and unavoidable in a society in which no one has time to cook.

Here the writer uses a hypothetic, humorous, and very specific example to make a real, serious point.

Define Your Terms and Use Details

If the terminology is clear, don't bother telling your readers what they already know. If, on the other hand, you think that a closer look at a word or phrase that is part of your topic will help your case, draw their attention to it.

Example   Although frozen dinners claim to be made of frozen food, the claim is debatable. Take, for example, what passes for dessert in one of these trays. Gustatory delight is expected because of a tantalizing picture on the box and an imaginative description—spiced apple supreme, for instance. Alas, the unsuspecting fruit has met a fate similar to that of the potatoes. Magnificent, tart, crunchy apples have been reduced to apple-facsimile chunks, improved by the thoughtful addition of a charming artificial flavour mixed in with a gelatinous goo. When the fruit is eaten, the fleshy texture is so odd that, except for the absence of pain, the consumer cannot be sure he is not happily chewing on his own tongue.

The focus here on something small and specific makes the point memorable.

Call in an Expert or Cite a Source

Convince your reader by turning to an expert for support. Don't expect readers to take your word for something if the words of a specialist in the area are available to buttress your own. If the person to whom you refer is a respected authority, your argument will be enriched by his or her utterance.

> The sad truth is that diners everywhere exist on frozen food because no one has **Example**
> time anymore for home cooking. While we all still have to eat, none of us is eager
> to prepare dinner—for ourselves or for others. Because time is precious, and frozen
> food is ubiquitous, we do not rebel against the horrors of monosodium glutamate,
> salt, and artificial colouring. As Shirley Conran says, "Life is too short to stuff a
> mushroom."

If you can find a quotation that fits neatly into your argument, take advantage of it. It will strengthen your case.

Note that the source of this quotation would have to be acknowledged, using some consistent form of documentation—a subject covered in detail in Chapter 23.

Unity

A paragraph, like the essay itself, should have demonstrated the development of your thought by the time your reader finishes it. Each paragraph should lead the reader along in a logical and coherent manner. If your outline has been well planned, the progress of your thinking should be orderly and your conclusion clear. Your paragraphs should each form a discrete unit, and each paragraph should be clearly connected to what precedes and to what follows.

> It is interesting that beets are rarely offered in these frozen dinner simulations. **Example**
> Possibly that is because beets stubbornly insist on having a beet-like tang no matter
> how they are diced, sauced, or otherwise adulterated. Such a renegade authentic fla-
> vour might take the targeted "average consumer" by surprise. He or she might then
> realize that the other items on the slab are pale imitations of the real thing. Since
> that realization could have dire consequences for the manufacturer's cash flow, only
> cooperative vegetables grace the microwaveable plastic tray.

In this example, the author discusses the quality of vegetables normally used in frozen dinners by pointing out one variety that never appears. The paragraph then goes on to offer a theory for the beet's conspicuous absence, one that connects this paragraph to the overall notion of the lack of flavour found in frozen dinners.

Pinning the Pieces Together—Transitions

Despite the basic structural independence of the paragraph, the reader must be able to appreciate how it fits into the whole essay. To make the connections clear to the reader, an essayist must use appropriate transitions and linking devices.

Transitions are signals of a turn in thought. They often pose a problem for the novice essay writer simply because our methods of changing or developing the subject in conversation are much less formal and much more spontaneous than in written, rhetorical form.

Ask yourself what your favourite techniques of transition in speech are. Then try to categorize the situations that prompt you to use them. You may find that your list of transitions includes such statements as "And you know what else?" to add to or elaborate on a point; "You see," to explain in greater detail; "Sure, but," to disagree with another's argument, at the same time conceding to some degree; "What if . . .?" to put forward a hypothesis; "Anyhow," to dismiss the view of your interlocutor; or "As I said before," to reinforce an earlier point.

Many of these transitions cannot be easily transferred to the printed page. They are too casual to suit the public occasion of the essay. In their stead, the writer must become familiar with and use more formal transitions to enhance the power of his or her rhetoric.

Transitions have many uses. Here are some examples of various transitions:

TO ADD	TO CHANGE DIRECTION
and	but
also	however
in addition	conversely
furthermore	although
as well	whereas

TO ILLUSTRATE	TO SUMMARIZE
for example	to conclude
for instance	in short
in other words	finally
that is	

TO QUALIFY	TO CONCEDE A POINT
often	although
generally	though
specifically	whereas
usually	

TO ENUMERATE	TO ESTABLISH CAUSE
first, second, third . . .	because
first, next, last	for

TO STATE A REASON

because

since

for

TO DRAW A CONCLUSION

thus

finally

hence

therefore

as a result

consequently

TO POINT AT A PREVIOUS
REFERENCE

this/these

that/those

who/whom

which/what

few

many

Good transitions are like carefully sewn seams. Although not readily noticeable, they are the means by which the garment is held together. Vague or unclear transitions may cause your essay to fall apart—an embarrassing state for something that is appearing in print and is being presented to someone you wish to impress.

Here are some body paragraphs from an essay about autism.

Example

This word indicates a time sequence.

When I was young, my little brother David's autism led him to regularly exhibit repetitive stereotypic behaviours in order to cope with his anxiety. Any time he felt overwhelmed or he simply wanted to block out the world around him, he would begin to play his favourite films over in his head, reciting each character's lines in the movie aloud. My family referred affectionately to these moments as David's retreat to what we called 'the fifth,' as in the fifth dimension. He had created this alternate universe completely separate from our world. The problem was that he would remain locked for long periods in the fifth, and his lack of desire to interact with others was severely hindering his development.

This transition indicates the first response.

The repetition of the word "behaviour" helps with paragraph unity.

At first my parents blatantly discouraged any behaviour that they deemed socially inappropriate for David's age group. Telling him to stop 'talking to himself' proved unsuccessful and left my parents feeling insecure, not knowing how to best help their son. In time they began to accept that although David's behaviour was not socially acceptable, and rather than discouraging his tendencies entirely, we all played along as a more effective way for everyone to adapt. As my brother learned lines in films he was fixated on, my parents and I would also learn the corresponding lines to those films. When he jumped into character, we

This transition indicates a later development.

The repetition of the word "films" helps keep things connected.

did the same and, eventually, rather than using films as a way to withdraw in order to cope with anxiety, David modified his behaviour to engage more with his family and eventually with his peers. It began with David in a corner reciting lines to Jim Carrey movies by himself. My parents and I would become one of the characters in the scene he was reenacting, and as we learned the corresponding lines he incorporated us into his world.

For my family, this method of play functioned as a social platform enabling us to bond while also facilitating the development of David's social skills. This approach took into account David's unique needs while also encouraging us to participate in a fun family activity. By learning how to participate as actors in David's world theatre, we found an unconventional yet effective way to bring him out of his world and into ours. When my parents initially wanted to discourage this behaviour entirely, they had feared David would be judged for being different. Walking around reciting film lines to oneself is socially unacceptable or abnormal, for it is stereotypically viewed as a sign that the person is mentally unsound.

A word like "this" makes a clear connection to what has gone before.

Repetition of the word "actors" helps keep the connection.

Becoming actors on David's stage brought him closer to us. We chose to identify with him and became part of his in-group. As Wendell discusses, "Emphasizing similarities between people with and people without disabilities seems to hold the promise of reducing the 'Otherness' of those who are non disabled by enabling the non-disabled to identify with them" (2006, p. 74). Rather than focusing on the differences between us, we reinforced our similarities. If my parents had remained rigid, forcing my brother to conform to social norms, he would have further withdrawn into his own world. We embraced difference by working with David's interests. By participating in activities he enjoyed, we not only interacted with him in a way that made him feel comfortable, but we also found a way to make David's therapy something fun for the whole family. This ability for everyone in the family to connect with one another is key to successful therapy as it facilitates the autistic child's desire to develop social connections.

Repeating "similarities" connects it with the quotation previously given.

Transitions like "this" help connect the paragraphs.

Checking the Overall Pattern of Your Paragraphs

There are two basic tests for the aesthetic appeal of the paragraph. One test is to read the first sentence of each paragraph to check whether the line of thought is clearly maintained throughout the entire work. That is, do the sentences themselves act as subheadings to guide the reader through your design? (*Note*: This test assumes that most paragraphs begin with a topic sentence. Sometimes, however, the topic sentence may appear at the end.) Another test of effective paragraphing involves looking at the length of the paragraphs themselves on the printed page. Is each paragraph a manageable length? Note that the length of paragraphs is typically governed by some basic guidelines. You need to make sure that all the essential elements are included; that is, there must be a topic sentence, some support for it, and some elaboration of that support. That generally means that a paragraph in a scholarly essay is usually at least three sentences long, and given the need for definitive explication of support, usually much longer. Occasionally, you may see a one-sentence paragraph used for its startling effect, most often in less scholarly material.

The layout counts too. As a rule, it is wise to include at least one paragraph break per printed page, and no more than about three. To have no breaks is to invite boredom on the part of the reader; to have more than three breaks is to suggest your thoughts lack integration. Paragraph length, in other words, is often fairly arbitrary: witness how newspapers often use one-sentence paragraphs simply because they look better in column form. Break your paragraphs with an eye to avoiding a "choppy" page or one that presents a daunting block of type. That said, internal logic is the main determinant of paragraph length.

CHAPTER 12 EXERCISES

1. Look at a paragraph in one of your textbooks. Does it conform to the principles of paragraph writing that are discussed in this chapter? Does it have a topic sentence, adequate support, some sense of unity and coherence, and useful transitions?

2. Now look at one of your own paragraphs in the draft of a recent paper. Can you find a topic sentence, adequate support, unity, coherence, and good use of transitions? Edit your paragraph to see if you can make any improvements in these items.

3. Develop a paragraph using your own definition of a term. Compare it with the definition you find in the dictionary. Try one of these words:

    responsibility

    guilt

    freedom

    happiness

4. Develop a paragraph using a statistic or a quoted authority as support. Look through newspapers or weekly magazines for topics, or try these:

    marriage

    children

    crime

    obesity

    weather

    a medical breakthrough

5. Write a paragraph establishing a connection or making a comparison. Develop your own comparison, or work with one of these:

    DVD vs. the big screen

    love vs. infatuation

    herbal medication vs. drugs

    habit vs. addiction

6. Develop two paragraphs, one using an example from your own experience and one paraphrasing a case study or a news report. Find your case study in a magazine or a textbook, and make up another on the same subject. Try one of these subjects:

someone who has an illness

someone who is being treated unjustly

someone who triumphs against the odds

7. Write two paragraphs, one using a series of small examples to make a point and one using an extended example to support the same point. Pick any one of these subjects:

how to win someone over

how to memorize facts

how to be assertive

how to make a speech successfully

how to develop muscles

how to overcome a setback

8. Use the following quotations in paragraphs that you devise:
   a. "In the confrontation between the stream and the rock, the stream always wins—not through strength, but through persistence."—*Anonymous*
   b. "It's not how smart you are, but how you are smart."—*Howard Gardner*
   c. "If you aren't the lead dog, the view never changes."—*Unknown*

CHAPTER 13

Perfecting the Essay

1. Out of clutter, find simplicity.
2. From discord, find harmony.
3. In the middle of difficulty lies opportunity. (Three rules of work)

—ALBERT EINSTEIN

In this chapter:

- How to revise your essay
- How to review the argument
- How to revise the sentences
- How to revise the words

Tips on Revising

The revision process involves more than fussing over a few typographical errors; it should ideally be a process that reconceives and reviews the entire essay: not only its mechanics, but also its structure and its thought. While it is usually valuable to proceed as this book recommends—from thesis to outline, to research (if required), to first draft—the first written draft you produce is unlikely to be the clearest version of your thinking on any given subject. Bearing in mind your own shortcomings as a writer, as you have come to know them in your writing experience, prepare yourself to judge your own work in its entirety. Much of your real writing will be done at this stage, now that you are free to put yourself in the reader's position and imagine your paper's impact on him or her.

Remember that an essay has a duty to be unified, clear, and coherent. Accordingly, judge your work by the relevance of the information you have provided, by its ability to explain itself fully and clearly, and by its ability to make connections in the reader's mind. Putting yourself in the reader's position means that you must re-examine your assumptions about the subject matter and the reader's knowledge of it, and you must be willing to query the things that strike you as doubtful or awkward as you read. Detachment is crucial here, as is the time to do a good job.

Word processors make revision a simple matter. It is usually best to print out a first draft and then make corrections on paper before making another pass through the paper. Compare the first draft on pp. 126–129 to the final wording of the essay on pp. 130–133.

Even after all your hard work, some minor but significant details may affect the reader's perception of your paper. Often these errors are the most embarrassing ones, errors that undercut your effort and distract the reader's attention from the elegance of your essay's form and the substance of its content. Like the emperor with no clothes, you and your work may be easily subjected to ridicule or to charges of arrogance if you neglect responsible proofreading and stringent self-criticism. To ensure the quality of your work, follow these steps:

EXAMPLE OF REVISION IN PROGRESS

Although they agree that the story with animals is the better story, the last word is given to the other, worse story, minus the animals except for the incontrovertible Bengal tiger. The leap of faith, in Martel's estimation, requires that we

spelling

chose the better story, select the one more aesthetically pleasing, perhaps the one easier to live with. This view of reality accords with something that Martel explains in one of his interviews: "To me a belief is something you cling to and faith is a letting go. Not only in religious terms—when you love someone, you let go, you trust them. When you love a system or anything, you let go—that's faith.

shorten

When you have a belief you cling" ("Ask"). It is in this way that Martel brings the reader round to the kind of faith that involves letting go, but to no particular

combine

system of belief. Explaining the point in the same interview, for him, each religious

tense

perspective was a kind of cuisine, any of which could sustain life. All the possible cuisines, however, were very different.

1. MOVE FROM THE WHOLE TO THE PARTS.

Revising needs a clear eye. To make sure you are seeing the paper's flaws, try to read it cold—that is, a day or so after you have written it. That will enable you to see more clearly just how persuasively argued and well expressed your paper actually is. You want a paper that is consistent, clear, and convincing. The process involves more than superficial corrections of mechanical errors. It involves a careful reconsideration of every part of your draft. Try to follow this sequence, or one adapted to suit you, when you revise your papers.

   a. Check your facts. Does anything need to be added or changed?
   b. Rethink your scheme of organization. Does the order make sense?
   c. Test the paragraph structure. Are your ideas developed and linked properly?
   d. Read over your sentences, aloud if possible. Are they clear, smooth, varied?
   e. Examine your word choice. Is it accurate, suitable, effective?
   f. Check your grammar and spelling. Is the paper free of errors?

2. REFLECT ON YOUR IMAGE.

Just as you wouldn't buy an item of clothing without first looking to see if it suited you and fit properly, don't write a paper and then submit it without first assessing its immediate impact on its readers. Reread the paper, scrutinizing its details very carefully—preferably a few days after you have written it. Reading aloud will help you find any awkward instances of grammatical construction and style. Ask a friend to read it too. Peer editing is a good way to improve your writing skills, and simple comments, such as "I don't get it," may help you or your friend get an essay back on track.

3. IF YOU CAN'T BE PERFECT, BE CAREFUL.

Some errors, in this imperfect world, may still creep in. Make necessary corrections as unobtrusively as possible. Resist the impulse to redo the whole paper (possibly introducing new errors), and instead make the corrections neatly in black ink—above the line. Stroke out unwanted letters with a small vertical line, and remove repeated words by the judicious use of "white-out" (Liquid Paper) or the simple horizontal stroke of a pen.

4. MAKE YOUR PAPER "EASY ON THE EYES."

Don't allow your essay to offend the eye. Avoid a printout so faded that you develop cycstrain trying to read it. Make your handwriting bold, large, and neat. If you submit a computer printout, take special care in proofreading to avoid errors that may have been introduced in production. Submit the paper in a tidy folder, neatly stapled or paper-clipped (as your instructor may prefer). Even if neatness is not an acknowledged criterion of excellence, there is no question that first impressions have a lasting effect.

5. TIE UP ANY LOOSE THREADS.

Don't submit your paper without checking such details as page numbers, exact quotations, bibliographical information, doubtful spellings, word divisions, and grammatical constructions.

6. FOLLOW THE "DRESS CODE."

Make sure that your assignment adheres to any conditions explicitly stated by the instructor, however arbitrary or trivial such matters may seem to you. Check to see that the mechanical format of your paper conforms to the expected standards of the instructor. Such items as the treatment of abbreviations, bibliographical arrangement, and even the format of the title page and the position and form of page numbers need careful attention. Although you may have already invested considerable time in these matters, a last-minute check is a good idea.

7. USE EVERY MEANS AT YOUR DISPOSAL.

Don't hand in a word-processed paper that hasn't gone through the spell-checking process. Spell checkers can't catch every mistake. Simple homonyms like "hear" and "here" are indistinguishable for them. With most spell checkers, American spelling is still the norm, and "our" at the end of words will be considered an error. For all that, computers are remarkably thorough in catching small errors that your tired eyes may miss. It is worthwhile to follow through on the advice of spell checkers and even of grammar checkers, though you may occasionally have good reason not to follow it. Not every use of the passive voice is reprehensible; not every fragment is unjustifiable. Still, word-processing spell checkers and grammar checkers do oblige you to look more closely at what you are saying and how you are saying it. Don't skip this step, and don't forget that a good Canadian dictionary is an important resource too.

Use the following checklist to see if your paper does what you intend it to do:

Revision Checklist

THE WHOLE—THE ARGUMENT

Does your paper have a suitable title that makes its focus clear?

Does your introduction tell your reader what he or she needs to know?

Can you find your thesis statement somewhere in the introduction?

Does every point you raise relate clearly to the thesis?

Is the point of every paragraph and its connection to your argument clear from its beginning?

Are there enough paragraph breaks (and not too many) for ease of reading?

Is your argument as persuasively ordered and worded as it can be?

Do you conclude by moving from the specific to the general?

Are there any fallacies in your reasoning or easy objections to be made?

Would your argument help to convince those who disagree?

THE PARTS—THE SENTENCES

Do you avoid sentence fragments?

Do your sentences show variety in their structure?

Do you use passive voice sparingly and only justifiably?

Do you keep your sentence length manageable?

Do you use colons, semicolons, and commas correctly?

Have you checked to see that wordiness and redundancy are at a minimum?

Is your meaning clear without rephrasing—even when revised some time after the first draft?

THE PARTS—THE WORDS

Do you use diction that is straightforward, clear, and unpretentious?

Do you avoid slang or excessive or unnecessary jargon?

Do you use terminology with expertise?

Do you avoid contractions?

Do you spell correctly?

General Advice

Does your essay read well, even aloud?

Can friends read it easily without questions or problems?

Have you checked specifically to eradicate the mistakes you typically make?

Sample Student Revision Process

First Draft

This is a good paper, with a strong structure and an informal, slightly journalistic tone, as the assignment suggested. It still benefited from careful revision to catch tiny errors, improve clarity, and reduce wordiness. Note the comments that summarize changes made.

Dustin Manley

June 17th, 2010

When I told people during the 2010 Vancouver Winter Olympics that my 26 year old cousin, Graeme Murray, plays defence for Canada's Paralympic Ice Sledge Hockey team, I generally received questions about what sledge hockey and the Paralympics even were. When I tell people outside of the Olympic season, even more are completely unaware of the Paralympics or Canada's Sledge Hockey team. Reasons for this could be due to people assuming that the Paralympics are not as athletic or competitive; however, the main reason could be because there is not enough sufficient media coverage on the event.

The 2010 Vancouver Olympic Games cost $1.76 billion dollars to operate (The Tyee), and were broadcast worldwide to hundreds of millions of viewers. Canadians along with the rest of the world were ripe with 'Olympic fever' and our nation cheered its athletes on to win 26 medals—14 of which were gold, in 15 different events. However, after the closing ceremonies of the Olympics, most of the world including Canada left Vancouver just as the Paralympics began. The Paralympics may not last as long as the Olympics, and only have a third of the events, but there are still Olympic-level athletes competing. The Paralympics are not a policy of sport equity where disabled persons compete after the 'real' Olympic Games are finished. Canada displayed an enormous amount of national pride during the Olympic Games; why did the fire burn out for our Paralympic athletes?

Governed by the International Paralympic Committee (IPC), the Paralympic games originated from a small group of British WWII veterans in 1948. It is now the second largest international sport event, with 39 countries represented by 506 athletes as of the 2010 Winter Games. There are Winter and Summer Paralympics which are held immediately following the Olympics, where athletes with physical disabilities including mobility disabilities, amputations, blindness, and Cerebral Palsy compete. The five Winter events consist of: Alpine Skiing; Biathlon; Cross-Country Skiing,

Manley 2

Wheelchair curling, and Ice Sledge Hockey. Despite being the second largest international sport event, there is a wide funding gap between the Olympic and Paralympic games, a leading factor to the lack of media presence in the games.

Television broadcasts of the Paralympics began in 1976; however, the Paralympic games have had difficulty maintaining a consistent international media presence until the 2000 Paralympics in Sydney, Australia which were broadcast to 300 million people (Cashman). Despite the recent improvement of global media exposure, my family still had to Graeme and Team Canada win the Gold Medal streamed online via the Paralympic Sport TV website (paralympicsport.tv).

During the 4th IPC Ice Sledge Hockey World Championships held at the lacklustre New England Sports Centre in Marlborough Massachusetts, USA, 2008 media coverage and awareness of the sledge hockey event was clearly lacking. There were 200 athletes from 10 countries participating in this event, and although it was the World Championships, it was evident the audience was mostly made up of family and friends of the athletes. Footage for "Sled Head", winner of "Best Documentary" award at the DeREEL INDEPENDENT FILM FESTIVAL (SledHeadMovie.com) among many others, was shot here to highlight Canada's Paralympic Sledge Hockey team and its members.

The biggest highlight of the footage was when Canada scored the winning goal with 10s left in the final period and all of the Canadian audience ran onto the ice to celebrate the victory of the World Championships.

In 2010 Canadian Paralympic media exposure grew immensely. Instead of having to watch games streamed over the IPC website games were broadcast by Canada's Olympic Broadcast Media Consortium, a joint venture between CTVglobemedia and Rogers Media (CTVOlympics.ca). CTV planned a record of 50 hours of television coverage which included a 90-minute daily highlight program, as well as live coverage of Canada's sledge hockey games and the gold medal game (which Canada was unfortunately not participating in).

Courtesy of Dustin Manley

Outside of the games, the Paralympics have raised tremendous awareness for disabled persons in the public. A 2010 study of the Olympic Global Impact (OGI) by the Paralympic Winter Games conducted by the University of British Columbia (UBC) showed that of approximately 1,600 Canadians surveyed, 41-50% believed that the games "triggered additional accessibility of buildings, sidewalks and public spaces...23 percent of employers, said the Games had increased their willingness to hire people with disabilities" (University of British Columbia). While accessibility of public spaces and hiring of disabled people shouldn't be increased solely because of the Paralympic Games being in town. This rising awareness is a tremendous sign of success.

Awareness of the Paralympic games has been rising—the fact that I was able to watch my cousin play with Team Canada live on CTV, while 4 years previous the family was huddled around a computer screen is proof of this. 50 hours of coverage is a huge improvement, but this coverage and media awareness needs to continue growing. Hopefully, with the dramatic rise in awareness and media presence over the past decade in the Paralympics, come 2014 I won't get blank faces when I tell people that my cousin, Graeme Murray, is number 29 on Canada's Ice Sledge Hockey team; Hopefully because they will be cheering on Canada's Paralympic athletes as well.

Manley 4

Bibliography

Cashman, Richard and Simon Darcy. Benchmark Games: The Sydney 2000 Paralympic
Games. Petersham, Australia: Walla Walla Press, 2008.

Web. 10 June 2010. <http://www.sledheadmovie.com/Sledhead_Movie/SLEDHEAD_.
html>.

"Record hours of coverage for Paralympic Games." CTVOlympics.ca. June 16, 2009.
http://www.ctvolympics.ca/news-centre/newsid=11882.html. Retrieved 14
February 2010.

Thomson, Hilary. "Paralympics a Force for Change." *UBC Public Affairs*. 4 Mar. 2010.
Web. 20 May 2011. <http://www.publicaffairs.ubc.ca/2010/03/04/paralympics-
a-force-for-change/>.

Revised Draft

Dustin Manley

June 17th, 2010

When I told people during the 2010 Vancouver Winter Olympics that my 26-year-old cousin, Graeme Murray, plays defence for Canada's Paralympic Ice Sledge Hockey team, I generally received questions about what sledge hockey and the Paralympics even were. When I tell people outside of the Olympic season, even more are completely unaware of the Paralympics or Canada's Sledge Hockey team. People may be assuming that the Paralympics are not as athletic or competitive; however, the main reason could be a lack of sufficient media coverage on the event.

The student changed this to reflect that "compound" adjectives that precede the noun take a hyphen.

The student made this less wordy by starting with the subject and verb and by searching for redundant wording.

The 2010 Vancouver Olympic Games cost $1.76 billion to operate (The Tyee), and were broadcast worldwide to hundreds of millions of viewers. Canadians along with the rest of the world were ripe with 'Olympic fever', and our nation cheered its athletes on to win 26 medals—14 of which were gold, in 15 different events. However, after the closing ceremonies of the Olympics, most of the world including Canada left Vancouver just as the Paralympics began. The Paralympics may not last as long as the Olympics, and only have a third of the events, but there are still Olympic-level athletes competing. The Paralympics are not based on a policy of sport equity that allows people with disabilities to compete after the 'real' Olympic Games are finished. Canada displayed an enormous amount of national pride during the Olympic Games; why did the fire burn out for our Paralympic athletes?

The student made this sentence clearer and more sensitive by putting "people" first.

Governed by the International Paralympic Committee (IPC), the Paralympic games originated from a small group of British WWII veterans in 1948. It is now the second largest international sport event, with 39 countries represented by 506 athletes as of the 2010 Winter Games. There are Winter and Summer Paralympics held immediately following the Olympics, where athletes with physical disabilities including mobility disabilities, amputations, blindness, and Cerebral Palsy compete. The five Winter events

Manley 2

consist of Alpine Skiing; Biathlon; Cross-Country Skiing; Wheelchair Curling; and Ice

Sledge Hockey. Despite being the second largest international sport event, there is a

wide funding gap between the Olympic and Paralympic games, a leading cause of the

lack of media presence in the games.

> The student changes here reduce foggy language and wordiness.

Television broadcasts of the Paralympics began in 1976; however, the

Paralympic games have had difficulty maintaining a consistent international media

presence until the 2000 Paralympics in Sydney, Australia which were broadcast to

300 million people (Cashman). Despite the recent improvement of global media

exposure, my family still had to watch Graeme and Team Canada win the Gold Medal

streamed online via the Paralympic Sport TV website (paralympicsport.tv).

During the 4th IPC Ice Sledge Hockey World Championships held at the lacklustre

New England Sports Centre in Marlborough Massachusetts, USA, 2008 media cov-

erage and awareness of the sledge hockey event was clearly lacking. There were 200

athletes from 10 countries participating in this event, and although it was the World

Championships, it was evident the audience was mostly made up of family and friends

of the athletes. Footage for "Sled Head", winner of "Best Documentary" award at the

DeREEL INDEPENDENT FILM FESTIVAL (SledHeadMovie.com) among many others, was

shot here to highlight Canada's Paralympic Sledge Hockey team and its members.

The biggest highlight of the footage was when Canada scored the winning goal

with 10 seconds left in the final period, and all of the Canadian audience ran onto

the ice to celebrate the victory of the World Championships.

In 2010 Canadian Paralympic media exposure grew immensely. Instead of

having to watch games streamed over the IPC website, we could now watch games

> The student caught a dangling modifier here.

broadcast by Canada's Olympic Broadcast Media Consortium, a joint venture between

CTVglobemedia and Rogers Media (CTVOlympics.ca). CTV planned a record of 50

hours of television coverage which included a 90-minute daily highlight program, as

well as live coverage of Canada's sledge hockey games and the gold medal game

(which Canada was unfortunately not participating in).

Courtesy of Dustin Manley

Manley 3

Outside of the games, the Paralympics have raised tremendous awareness for disabled persons in the public. A 2010 study of the Olympic Global Impact (OGI) by the Paralympic Winter Games conducted by the University of British Columbia (UBC) showed that of approximately 1,600 Canadians surveyed, 41-50% believed that the games "triggered additional accessibility of buildings, sidewalks and public spaces . . . [and that] 23 percent of employers said the Games had increased their willingness to hire people with disabilities" (University of British Columbia). While accessibility of public spaces and hiring of disabled people shouldn't be increased solely because of the Paralympic Games being in town, this rising awareness is a tremendous sign of success.

Awareness of the Paralympic games has grown—the fact that I was able to watch my cousin play with Team Canada live on CTV, while 4 years previously the family was huddled around a computer screen is proof of this. Fifty hours of coverage is a huge improvement, but this coverage and media awareness need to continue growing. I hope that with the dramatic rise in awareness and media presence over the past decade in the Paralympics, come 2014, I won't get blank faces when I tell people that my cousin, Graeme Murray, is number 29 on Canada's Ice Sledge Hockey team because they will be cheering on Canada's Paralympic athletes as well.

The student adjusted the wording of the quotation to make it clearer by adding square brackets to add his own words.

The student caught a subject and verb agreement problem here.

The student eliminated "hopefully" because it is a dangling modifier.

Courtesy of Dustin Manley

Manley 4

Works Cited

Cashman, Richard, and Simon Darcy. *Benchmark Games: The Sydney 2000 Paralympic Games*. Petersham, Australia: Walla Walla Press, 2008. Print.

"Record Hours of Coverage for Paralympic Games." CTVOlympics.ca. 16 June 2009. Web. 14 February 2010.

Sledhead. Web. 10 June 2010.

Thomson, Hilary. "Paralympics a Force for Change." *UBC Public Affairs*. 4 Mar. 2010. Web. 20 May 2011.

Student made changes to conform to MLA format.

Courtesy of Dustin Manley

CHAPTER 14
Mending the Essay

Blot out, correct, insert, refine,
Enlarge, diminish, interline;
Be mindful, when invention fails,
To scratch your head, and bite your nails.
—JONATHAN SWIFT

In this chapter:

- How to make sense of instructor comments
- How to grow as a writer

If, when you get an essay back, you find that your work has been disappointing, there are still some things you can do to redeem yourself. It may be too late to get the kind of grade that you had in mind on this particular paper, but some of the tactics proposed below ought to make the next essay better.

First, don't throw the paper away in a fit of glee or gloom. You write essays not only to get grades but also to learn how to write. Long after you have forgotten the facts and figures involved in writing your paper, you will still have the writing skills that were developed in its preparation. Your reading, writing, and research skills are the most visible parts of your education long after you graduate.

Deciphering Comments

1. READ THE GRADER'S COMMENTS WHEN YOUR ESSAYS ARE RETURNED TO YOU—REGARDLESS OF THE GRADE YOU RECEIVE.
Don't read only the comments accompanying the grade at the end of the paper, but also any questions or hints dropped in the margins or within the text of the paper.

2. NEXT, SEE THAT YOU UNDERSTAND WHAT THE COMMENTS AND QUESTIONS MEAN.
The list below should help, though your instructor may use different abbreviations when he or she gives you feedback:

#	add a space
agr	error in agreement (subject/verb or antecedent/pronoun)
apos	indicate possession or add apostrophe

awk	awkward wording
bib	error in bibliographical form
◯	close up space
=	correct letter case
case	error in pronoun case
coh	problem with coherence
cs	comma splice
d	problem with diction or usage
dev	inadequate paragraph development
div	incorrect word division
dm	dangling modifier
doc	error in documentation
frag	sentence fragment
gr	error in grammar or usage
log	logic
mm	misplaced or misrelated modifier
p	error in punctuation
par	problem with paragraphing
pass	overuse of the passive voice
?	unclear, doubtful, or unreadable
ref	problem with pronoun reference
rep	repetition
rev	revise or proofread
run-on	run-on sentence
shift	shift in verb tense or logic
sp	spelling error
ss	problem with sentence structure
stet	keep as it was
sub	faulty subordination
t	error in verb tense
trans	transition
ts	problem with thesis statement
//	faulty parallelism
∧	something missing
wdy	problem with wordiness
ww	wrong word
X	obvious error

3. ASK YOUR INSTRUCTOR TO EXPLAIN A PARTICULAR COMMENT IF YOU DO NOT UNDERSTAND IT.

4. WHEN YOU HAVE READ THROUGH THE COMMENTS, TRY TO ANALYZE THE KIND OF MISTAKES THAT YOU MAKE MOST FREQUENTLY AND DETERMINE THAT YOU WILL TAKE STEPS TO ELIMINATE THEM.

5. NEXT, CONSULT A RELIABLE GUIDE IN ORDER TO CORRECT YOUR MISTAKES.
Such guides include a dictionary (for spelling errors and errors of usage), a writing/ grammar handbook (such as this one), or a guide to proper format of notes and bibliography (such as the *MLA Handbook*).

Learning from Experience

1. ANALYZE THE STRENGTHS AND WEAKNESSES OF YOUR STYLE.
At first, this may seem a puzzling endeavour, but after a time you should be able to discern changes in your writing—not only in its mechanics, but in the development of its thought as well.

2. ANALYZE YOUR WRITING HABITS.
Do you find that you have certain favourite expressions that crop up too often? Do your readers frequently comment that your sentences are too complex or too simple? Do certain tactics in your argument often meet with an unfavourable response? Paying attention to these trends in your collected essays will enable you to become more sensitive to your patterns of self-expression and more able to prevent problems in the future.

3. KEEP A LIST OF YOUR MOST COMMON SPELLING AND GRAMMAR ERRORS FROM PAST WORK.
Refer to this list when you are about to write the final draft of your next paper. It may help eliminate some pitfalls.

4. EXERCISE YOUR WRITING SKILLS.
Reading is probably not a strong enough remedy to cure you of some errors; writing is the recommended therapy. If possible, set yourself the task of completing some exercises aimed at a specific problem diagnosed by your instructor. If, for example, dangling modifiers are a persistent problem, consult the section in this book on their diagnosis and treatment. Your instructor may agree to check your answers afterwards.

5. REWRITE.
Rewriting is also a good way of curing some of the ills of essay writing. Try, for example, to recast a troublesome paragraph in clearer, smoother prose, incorporating your instructor's suggestions. Remember, though, that no writer ever developed a style mechanically; it is intimately related to thought. Rethink your thoughts as you rewrite. You will learn a great deal about the impact your writing has on its readers if you remember the grader's comments.

6. WORK THROUGH APPROPRIATE SECTIONS OF THIS BOOK WITH AN ESSAY THAT HAS JUST BEEN RETURNED.

This exercise will help you in your next essay assignment.

7. EXPERIMENT.

Writing should not always be a chore. Sometimes, when you find yourself able to express something exactly the way you want to, writing becomes play. Allow yourself to become comfortable as you write. Remember that your real writing purpose, grades and completed assignments aside, is to say what you want to say. Practice will make writing a satisfying form of self-expression.

8. ANALYZE YOUR OWN WRITING PROCESS.

What part of composing an essay could you improve for next time? Would you start sooner? Take better notes? Use more paraphrase? Use more positive language? Think about the entire process so that you can modify it for better results next time, or just to figure out what works best for you.

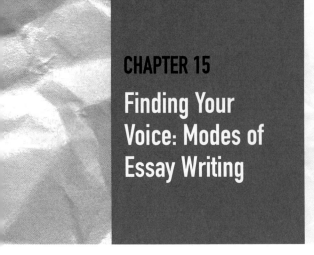

CHAPTER 15

Finding Your Voice: Modes of Essay Writing

The essayist . . . can pull on any sort of shirt, be any sort of person, according to his mood or his subject matter.
—E. B. WHITE

In this chapter:

- How to write an expository essay
- How to write an argumentative or persuasive essay
- How to recognize and avoid fallacies in argument

Role playing is a vital part of the skill of essay writing. You must write the essay confident of your role as an expert. In this chapter, we will modify the general principles of essay writing according to the various purposes of different types of essays, and describe a role you might adopt as the author of one of these types. In addition, the chapter emphasizes the kind of reader or audience that each of the different essay types has. All of the types described share the general characteristics that we have already discussed:

1. a narrow thesis statement
2. a clear outline
3. carefully delineated patterns of development
4. a unified structure—introduction, body, and conclusion
5. a coherent approach to the integration of support materials
6. an attention to sentence structure, emphasis, and tone

Remember that many of the steps involved in writing the different types of essays described in this chapter overlap. But whether an essay is meant as an informal discussion or as a formal research paper, the steps outlined above are essential. No less important are the steps in revision described in Chapter 13. This chapter will show you how to prepare yourself for certain specialized types of essay writing. Consult it for advice geared to the particular task at hand.

The Expository Essay

You shouldn't pay very much attention to anything writers say. They don't know why they do what they do. They're like good tennis players or good painters, who are just full of nonsense, pompous and embarrassing, or merely mistaken, when they open their mouths.

—John Barth

Expository essays teach, clarify, show, illustrate a less controversial subject. Persuasive essays argue, claim, defend, debate a more controversial subject. The expository essay is the most common essay assignment. It is based on the premise that you learn best about something by trying to teach it to someone else. In other words, the expository essay asks you to play the role of teacher, by presenting your chosen material according to your sense of its meaning and structure.

The expository essay exposes: it shows your approach to a particular subject. As in all essay writing, you must develop a general topic into a specific thesis statement, you must prepare an outline, and you must determine the patterns of development appropriate to your discussion. The expository essay is different only because its object is primarily to *teach*, rather than to persuade, to present research material, to review, or to express personal conviction.

Four stages are involved in writing the expository essay:

1. finding your focus
2. planning your structure
3. adjusting your level of language
4. testing your results

These stages, while much the same as those outlined in the sections on developing, designing, and drafting the basic essay, are all affected by your role as teacher, and hence they need special consideration.

The Role of the Expository Essay

Before you begin, try to see your task in terms of its audience and its purpose.

AUDIENCE: a curious, but uninformed, reader you address in a professional but approachable way

PURPOSE: to present some important idea in a way that clarifies it, shows your attitude toward it, and answers questions the reader might have

With these criteria in mind, you can now adjust the stages in writing to suit the occasion.

Finding Your Focus

1. Find a subject that you know something about and are genuinely interested in, if possible.
2. Establish your objectives. Like a teacher, you should know what you want your reader to learn from your work.
3. Limit your subject to what can be thoroughly explained within the word length of the assignment. What you propose to show or explain is, in this case, your thesis statement.

SUBJECT: Forest-fire management   **Example**

OBJECTIVE: To show how it is done

LIMITATION: The step-by-step process of forest-fire management: prevention and control

Planning Your Structure

1. Break down the parts of your subject clearly in an outline.
2. Choose the pattern(s) of development that will allow you to explain most clearly.
3. Connect the steps in your thought logically and clearly.

Example

PATTERN OF DEVELOPMENT: Process: how forest fires are managed

BREAKDOWN OF IDEAS: Rough outline

THESIS: The Ministry of Natural Resources annually sets in motion a regular plan by which to combat forest fires that threaten to destroy Canada's natural resources.

BODY: The Ministry does several things to control forest fires:

1. It establishes central locations where firefighting begins.
2. It predicts what areas are most endangered and maps these areas in detail.
3. It monitors weather conditions and keeps records of soil moisture and amounts of precipitation.
4. It monitors weather predictions.
5. It uses aerial patrols and lightning towers to keep watch.
6. It mobilizes fire crews when fire or smoke is reported.
7. It dispatches water bombers and erects fire camps in crisis situations.
8. It supplies all types of firefighting equipment.

CONCLUSION: Firefighting in Canada's forest regions is a careful process, dedicated to ensuring the protection of precious natural resources.

Adjusting Your Level of Language

1. Keep your reader's level of knowledge in mind.
2. Define all terms likely to be unfamiliar to the reader.
3. Make language concrete, concise, and clear.

LEVEL OF KNOWLEDGE: Provide enough background in the introduction so that the reader will know why forest-fire management is important.

Example

In 1996 alone, despite preventive measures, a total of 1356 forest fires ravaged 371 358 ha of prime timber.

USE OF TERMS: Explain terms like "water bombers" and any other terms unlikely to be familiar to a reader.

Example

A water bomber is a large and cumbersome government-owned plane that can douse a fire with 5400 L of water.

CONCRETE, CONCISE, CLEAR LANGUAGE: Tell what a firefighter does, rather than what fire management is in the abstract. Include plenty of detail.

Maps that show area landscapes precisely enable officers to see what sort of timber **Example** may be threatened by forest fires and what buildings, such as summer cottages and outpost camps, are in immediate or anticipated danger.

Testing Your Results

1. Check your work to see that it is as clear as possible. Put yourself in your reader's place: would you learn from the essay?
2. Have someone else read your work to see that it is readily understandable.
3. Proofread carefully to see that your writing does justice to your thoughts.

The Argumentative Essay

Use soft words and hard arguments.

–English Proverb

The argumentative or persuasive essay aims at convincing the reader of the truth and validity of your position. Its subject matter is controversial, its thesis one view of the issue. Your task is to win your reader over with your credibility, your wealth of support, and your good reasoning.

Unlike the expository essay, which simply aims to *show* the reader something, the argumentative essay, by taking one side of a controversial issue, aims to *convince* the reader.

Prepare the argumentative essay according to the following stages:

1. Study the issues.
2. Pick a side—your thesis statement.
3. Make a case for the defence—your support.
4. Consider opposing viewpoints, and qualify or refute accordingly. You need to take a side and stick with it, except in rare cases where you argue that some reconciliation is possible or occasionally that no choice need be made. Most often, you need to be aware of what your opponents will say in objection and try to anticipate challenges by showing weaknesses in thinking that are contrary to your point of view.
5. Test your argument for fairness and effectiveness.
6. Direct your argument, first in outline, then in final form.

An argumentative or persuasive essay may or may not demand that you engage in extensive research to support your case. It does, however, demand that you keep your writing role in mind.

The Role of the Argumentative Essay

Tailor your essay to fit its special demands.

AUDIENCE: readers who have not made up their minds about a controversial matter and who are willing to make a fair and impartial judgment

PURPOSE: to convince them that your informed opinion on a particular subject is the best one

With these points in mind, consider the stages of the argumentative essay. Suppose you are writing a paper on the accessibility of health care. Research is not always a major requirement; what is required is your independent, well-formulated viewpoint regarding this controversial subject.

Studying the Issues

Before you take sides, you must examine all the angles of the question. Make a list of pros and cons about any issue that must be decided or possible answers to any question that must be settled.

Example   Issue: Should the government continue to influence the distribution of physicians across the country in order to improve health-care access?

PROS

health care should be accessible to everyone

rural areas are underserviced; most specialists are located in cities

rural areas often lack hospital services

CONS

doctors, particularly specialists, must be near hospitals

the financial constraints of building and maintaining hospitals in rural areas are overwhelming

the cost of health care itself impedes access to it

Picking a Side

1. Choose the side for which you can muster the most support. If possible, choose a thesis that you genuinely believe in.
2. Define your position by making a claim or by arguing against another's claim.

Example   Side Chosen: The distribution of physicians has no real bearing on health-care access.

Position Defined: The current distribution of physicians does not affect health-care access. The high cost of health care is the main constraint to adequate access.

1. Physicians, particularly specialists, must be near medical facilities to run their practices effectively.
2. Physicians, therefore, should not be penalized for their decision to practise in cities, as they have been in Quebec, Ontario, and British Columbia.
3. The number of physicians should not be increased, as it has been in the rest of Canada, since that "solution" only increases the cost of an expensive health-care system.
4. More hospitals cannot be built and maintained in rural areas without increasing expenditures even more.

5. The current situation, where general practitioners tend to work in towns and rural areas and specialists choose cities, is the only workable way of balancing cost and access.

Making a Case for the Defence

1. Gather support for your arguments. In some instances, this support will come from books or journals, though it may also come from your own clear understanding of the issue.
2. Use your own reasons. In the case of a research essay like this one, also use statistics and expert opinion as further support. Remember to acknowledge sources.

Accessibility is a fundamental principle of Canadian health insurance. The 1966 *Medical Care Act* "requires insured services to be delivered in a manner that does not impede or preclude, either directly or indirectly . . . reasonable access."[1] In keeping with this principle, both federal and provincial governments have tried to change the geographic distribution of doctors in an effort to correct a perceived inequitable distribution of physicians. They hoped thereby to improve access to health services in rural areas.

Example

(Expert Opinion) Here the writer quotes an authority and comments on it, connecting it to the thesis of the paper.

In the 1960s and early 1970s, the federal government attributed the low physician-to-population ratio in rural areas to an overall shortage of doctors in the country. They believed that if there were more doctors, rural areas would no longer be under-serviced.[2] So, the Canadian government responded to the problem by increasing the capacity of domestic medical schools and opening immigration to physicians. Between 1968 and 1974, the number of physicians in Canada grew by 8151, or 36 percent;[3] however, the distribution of physicians between rural and urban areas remained disproportionate, and the gap even worsened in Ontario.[4] In fact, the growth in the number of physicians increased health-care costs, but it did not improve the accessibility of health services.

Example

(Statistics) Here the writer uses statistics to show that access to physicians in rural areas did not improve, though at first glance the numbers might have seemed encouraging.

Actually, the increase in the number of physicians to which governmental controls has led is responsible for increasing health-care costs; to build more hospitals would increase these costs even more. Given that funds are limited, if every small town were provided with a fully equipped hospital, then the more expensive equipment and treatments—like CAT scans and cancer treatments—would not be available anywhere in Canada. It might also become necessary to impose restrictions on accessibility similar to the rationing of health care in Britain, where—as a means of containing health costs—kidney dialysis is not available to National Health Service patients over 55 years of age.[5]

Example

(Reasons) Here the writer uses reasons to show that more hospitals is a facile answer since they would not improve access to new technology except through the imposition of more restrictions.

Considering Opposing Viewpoints

1. Anticipate objections to your arguments as you go along.
2. Treat the opposition fairly.

Example

Anticipated Argument: In spite of these arguments, the number of physicians in rural areas is still smaller than it should be to ensure access to health-care services.

Fair Treatment: a counterargument that analyzes the problem closely

Although rural areas tend to have fewer physicians per capita than cities, the difference in available medical services is not necessarily proportional to the difference in the respective physician-to-population ratios. Family and general practitioners gravitate toward smaller towns, while specialists tend to settle in cities.[6] The significance of this fact lies in the kinds of medical care these doctors provide. GPs perform a considerably wider range of services than do specialists. To some degree, then, one GP acts as a substitute for the many different specialists available in the city, so access to health care may not be as unequal as the present geographic distribution of physicians implies.

Here the writer shows that the research findings may be more complex than they first appear, so they may not lead to the conclusion that rural areas have poorer access to health care.

Testing Your Argument for Fairness and Effectiveness

1. Check for fallacies, or flaws, in your argument.
2. Weigh your words carefully, avoiding biased, vague, and unconsidered words.

When writing (or reading) any argumentative or persuasive essay, you may fall prey to a number of logical errors in your thinking. Remember that certain arguments are not in the spirit of fair play. Learn to recognize the following faulty arguments or fallacies and avoid them in your own writing:

1. ACCEPTING GLIB GENERALIZATIONS.

An argument that uses catch phrases like "Canadian identity" or "freedom of the individual" in an unthinking way may just be appealing to what the words conjure up, rather than to any thoughtful meaning assigned to them by the writer. Make sure such general appeals can be pinned down to specifics. If the mayor of your city argues that he or she will work to increase "civic pride," ask what specifics such a general statement entails.

Example

Women commit more crimes today than ever before; therefore, modern society has corrupted women.

I have a right to keep my gun even though I have anger issues; everyone has the right to own property.

2. ARGUING *AD HOMINEM*.

This kind of argument distracts readers from the issue being discussed and, instead, uses personal attacks against an opponent. For example, someone might argue that health-insurance fees should not go up because doctors are interested only in making money. Here the personal charge being made may have nothing to do with the issue.

That counsellor has no business giving advice to married couples; she has been divorced herself. **Example**

I do not believe that new employee will be hardworking; he has too many interests to devote himself to working at this job.

3. ESTABLISHING FAULTY CAUSE AND EFFECT.

This kind of faulty reasoning assumes that there is a connection between two events simply because one followed the other. For instance, if a political party claims that it is responsible for a drop in interest rates that occurred during its period in office, we need to ask if such a drop might have occurred regardless. After all, there may be many other ways of explaining changes in interest rates.

Since the new laws related to airport security were put in place, acts of terrorism have been less in evidence. **Example**

After the new government was elected, the commodity market recovered.

4. MAKING A FAULTY ANALOGY.

Often we make analogies, or comparisons, in order to show significant similarities between things. We must, however, always take care to make sure that such comparisons are fair. Commercials are often the chief offenders in this regard. Is a day without orange juice really like a day without sunshine? Check to make sure that your own comparisons are appropriate.

Children should not be expected to do homework every day. You would not expect a family pet to perform tricks every day. **Example**

Procrastination works like adrenaline; when you really need to finish something, you will find the time and energy.

5. ASSUMING AN "EITHER/OR" SITUATION.

One of our commonest assumptions is that there are always two sides to any issue. In fact, there may be many more than two sides. See to it that you do not phrase your arguments in such a way that they falsify the problem. It is probably not true that if you don't believe in free enterprise, then you are a communist. Be aware of other possibilities between extremes. This fallacy is also known as the false dilemma.

Example   If the doctor cannot diagnose my illness, I must have cancer.

We should close the prisons and open the treatment centres.

6. JUMPING ON A BANDWAGON.

When you deal with a controversial topic, make sure that you examine the issues carefully before arriving at your own point of view. The argument that something is right because it is "modern," "current," "up-to-date," or because everyone is in favour of it, will not stand up.

Example   Christianity has defied its opponents for centuries. How could it have survived if it were not the true word of God?

Facebook and Twitter give us the right to express our opinions even if the government opposes us; they are changing the way things are done in the world.

7. BEGGING THE QUESTION.

You beg the question when you assume the truth of what you are trying to prove. For example, if you argue that books should not be taxed, it is not enough to say that no one could possibly support a tax on books because it will lead to increasing illiteracy. The onus is on you to prove that illiteracy will increase; you cannot simply assume so.

You may want to argue against this stated position:

Example   Health-care access would be more equitable if physicians were more concerned with taking care of patients than with making money.

The government in power is worthy to rule. The people have spoken.

Checking for flaws: Look at the underlying biases of the statement.

This statement in the context of the essay it comes from assumes that doctors practise in cities in order to make more money than they would in rural areas, but no proof is advanced for the claim. Here, in other words, the argument begs the question.

It is important to find evidence to justify any claim that you intend to make. The argument above rests on an unexamined assumption.

8. THE SLIPPERY SLOPE.

This fallacy occurs whenever someone assumes that one event will follow inevitably after another, without any argument in defence of that position. Like the expression "Give them an inch and they'll take a mile," it's assumed that one thing leads to another as a matter of course. This fallacy is also called the domino theory.

Example   If we allow this student more time between his exams, all the students will want time off to rest between exams.

If the bookstore sells magazines and tabloids, soon the entire campus will be reading scandal sheets and believing everything they read with no critical awareness whatsoever.

Directing Your Argument

1. Remind your readers of the points you are making by reinforcing those points as you go along. Some artful repetition is useful in essay writing; summarize or echo your arguments. Don't assume that the arguments will ring true to your readers without adequate evidence in the form of examples, statistics, expert opinion, and reasons.

2. Engage your readers as comrades-in-arms, not as antagonists. Assume that they are reasonable and open-minded about the issue. Do not assume that they are antagonistic even though they disagree with your point of view.

Look at these techniques in the following paragraph that concludes the paper on access to health care:

Since every small town does not have a hospital and physicians are not located in proportion to demand, barriers to access to health services unquestionably exist; however, the cost of breaking down these barriers is higher than the cost of their presence. Ultimately, then, it is the cost of health care itself that impedes equal access. With limited government funds, equality of accessibility to health services is little more than an idealist's dream. So far, measures to make such services more accessible have invariably increased costs by more than they have improved access. Policies aimed at changing the distribution of physicians and hospitals are not the solution. Clearly, the federal and provincial governments need to change their approach to the issue of health-care access.

REINFORCEMENT: Summary of the line of argument

CHAPTER 15 EXERCISES

1. Make a case for the defence for each of the following statements, using Expert Opinion, Statistics, and Reasons as support.
   a. Taser guns should be banned.
   b. Canada has the best economy in the world.
   c. Extra-curricular activities will deflect from your academic success.
   d. Pets have therapeutic value.
   e. Social media are a waste of time.

   Now take each of these statements in turn and make one good argument on the side of the opposition.

2. Identify the fallacies in the following examples:
   a. Of course Father Whiteford opposes abortion. He's a priest and believes that the Pope is infallible.
   b. Teens should not participate in chat rooms because abduction of minors is on the rise.
   c. I fixed the picture on the TV by hitting it on its side. The picture improved immediately.
   d. Women do not belong in boardrooms; they are indecisive and emotional.
   e. Lying on your résumé shouldn't matter if you don't get caught. It is the company's responsibility to check the applications it receives.

f. If you allow students to hand assignments in late, they won't ever hand anything in on time.
g. Since she has been carrying that good luck charm, she has won two lottery prizes.
h. What does Martha Stewart know about homemaking? She was trained as a stockbroker.
i. We must oppose the war for the good of the nation.
j. Anyone who seriously believes that plastic surgery is acceptable is making a big mistake.

CHAPTER 16

Collaborative Writing

"A camel is a horse designed by a committee."
—SIR ALEC ISSIGONIS

In this chapter:

- How to work well with others on writing projects
- How to use technology effectively in group work

As this saying suggests, collaboration can produce some unintended results. Writing collaboratively is no exception. Exerting control over the design and execution of a paper is complicated when you are working with other people. If you want to make sure that the essay you produce has unity and coherence, you will need to start with a plan, divide the work wisely, and edit for a smooth and seamless final product. Although it may be a complicated process, collaboration is frequently involved in work settings, and many instructors have turned to it as a teaching method not only because it imitates the real-life conditions in the contemporary workplace, but also because it promotes learning among peers. The object of collaborative writing is to learn from other members of your team and ultimately produce a better and more sophisticated final work than would be possible on your own.

More and more, projects are pursued by groups rather than individuals. Witness the popular success of online projects like Wikipedia, where the materials that make up an ever-evolving encyclopedia are daily changed and amended by a multitude of hands. Some may argue that this peer-centred approach to education lacks authority, but it gains in speed, in evolution, and in the power of consensus. Authority need not be a centralized thing, and indeed, innovations like the Internet argue that a multiplicity of voices is a better approach to getting at the truth about any subject as it changes and as it is accepted or rejected by numbers of readers and writers.

Group Work

To make the most of a collaborative writing experience, think about the group dynamics. You need to be able to get along with other members of your group, whether it is selected for you or you have a hand in its formation. Here are some tips for working in a group:

1. Be sensitive to others' feelings. You need to be able to handle disagreements, achieve consensus, and discuss openly any issues that come up.

2. Be willing to play more than one role in the group. Groups need leaders, but they also need people willing to act as secretaries or note-takers, people who ask questions or formulate objections, people who offer support, and others who manage the group's time. Don't fall into the habit of playing just one role. If you need to, it might be useful to delegate responsibilities in a group, so that for each meeting, you have a different leader, a different secretary, a different supporter, and a different objector. Creating roles like this will help you sort out your ideas without too much personal attachment to them.

3. Have an agenda. Make sure at the outset of each meeting that you know what you want to accomplish before the next meeting, so that the work goes forward.

4. Establish clear goals and schedules for the group, and do everything you can to stick to them.

5. Keep track of your progress. It is a good idea to submit comments on your own performance and your group's performance in writing at the end of each meeting. That way, your instructor can monitor your progress and make suggestions to help you achieve your goals.

6. Be present. Attendance is a crucial part of group work. Although there are many technological advances that make collaborative work possible and even easy, face-to-face meetings are an important part of the process.

7. Use support systems, like MSN or Track Changes (under the Tools menu in Microsoft Word), to register the contributions and changes that each member of the group makes. E-mail and collaborative software like Track Changes make it easy for more than one person to write and edit documents since a record of each change, pertinent comments, the authors, and the dates the changes were entered are easy to find and can be colour-coded for improved visibility.

8. Divide and conquer. Remember that your group should ideally produce something exponentially better than any one individual could create for an assignment. While the extra communication can be complicated, the result is usually stronger for it. Two heads are better than one.

9. Allow extra time to assemble all the parts of the work into the whole. The final editing process is more complicated when many hands are involved in the writing and research, so more checking and more focus on the overall goals of the project are essential.

10. Remember that the process is almost as important as the final result. How you create this work is often part of the assignment, not just what you create. Use the group work situation as a means of learning from each other, not only in terms of the subject matter, but also in terms of project management itself.

A SAMPLE COLLABORATIVE PARAGRAPH USING TRACK CHANGES

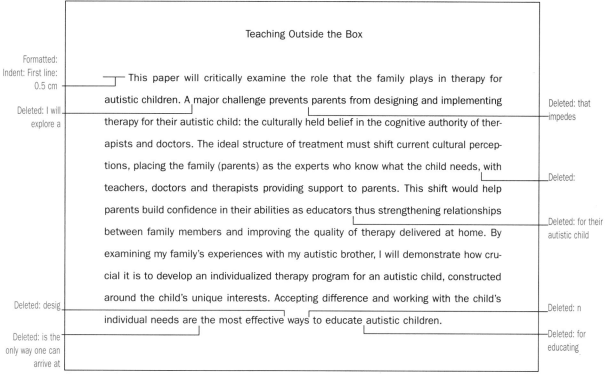

Courtesy of April Beresford

CHAPTER 16 EXERCISES

1. Start a blog, that is, a Web log. You can often get a free account provided through a search engine. For example, Google offers space on <http://www.blogger.com>. You can start a blog on any subject you like, provided you adhere to the standards that the search engine sets. There you can publish on the Web your comments or questions on any subject you like and invite others to join your blog and participate in it.

2. Investigate some existing blogs on the Web. Many blogs allow you an opportunity to post comments on them and engage in the online conversation. This is an excellent way to improve your writing and your sense of audience.

3. Use a blog as a means of collaborating on a project with classmates. Each one can write and publish a particular section of the assignment, and all members of the group may edit the materials, if so desired.

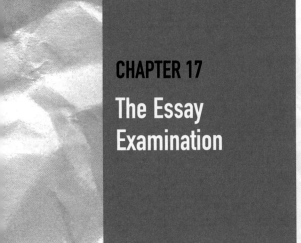

CHAPTER 17

The Essay Examination

Eighty percent of success is showing up.
—WOODY ALLEN

In this chapter:

- How to study for essay exams
- How to interpret essay questions on exams
- How to improve your essay writing on exams

Essay examinations are frequently a source of panic because they strip the writer down to the bare essentials. Without hours of preparation to cover your flaws, whether in knowledge or fluency, you may feel exposed—unless your work is genuinely in good shape. An essay examination, because of its time limitations, is brief but not without style.

   The advice that follows will help you write a better examination, if you approach it in stages:

1. Getting in shape
2. Coping with exam shyness
3. Making the material fit
4. Taking the plunge
5. Standing out in a crowd

The Role of the Essay Examination

Remember your reader and your aim:

   AUDIENCE: an expert (not an antagonist) who wishes to test your knowledge and
                 facility in his or her discipline

   PURPOSE: to show what you have learned and how you can apply it

Getting in Shape

An examination is only the product. What determines its outcome is your preparation, not only in the nervous hours immediately before it, but in the days and weeks preceding it as well.

To make your performance on the exam less fraught and more predictable, prepare for it gradually. If you have faced your fears throughout the year, the final countdown should not be anxiety-ridden. At least your conscience will be clear if you have attended class, read the textbooks, and completed the course work.

Coping with Exam Shyness

ANALYZE THE SHAPE YOU'RE IN. Be brave. Take a good hard look at yourself. Judge your past performance in the course. Consider the amount of work you have done. If you're already in good shape, this step will increase your confidence. If not, read on.

LIMBER UP. Even a well-prepared student will need to warm up for the examination by conducting a review. Review course work by setting up a reasonable work schedule and then following it (with some flexibility, of course).

Review does not mean reread. Review should be refreshing, just as a warm-up exercise is meant to get you ready for more and not to drain you of energy. Review is just part of the routine. Look through your notes and your texts, as well as your past essays and tests. This process will be easier if you have highlighted important points beforehand (and if you have done all the required work in the first place).

LOCATE PROBLEM AREAS. To overcome shyness about the exam, you must confront your fears. Ask yourself, unflinchingly, "What am I afraid of?" If you find that you are worried about some specific problems in your understanding of the course, pay particular attention to these problems. The benefits will be twofold: you will conquer some of your fears, and you will learn something.

Making the Material Fit

In order to learn anything, you must make it a part of yourself. You must carry it away with you and get carried away with it (while still keeping your feet on the ground).

To gain full possession of the course material, you will use *memory, fluency, application*, and *imagination*. Here's how.

MEMORY. There is no learning without memory, though memory is just the first step in turning course material into something of your own. To sharpen your skills of recall, try reading aloud, so that both sight and hearing can register the information.

Concentrate on facts and significant details. Help your memory along by making associations or by visualizing material. These tactics will trigger memory when you're stuck for words.

If memorizing is not your strong point, don't despair. Although an essay exam demands that you have some facts at your fingertips, how the facts are presented, how they are used, and what you create out of them are equally important.

FLUENCY. To make yourself an expert in a discipline, learn how to speak its language as you master its content. Make the terms a part of your language by learning to define them, by including them in speech, and by using them in writing. When imagining how you would answer a question, talk to yourself. Jot down notes. The more conversant you are with specialized language in your subject area, the more grace-fully you will write under pressure.

APPLICATION. Make sure you can use what you know. To apply your knowledge, you need to supply a context. Don't just repeat the facts: question the material. As you review, note questions that the textbook may have raised. Keep in mind any questions raised in class or topics distributed for review that strike you as pertinent. These questions may prove useful when exam time comes.

IMAGINATION. All work and no play would make a dull examination and certainly a grim study period. Approach the test and your preparation for it with a sense of play, if at all possible. Wonder about its potential. Don't confine your imagination to the tried and true; experiment with some ideas of your own. Develop a theory or two, as if you were preparing for a formal essay. You may well get a chance to try them out on the examination. The difference between an A and a B is often a desire to develop your own ideas and to create something new out of the material.

Taking the Plunge

Writing an examination successfully depends on two factors: what you know *and* what you can say about it in a limited time. To make the best use of your time, follow this basic pattern: *read, sketch, write, skim.*

READ THE QUESTIONS CAREFULLY. Before you get your feet wet, so to speak, read over the entire exam. Take careful note of the instructions. If you are given a choice of questions, devote a few minutes to their selection. Allot an appropriate amount of time for each question and *adhere to that schedule.* It is wise to begin with the ques-tions you know best.

Look for questions to challenge you. Remember that an essay question does not necessarily have a correct answer. An essay simply tries, as its name suggests, to come to terms with a provocative, perhaps troubling, question.

Become familiar with these common examination terms:

Explain. If you are asked to *explain,* be thorough in your approach and ready to clarify in detail, as though you were teaching the reader. Both structure and sub-stance are needed, so be prepared to show both breadth and depth in your treatment of the question.

Example   The federal New Democratic Party has been called the "normal opposition party." Explain. What must the federal New Democratic Party do to become the "normal gov-ernment party"?

Begin by using facts to explain the label "normal opposition party." These facts should be available to you from the course material. Then, making sure to refer to appropriate sources, discuss various theories of what is needed to ensure NDP suc-cess at the polls.

Discuss. If asked to *discuss,* use the latitude of the question to focus on some part of the problem that captures your attention and allows you to present a lively, informative, and thoughtful consideration of the problem. Treat the question as if you were writing a less than formal essay—as indeed you are.

Discuss the ways in which family ties and loyalties dramatically expand the inner conflicts and crises of conscience in *Huckleberry Finn* and *King Lear*.   **Example**

Begin by focusing on the conventional bond between parents and children. Show how the bonds are broken in both works. Then you could go on to show how a new sense of family is created for both Lear and Huck in the levelling process that occurs in both works. Remember to include many examples to support your points.

Outline. If asked to *outline*, put your emphasis on the bare bones of the argument—the facts—rather than the flesh. An outline will require you to place more stress on the shape and the sequence of your subject, rather than the substance.

Outline how and why geographical factors are so strongly evident in classical mythology.   **Example**

Your outline should be broadly based, isolating a number of examples of geographical factors in a variety of myths, rather than in one or two. Follow these examples with a discussion suggesting some of the reasons for this phenomenon. Aim at broad coverage rather than deep analysis.

Compare and Contrast. If asked to *compare and contrast*, or simply to *compare*, remember that the object is to show the relationship between two things. Focus the essay on the connections and differences you find by setting two things side by side in your sketch.

Compare and contrast the women's movement of the late nineteenth and early twentieth centuries with the women's movement that began in the late 1960s.   **Example**

Begin by making an outline to discover the main similarities and differences. Say, for example, that the main similarities include the desire to change attitudes toward working women and the desire to gain more influence in the workplace. The differences might include the earlier movement's focus on political rights and the later movement's focus on issues relating to sexual harassment on the job. You could compare and contrast not only the goals of the movements, but also the relative success of each of them. Then you need a summary of your findings in order to compare these two movements more generally.

SKETCH. Sketch out your answers to the questions chosen. First, let yourself go. Jot things down as they occur to you. One good approach to quick brainstorming is the use of a concept map. A concept map allows you to draw the idea, usually from a central point. Connected ideas branch out from the centre, and sometimes branches grow new branches. This method allows you to group concepts together quickly and to explore their relation to each other better than a mere "laundry list" can do. You can see on one page the connections you are discovering as you explore the topic, and you can group them together more easily in visuals than in words. Avoid getting embroiled in outlines, whether visual or verbal, which are too complex or too demanding for the time allowed.

Sketch your answers in the briefest possible form. As you do so, use key words in the question to guide your responses. Above all, obey the terms of the question as you work in the things you want to say.

WRITE. Sketching your material enabled you to get warmed up. Therefore, the writing process itself should be more graceful and more organized. To ensure an organized presentation, fall back on established essay-writing habits. Begin at the beginning. Make sure your answer has an introduction, a body, and a conclusion. While these sections will be hastier and less polished, do not abandon structure entirely.

The main thing to keep in mind is the connections you are making between the question and the knowledge you brought with you into the exam. Refer to your sketch and to the original question as you write, but also allow yourself the freedom of an unexpected idea or a unique turn of phrase, as long as it doesn't interfere with the basic flow of your answer.

Let the words flow quickly, but keep the writing legible. Write on every other line as a courtesy to your reader.

SKIM. Force yourself to read your answers quickly and to make small changes. To neglect this stage is to force your instructor to become the proofreader—a proofreader who might become annoyed at your carelessness. A small mistake is forgivable; reckless abandon is not.

Standing Out in a Crowd

Now that you know how to pass an essay examination, you may well wonder how to surpass expectations. Though you are writing the examination along with perhaps hundreds of other students, there are ways of making your exam style unique without defying the conventions of test writing.

What does a bleary-eyed instructor, marking 200 essay questions, look for in an answer?

DEFINITION. An essay examination is your chance to show your understanding of how some terminology in the subject area works. Unlike a multiple-choice exam, this kind of test will allow you to use the language of the discipline precisely and fluently.

DIRECTION. Your answers should be pointed directly at the questions. Don't make the mistake of trying to say everything; you can't assume that the instructor will give you credit if he or she can find the right answer somewhere in your paper. You also can't assume that your instructor will want to look for your answer. Make your answer easy to find.

DETAIL. While even an exceptional student cannot remember all of the fine points in a complex body of work, it is certainly possible to learn a smattering of appropriate details on a variety of subjects. Such details may be inserted, where applicable, as you are writing the exam. Details have the effect of a close-up. They allow you to focus on something precise, and they reveal your careful reading of your subject matter.

DEPTH. To demonstrate depth of knowledge, an examination must show that the writer has thought about the implications of the subject and of the specific question. Dive in. Don't avoid entirely the deeper complexities of a question in favour of its superficial requirements. Where possible, do more than you need to do. Answer questions seriously; you are writing as a curious and concerned expert. Address your subject, not as an illustration of how well you have learned it, but rather as a serious attempt to advance the subject matter itself.

DISCOVERY. A brilliant exam will show what a student has learned above and beyond what the instructor has taught. If you have some insight or even some questions about the material that you have not raised in class, this is your opportunity to voice your concerns. Never recite the answer to a question based on your memory of a lecture unless you have, sadly, nothing of your own to add to the material. An exam should occasionally allow you to take intelligent, calculated risks.

If you stay on topic, actually answer the question that is being asked, and structure your essay with an introduction and a conclusion—no matter how short of time you are—your exam will be a success.

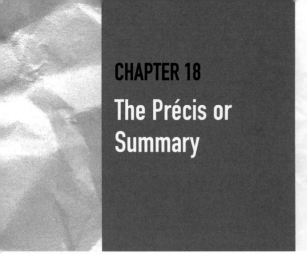

CHAPTER 18
The Précis or Summary

When you catch an adjective, kill it.
—MARK TWAIN

In this chapter:

• How and why to write a précis

A précis is a concise summary of a longer passage. Sometimes, a précis will be an assignment in its own right; on other occasions, it will be something that you prepare as part of writing a larger essay of your own. The ability to summarize one's own or others' work is important: often, you will be asked to provide short summaries of your written material, whether in abstract form, as is the case with dissertations, or in executive summary form, in the case of reports. Sometimes, too, a précis will provide you with a short memo about what you considered the key features in a work central to your research. The task of writing a précis will help you learn to focus on the line of argument in a passage and will oblige you to reconsider it in your own words; this kind of engagement with source material, or even with your own writing, can be invaluable in honing your critical abilities. In addition, précis writing can help make your writing more concise.

The Role of the Précis

Before you start, conceive of your task in relation to its audience and its purpose.

AUDIENCE: someone who wants you to give a quick overview of a detailed piece of writing without sacrificing central content

PURPOSE: often to reduce a passage to one-third or even one-quarter of its original length, occasionally even shorter, in a way that keeps the original focus and does not obfuscate ideas

Assuming that your task is to reduce a passage to one-third of its original length, you can now follow these guidelines:

Reading the Original Passage
1. Read the passage to ferret out its main focus.
2. Try to reconstruct the organization of the passage as you read through it.

3. Jot down the main idea of the passage, and mark ideas that are central to it, or peripheral to it, as you go along.
4. Reduce the passage to an outline that constitutes its line of argument.

Condensing Sentence Structure

Many constructions in English are redundant and can be substantially reduced without adversely affecting content. Here are some suggestions about how to reduce the sentence structure you find in a longer passage:

1. LEAVE OUT APPOSITIVES, WORDS OR PHRASES THAT RENAME OTHER WORDS.

✗ Socks, his cat, caught her third mouse this week.　　　　　**Example**

✓ Socks caught her third mouse this week.

2. LEAVE OUT WORDS THAT ARE INCLUDED ONLY FOR EMPHASIS.

✗ Bill was very disappointed.　　　　　**Example**

✓ Bill was devastated.

3. CHANGE FIGURATIVE LANGUAGE, SUCH AS SIMILES AND METAPHORS, OR OMIT THEM.

✗ Tilly worked like a dog on the project.　　　　　**Example**

✓ Tilly laboured on the project.

4. LEAVE OUT INTRODUCTORY CONSTRUCTIONS LIKE "IT IS . . . WHO" OR "IT IS . . . WHICH."

✗ It is Cathy who works in the library.　　　　　**Example**

✓ Cathy works in the library.

5. FIND ONE WORD THAT WILL DO THE WORK OF SEVERAL.

✗ Cole is a man who had once taught school.　　　　　**Example**

✓ Cole is an ex-teacher.

✗ Dil left the room without a sound.

✓ Dil left the room silently.

6. FIND WORDS THAT ALLOW YOU TO GENERALIZE RATHER THAN PARTICULARIZE.

✗ Nelly bought hamburgers, French fries, and soft drinks. **Example**

✓ Nelly bought fast food.

7. TURN RHETORICAL QUESTIONS INTO STATEMENTS.

✗ What kind of person would be interested in yet another situation comedy? **Example**

✓ Few people would be interested in yet another situation comedy.

8. COMBINE SHORT SENTENCES TO REDUCE WORD LENGTH.

✗ In the beginning of the twenty-first century, more unrelated people are living **Example**
together under the same roof. These people may be joined together for love. They
may be joined for convenience. Or, they may be joined out of necessity. Whatever
the reason, choosing a roommate is one of the most important decisions you will
make. If two people are united for love, then choosing a roommate is a very personal decision. If two or more people are going to live together for convenience,
or out of necessity, then choosing roommates is an important decision. This decision must be well thought out because choosing the wrong roommate could cost
you financially, physically, and mentally. Choosing a roommate is difficult, but the
process you use in choosing a roommate is as important as the roommate you
choose, because the process you choose will lead to your roommate, and your new
roommate will have a significant effect on your life.

✓ In the beginning of the twenty-first century, more unrelated people are living
together under the same roof for love, for convenience, or out of necessity. If two
people unite out of love, then the choice of a roommate is personal; however, if you
live with someone for convenience or out of necessity, you must choose cautiously.
The wrong roommate could cost you financially, physically, and mentally. Choosing
a roommate, though difficult, is crucial because the roommate chosen will have a
powerful effect on your life.

Writing the Précis
1. Write out in your own words the main points in the passage.
2. Check that words you substitute are appropriate to their new context. Check the precise meanings of words.
3. Keep the original paragraph structure unless the piece is short.
4. Try to keep the tone and style of the original intact.
5. Do not add anything as you interpret the passage.
6. Keep the word length to approximately one-third of the original, unless other-wise instructed, but don't cut out essentials.
7. Read the passage again and revise carefully.

CHAPTER 19
The Informal Essay

All writing is communication; creative writing is communication through revelation—it is the self escaping into the open. No writer long remains incognito.
—E. B. WHITE

In this chapter:

- How to write an informal essay
- How to engage your audience in an informal piece of writing

In most cases, the essays you write as part of your course work will be formal in tone. When you are allowed the luxury of writing an informal essay, follow these basic suggestions:

1. Be yourself.
2. Choose a comfortable subject.
3. Experiment with style and subject.
4. Shop around.

The Role of the Informal Essay

The informal essay affords you greater freedom and a more casual approach than the formal essay. Although the same writing process is demanded in the informal essay—it too needs a thesis statement, a typical essay shape, and a command of the mechanics of writing—what you say and how you say it are a matter of invention rather than convention.

AUDIENCE: friendly company who find your perspective stimulating

PURPOSE: to talk about anything that appeals to your imagination

Be Yourself

The informal essay should let the reader learn about you and about your subject. Whereas you are obliged to keep a restrained and professional distance in the formal essay, you should maintain a casual and personal tone in the informal essay. Someone reading your paper will learn not only the facts and figures of your subject, but also some of your characteristics and your attitudes.

You will necessarily be more exposed: flaws in your arguments, biases in your attitudes, and unattractive aspects of your personality may show. The informal essay is by definition a face-to-face meeting between you and the reader. To prevent excessive vulnerability, you must examine your attitudes scrupulously, and be prepared to face your reader's reaction—alone.

Choose a Comfortable Subject

Whereas a formal essay must be logical, objective, tight, and well supported, an informal essay allows you to be more subjective in your viewpoint, more personal in your selection of supporting material, and more idiosyncratic in your approach.

The formal essay may argue a life-and-death matter; the informal essay is, by contrast, an intellectual exercise for its own sake. This characterization does not mean that the informal essay cannot be heartfelt or deeply important—but its tone is less public, its argument closer to your personal interests, and its value less dependent on knowledge of facts than on grace and eloquence.

Experiment with Subject and Style

You must draw the material and the viewpoint from your own sense of the subject, rather than looking to authorities for defence.

In an informal essay, your object is to keep your reader interested in what you have to say. You cannot assume that the subject is intrinsically appealing to the reader from a professional standpoint, as you do in the formal essay. Since the material you choose in the informal essay reflects you and your personal understanding of the matter, you must appeal to your reader personally and share your opinions enthusiastically.

The informal essay allows you the opportunity to experiment with language in a way that would not be appropriate in a formal or research essay. Try writing as you speak—without lapsing into grammatical and structural errors. For example, in an informal essay, you can use contractions (don't, can't, etc.), which are generally not acceptable in a formal essay.

Shop Around

Make an effort to read some personal essays, whether newspaper editorials or in magazines or the "collected works" of a classmate. Here are some choices for stylistic study:

Barbara Amiel	Michele Landsberg
Russell Baker	Fran Lebowitz
Harry Bruce	Joey Slinger
Allan Fotheringham	Lewis Thomas
Ellen Goodman	James Thurber
Peter Gzowski	Jan Wong

CHAPTER 19 EXERCISES

Read the following informal essay and answer the questions that follow.

What I Learned by Watching TV*

Some say that television cannot teach me anything about real life, and that is the reason why I am currently engaged in a staring competition with my set. So far, the tube has won best three out of five, but as Dr. Schuller says, "If it's going to be, it's up to me." That TV has to blink sometime. So, while I wait for sweet victory against the naysayers of educational TV, I will set my mind to learning and become a couch potato.

Channel 57, Women's Television Network, will be the genesis of my education. This week's Friday night "Girl Movie," *Indiscretion of an American Wife,* launched me into a convertible Mercedes and down the streets of Rome to rendezvous with the heroine's Italian lover, Matteo. He is a splendid chap with dark, mysterious eyes, lusty eyebrows, and a five-o'clock shadow that never grows. He owns a vineyard in a gorgeous location where he and Julia make love under the warm stare of an Italian sun.

I quickly realize that if I am ever going to get the girl who drives the Mercedes and never have to shave again, then I better learn how to grow grapes. Where to go? Where to go? I know, Channel 39, Home and Garden Television. Here, Mike Holmes, endlessly cautions against unprofessional contractors and demonstrates his own prowess, touting the satisfaction of building my own Italian villa; *Landscape Smart* next reveals the secrets of a rigorous vineyard. I will stand back in amazement as three or four of my neighbours' lonely and ignored housewives come to comment on my earthiness.

But wait, that home wrecker, Matteo, was a marvellous lover. He wooed Julia. She felt special. He fed her grapes. They lived happily ever after. Where does a fellow learn those kinds of sensitive manoeuvres?

Channel 60, of course. If such a gentleman is so inclined, he may stay up far into the wee hours of Saturday morning to watch the Showcase Late Revue. They always show second-rate, low-budget porn with frequent nudity and gratuitous sex. Add in The Learning Channel's (TLC's) objective and mechanized educational program *The Sex Files,* and a fellow will be well on his way to developing some top-notch manoeuvres. The sensitivity part is easy: a season of *Dr. Oz* (ABC, Channel 10) and *I Dream of Jeannie* reruns (Family Channel, 37) is enough to earn any boy scout his sensitivity badge.

Now the next logical step is to apply all of this wonderful learning in the real world. Not so. Upon rousing himself groggily at one in the afternoon, the aspiring Matteo plunks himself back on the couch. Victory is mine. The television begs permission to be allowed to answer all of life's pressing questions.

How am I going to propose?—Life, Channel 56, *A Wedding Story*. What about divorce?—NBC, Channel 8, *The Good Wife*. What if my indiscreet housewife gets pregnant and goes into labour in a taxicab?—TLC, Channel 41, *Paramedics,* or perhaps *Trauma: Life in the ER.* What if she sleeps with my brother?—Global, Channel 5, *Jerry Springer,* or TNN, Channel 17, *WWF.* Gosh, I am set. I have got the answers to the world and to a woman's heart right here at my fingertips. Now it is really time to put my research to work.

---

* Reprinted with permission by Jeremy Cooper

Blink.

I uprooted my tubers from the fertile furrow of my couch and headed out into the real, non-televised world. What a shock. Can you believe that no one wants to hire a paramedic whose primary work experience is eight hours per week watching TLC, and whose best reference came from the cable company? And did you know that not a single construction company would apprentice me, not even when I showed them my autographed portrait of Mike Holmes? Frankly, I was stunned.

I was so bewildered, in fact, that I even stopped to talk with some of the other folks in the unemployment line. Trade tickets and diplomas and bachelor degrees and hours upon hours of work experience came flying out from under hats and pocket flaps. They weren't the send-away kind of certificates either; they were the real thing. Just about every person in the line had gone to school and bled over exams or term papers. What an epiphany. (I learned that word from *Spelling Bee*. Do you think those kids got so smart by watching TV?)

Apparently, asides and interior monologues do not work off-screen: someone was shaking me and slapping me in the face. The girl with the plumber, pipe fitter, butcher, and hairdresser tickets was pulling her hair out and yelling in my face, "No! Get a grip, man. Get a life. Kids don't learn that stuff from watching TV. They have to internalize their knowledge and put it to use; television just puts *it* out." (*It*? Is *it* like how a fire extinguisher puts fires out? Television likewise puts kids' ability to learn out; and just like how evangelists disseminate tracts, television puts knowledge into the minds of kids.) She was very enigmatic.

I changed the channel on her, set my mind to vineyards, and started to crawl toward the curb, out from under the unemployed, enraged, ex–television junkies. By the time I struggled to my knees, the crowd was chanting, "Books, man, books. You gotta read books." It was very Gregorian. (Those monks were on Vision, Channel 16, last night.)

For some reason, maybe the rhythm, the chant stuck with me, or maybe I felt compelled to solve the butcher's riddle. I lack faith in the written word, but I decided to allow a few books my meagre reverence. I discovered Arnold Bennett has some interesting things to say about books:

> Study is not an end, but a means. I should blush to write such a platitude, did I not know by experience that the majority of readers constantly ignore it. The [person] who pores over a manual of carpentry and does naught with it is a fool. But every book is a manual of carpentry, and every [person] who pores over any book whatever and does naught else with—deserving an abusive epithet. (118)

The plumber's words came flooding back to me. I imagined that she and Bennett were like a diamond ring lodged in a sink's drainpipe waiting to be recovered. If they are right, I can watch all the Home and Garden Television I want, but if I do not swing a hammer, then I will never get my Italian villa. Internalizing began to sound like a lot of work, so I read on.

Bruce Hutchison wrote a short essay entitled "The Shadows," which uses Plato's Simile of the Cave to illustrate what has happened to the couch potato. Hutchison argues that television "is the great current illusion. The shadows are mistaken as things" (143). Indeed, as a sofa spud, I would sit in my cave and watch the shadows being emitted from the screen. I interpret the images as reality not knowing that I am actually separated from true life, a spectator behind a "gaudy curtain," and unable to see, never mind make love under, an

Italian sun. I had the slightest urge to go get a pipe wrench and a hammer, but the thought of losing a fingernail made me turn another page.

Apparently, when a philosopher leaves the confines of the cave and steps into the sun, Plato calls this understanding. Hutchison agrees: "the grim inescapable fact of human understanding is that it must be private, must come from within….Though [knowledge] is presented in a million different versions, the paramount problem of modern [people] is to find a satisfactory participation in modern life" (144).

Internalize? Participate? Philosophy? Understanding? I am going to have to watch some more *Spelling Bee,* but then again, why did that plumber slap me? Oh ya, those smart kids.

Children participate in the adult world through a sense of wonder. They wonder why the sky is blue, how babies are made, if the fridge light stays on when the door is shut; they wonder why wars start, how people die, and if all families have two fathers. Neil Postman, as quoted by Matthew Stevenson, states, "children must enter, through their questions, into the adult world. As media merge the two worlds, the calculus of wonderment changes. Curiosity is replaced by cynicism, or, even worse, by arrogance. We are left with children who rely not on authoritative adults but news from nowhere" (3). And these cynical children grow up too. When they are eighteen, average American children have seen 17 000 murders, spent 20 000 hours mesmerized by the TV's glow, as compared to the 11 000 hours spent in front of a teacher; and, if they were watching during the 1996 prime time season, children will have 65 000 sexual references to discuss at the dinner table or across the TV tray (Stevenson 3).

Again, I was stunned. With children watching so much television, they do not have to wonder about anything anymore. Television is putting it out, and by "it," I mean extinguishing wonder. When I was a kid, I used to wonder what it would be like to kiss a girl. Sure, my first kiss was not as graceful as the last kiss of *The Princess Bride,* and sure, there were no violins playing in the background. But if I may, I will quote a fitting piece of literature to describe the experience:

A pear's a pear

A plum's a plum

But a kiss ain't a kiss

If it ain't got the tongue.

Not even 65 000 sexual references could convince me to trade in that first kiss, even if she did throw up two minutes later.

With that, I closed my books, collected a tin can full of nails and a hammer, and headed outside. Now, there is bamboo lattice on my front lawn, but no grapes are growing yet. Bruce Hutchison is riding his garden tractor trying to put the fear of God into some stubborn cucumbers. Arnold Bennett is planting begonias in our new television planter box. And I? I am dangling from the eaves of my very crooked house where we are about to break for a barbeque. There are no lonely housewives banging down my door, and if they did, I am afraid they would knock the humble beginnings of my Italian villa over. If you want to drop in, I will have to ask you to do me a favour before you come over. Read Seamus Heaney's "Digging." It's about potatoes.

Bennett, Arnold. "Translating Literature into Life." *The Open Window: Essays and Short Stories.* Eds. W. F. Langford and Patrick J. Daniel. Toronto: Longmans, 1961. 117–120. Print.

Hutchison, Bruce. "The Shadows." *The Open Window: Essays and Short Stories*. Eds. W. F. Langford and Patrick J. Daniel. Toronto: Longmans, 1961. 143–45. Print.

Stevenson, Matthew. "America Unplugged: Giving Up TV Viewing." *The American Enterprise*. 8.5 (1997): n. pag. Web. 30 Mar. 2011.

1. How is word choice used to enhance the humour of this essay? Find examples to support your point.

2. How does the writer make the transition from TV to books to experience? By what techniques does the writer achieve these transitions?

3. Examine the introduction and conclusion. How is each of these made effective?

4. Find a copy of Seamus Heaney's poem "Digging." What is its relationship to the essay?

CHAPTER 20
The Literary Essay

I find television very educational. Every time someone switches it on, I go into another room and read a good book.
—GROUCHO MARX

In this chapter:

• How to write a literary essay

The Role of the Literary Essay

The literary essay requires you to read, to analyze, and to come to terms with the meaning of a piece of literature. Whether it demands secondary sources or simply focuses on the literary work itself, the literary essay demands that you show your understanding of how and why the work is put together the way it is. Note that an analysis of a literary work demands that you ask why it is told the way it is; it does not ask for plot summary. Your first assumption is that your readers have also read the work in question, and they do not need to know information about the story; they do, however, need help to appreciate how and why the story is told the way it is. Avoid the temptation to re-tell the story; that is out of place in a literary essay.

Write the literary essay according to the following stages:

1. Formulate a thesis about the work based on your first reading of it. Usually, you will explore an idea or theme that is a focal point of the work. Alternatively, you may explore the author's use of certain techniques in telling the story.
2. Reread the work closely.
3. Use secondary sources, if required.
4. Select only the best supporting evidence.
5. Quote often, but not at great length.
6. Write in the present tense.
7. Write with both the text and the argument in mind.
8. Revise with style.

AUDIENCE: someone who has read the novel, poem, or short story, but who wants to understand more about how it works (for example, its structure, its themes, its techniques)

PURPOSE: to interpret the meaning of a work and the techniques by which that meaning is revealed

Note that a literary essay may either explore an idea or theme and clarify the author's position on a subject or consider the use of certain techniques or elements and show how they help to tell the story. In a prose analysis, such techniques or elements may include plot, character, setting, imagery, use of dialogue, or type of narration. In a poetry analysis, by contrast, you focus on the relationship between the meaning of the poem and the poetic techniques (simile, metaphor, rhyme, alliteration, and so forth) by which the poem constructs that meaning. Your assumption with both prose and poetry is that every element contributes to the meaning, and you give examples that demonstrate how the author has chosen words and structures to convey his or her meaning.

Formulate a Thesis

The thesis of the literary essay should be something that helps the reader make sense of the work in question.

For example, in the essay that follows on pp. 173–179, the reader needs to know how Yann Martel's novel *Life of Pi* succeeds in allowing both the reader and the writer to make the leap of faith that is demanded by magic realism. The thesis statement thus is that Martel demands a leap of faith from both narrator/writer and reader.

Find your thesis by asking yourself what the important questions are about the literary work you have in front of you. Sometimes these will be assigned, but sometimes you will have to find your own questions, based on class discussion and reading.

Remember that you cannot conclusively prove your thesis statement. All you are expected to do is to show that your reasons for it are based on the text itself.

Read the Work Closely

With your working thesis in mind, read the work carefully. Underlining or highlighting the text as you go along is often a good idea (provided you own it, of course).

Note anything that might count as evidence for your analysis of the characteristics of a literary work. Don't, however, neglect passages that might support a contrary view. You will need to account for these as well.

Use Secondary Sources, If Required

Maintain your balance when using secondary sources. Use them to get some critical perspective on the work in question, but remember that your own task is no different from theirs. The main reason for writing a literary essay is to show your own powers of analysis.

Keep track of the sources you have consulted. The ideas you find must be acknowledged to avoid charges of plagiarism. Keep track also of the basic line of argument set forth by each critic you consult: it is unfair to take ideas or phrasing if you intend to use them out of their original context. Note that if you copy and paste material from the Internet, it is wise to do so in a different font from the rest of your writing, in order to be able to differentiate at a glance between your words and another's words.

Select Only the Best Evidence

After close reading, you need to "back off" from the work somewhat. Your task is not to summarize the work, or to explain every detail of it, but merely to present a viewpoint that suggests what the work means and how it is put together.

Skim through the work, noting down the most prominent support you have found. Then, categorize the material into sections appropriate for discussion in your essay. Fit these into a rough outline, and you are ready to write.

Example

> THESIS STATEMENT: Readers are asked to take a leap of faith to understand the meaning of the experience of the narrator in *Life of Pi.*
>
> A. Readers are asked to participate in a magic realism fable and suspend their disbelief accordingly.
>
> B. Readers are encouraged to embrace a faith in the god of their choice, as the narrator does.
>
> C. Readers are asked actively to choose the better story between the two that are provided in the novel.

This essay accumulates evidence of how the reader is asked to make a leap of faith in ways similar to those made by the narrator. As you gather support, try not to include everything. Pick only those passages central to an understanding of the work's meaning and those that work best as illustrations of your thesis.

Quote Often, but Not at Great Length

The best illustration of a point in a literary essay is a quotation. Whereas paraphrase may be a useful way of reporting research, the quotation is the most precise way to examine meaning in literature. Exactitude is important.

Remember, though, that you must *use* your quotations. Don't just copy them and assume that your point has been made. Focus in on them to show exactly how they work as support for your thesis. Don't assume that the meaning of the quotations or your purpose in quoting them is self-evident.

Write in the Present Tense

When discussing a work of literature, stay in the present tense—treat the work as a living thing.

Example

> When confronted by the priest, the pandit, and the imam when Pi is out walking with his parents, he explains, "Bapu Ghandi said, 'All religions are true.' I just want to love God" (*Life* 76).

History, on the other hand, and accounts of historical events, are written in the past tense.

Write with Both Text and Argument in Mind

Stay close to the text and to your argument at all times. But remember that you are not writing to record the plot or to state the obvious. Assume that the reader has read the work. Your job is to offer an interpretation of its meaning. Use the primary text to *demonstrate* your thesis and present your support for the argument at every step of the way.

Write an analysis, not an appreciation or a summary. Don't, for example, waste words admiring Sondheim's skill as a lyricist or Martel's gifts as a novelist. Instead, show how a particular literary work is put together and explain why it has the effect it does.

Assume that the work has unity and coherence, unless evidence shows otherwise. Take the text apart and show how some features of it work. Your job is to show how its synthesis is achieved.

When you are not working with a literary text alone but are instead analyzing a phenomenon, such as musical theatre, remember to keep your focus on the argument and your support for it.

Revise with Style

In a literary essay, style is crucial. Your grade will depend not only on what you say, but also on how you say it. Check for grace in style. Aim at writing smoothly and confidently. Find a critic you admire and emulate his or her method of proceeding. Your argument, no matter how cogent, will not succeed unless your paper is well written.

CHAPTER 20 EXERCISES

1. Examine the introduction of any short story to show how it works. How does it introduce themes that are picked up later?

2. Look at the concluding section of a short story you are studying. How was the conclusion set up in the earlier part of the story? What feeling does it leave the reader with?

3. Discuss the use of repetitive words or images in any short story you have studied. Why does the author deliberately stress these elements?

4. In any short story or play you are studying, what techniques are used to create the sense of a unified body of work?

Sample Literary Essay—MLA Style

The following is a sample literary essay whose format conforms to the new MLA guidelines. Refer to Chapter 23, Documenting—MLA, APA, and University of Chicago Guidelines, for more information. Study it carefully, noting the format and the method of documentation.

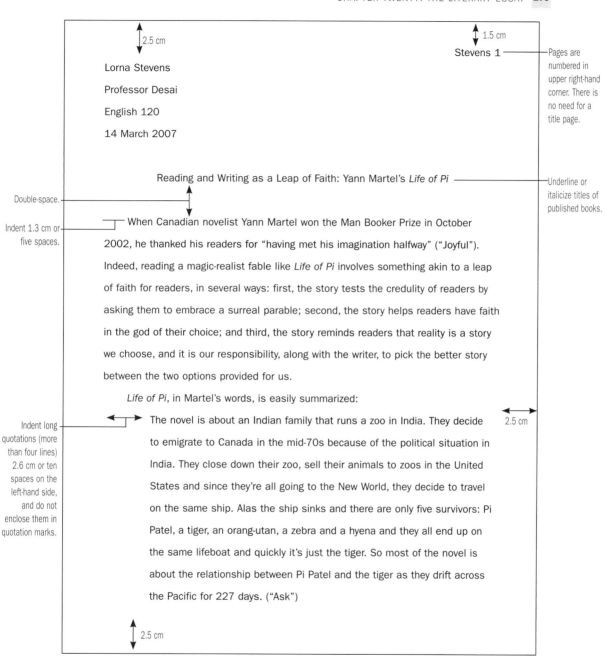

2.5 cm

1.5 cm

Stevens 1

Pages are numbered in upper right-hand corner. There is no need for a title page.

Lorna Stevens

Professor Desai

English 120

14 March 2007

Reading and Writing as a Leap of Faith: Yann Martel's *Life of Pi*

Underline or italicize titles of published books.

Double-space.

Indent 1.3 cm or five spaces.

When Canadian novelist Yann Martel won the Man Booker Prize in October 2002, he thanked his readers for "having met his imagination halfway" ("Joyful"). Indeed, reading a magic-realist fable like *Life of Pi* involves something akin to a leap of faith for readers, in several ways: first, the story tests the credulity of readers by asking them to embrace a surreal parable; second, the story helps readers have faith in the god of their choice; and third, the story reminds readers that reality is a story we choose, and it is our responsibility, along with the writer, to pick the better story between the two options provided for us.

Life of Pi, in Martel's words, is easily summarized:

Indent long quotations (more than four lines) 2.6 cm or ten spaces on the left-hand side, and do not enclose them in quotation marks.

2.5 cm

The novel is about an Indian family that runs a zoo in India. They decide to emigrate to Canada in the mid-70s because of the political situation in India. They close down their zoo, sell their animals to zoos in the United States and since they're all going to the New World, they decide to travel on the same ship. Alas the ship sinks and there are only five survivors: Pi Patel, a tiger, an orang-utan, a zebra and a hyena and they all end up on the same lifeboat and quickly it's just the tiger. So most of the novel is about the relationship between Pi Patel and the tiger as they drift across the Pacific for 227 days. ("Ask")

2.5 cm

Stevens 2

Martel explains the role of the reader in an interview conducted after he won the literary prize:

> When I started writing I didn't ever imagine that I would have readers. But once I met readers they are now essential. I think a book really comes alive only once it has met a reader. A book in that sense otherwise is 50%—the other 50% is what the reader brings to it—their imagination. ("Ask")

Use shortened title for Web pages if they are listed by title in the Works Cited.

For Martel, it is this interaction between readers and writer that is important. And the role of the writer in coming to grips with the story he is telling is similarly learning to leap into his or her own imagination. In an essay entitled "How I Wrote *Life of Pi,*" Martel describes the arduous journey by which he arrived at the novel as one in which he learned to blend the real and the imagined, the literary and the ordinary in a novel that transcends time and place, in the tradition of magic realism. Martel admits to finding the idea for the plot in a book review of *Max and the Cats,* a novel by Brazilian Moacyr Scliar, an idea which acted on him like "electric caffeine" ("How"). But in addition to this literary influence, Martel needed the inspiration of India, and the painstaking research he conducted in India and Canada, including interviews with zookeepers and zoological studies. For him, even the writing of a book begins first with the social and imaginative interaction of reading, as he recounts. Even though he claims that he began the day in the splendid imagination of asking "OK, what's happening today with my tiger?" ("Yann"), he also defines the work of the novel as fundamentally social.

The novel is a surreal parable that requires imagination on the part of the reader who makes the journey with Pi and Martel. Still, it is a journey grounded in two worlds: one real, the other literary. The real one is significant since Martel reported to interviewers that he "wanted to go against the maxim that writers should only tackle subjects they already know about" ("Martel's"). Besides that, Martel based his research on recognizable literary roots, running the gamut from

Stevens 3

the story of Noah's ark in the Bible through to *Robinson Crusoe* and *The Old Man and the Sea* and other stories of shipwreck and disaster, a combination that culminated in what Martel himself whimsically refers to as "Beckett in the Pacific" ("How"). Like Daniel Defoe's *Robinson Crusoe, Life of Pi* explores the journey of one soul towards God, a journey brought about through the catastrophe of shipwreck. Both Crusoe and Pi discover a kind of providence in the way they tell stories of their salvation. As Crusoe recounts,

> How wonderfully we are deliver'd when we know nothing of it. How when
> we are in (a Quandary, as we call it) a Doubt or Hesitation, whether to go
> this Way, when we intended to go that Way; nay, to go the other Way, yet
> a strange Impression from the Mind, from we know not what Springs, and
> by we know not what Power, shall over-rule us to go this Way; and it shall
> afterwards appear, that had we gone that Way which we should have gone,
> and even to our own Imagination ought to have gone, we should have been
> ruin'd and lost. (137)

Works of shipwreck and peril at sea, like Gerard Manley Hopkins's poem "The Wreck of the Deutschland," seem to lend themselves to explorations of doubt and despair and of the human being's place in the universe. The theme of faith is omnipresent in such literary precursors. Witness Hopkins's lines:

> Into the snows she sweeps,
> Hurling the haven behind,
> The Deutschland, on Sunday; and so the sky keeps,
> For the infinite air is unkind,
> And the sea flint-flake, black-backed in the regular blow,
> Sitting Eastnortheast, in cursed quarter, the wind;
> Wiry and white-fiery and whirlwind-swivellèd snow
> Spins to the widow-making unchilding unfathering deeps. (97–104)

References made in parentheses usually include page numbers. Omit authors' names if they are clear from the context.

Stevens 4

In his poem, Hopkins explores the mystery of suffering unleashed upon the faithful, who cannot escape the unfathomable wrath of the sea.

Martel's method may involve faith, but it is also his theme since he recounts his protagonist's conversion to Christianity, Islam, and Hinduism all at once, which Bryan Walsh, one reviewer of the novel, describes as "promiscuously religious." When confronted by the priest, the pandit, and the imam when Pi is out walking with his parents, Pi explains, "Bapu Ghandi said, 'All religions are true.' I just want to love God,' I blurted out, and looked down, red in the face" (*Life* 76). But in the course of researching his novel and reading the foundational texts of Christianity, Hinduism, and Islam, Martel himself arrived at something similar and made his own leap of faith: "I used to dismiss spirituality and religion as being mumbo jumbo for children. . . . However, there's more than just fundamentalism out there when you talk about religion. And that I'm more in tune to now" ("Yann"). Hence, the novel is itself profoundly ambitious and makes the claim that it is "a story that will make you believe in God" (*Life* viii). Indeed, the story of a boy fighting for survival in a lifeboat he shares with a tiger is one that reminds the reader of the importance of faith as a means by which to endure suffering and to understand one's place in the universe. Hence, the last part of Pi's inventory reads like this:

> 1 large bar of dark chocolate
>
> 1 survival manual
>
> 1 compass
>
> 1 notebook with 98 lined pages
>
> 1 boy with a complete set of light clothing but for one lost shoe
>
> 1 spotted hyena
>
> 1 Bengal tiger
>
> 1 lifeboat

Enclose short quotations (no more than four lines) in quotation marks, and include them in the body of the essay.

Use a period and three dots (with spaces between) to indicate words left out of the end of a sentence.

1 ocean

1 God (*Life* 162)

The inventory leaps from the mundane to the transcendent, but Pi is matter-of-fact in his approach to the list. There is in his view one God, even though he cries out in distress to "Jesus, Mary, Muhammad, and Vishnu" (*Life* 166).

Of course, the trouble with the leap of faith, even in the novel, is that not everyone is willing to make it. When Pi tells his fabulous story to Mr. Tomohiro Okamoto and Mr. Atsuro Chiba, they refuse to believe it, and they choose instead a "nasty, brutish and short" version that Pi makes up for their benefit. Pi challenges them with these words:

> "You can't prove which story is true and which is not. You must take my word for it."
>
> "In both stories the ship sinks, my entire family dies, and I suffer."
>
> "So tell me, since it makes no factual difference to you and you can't prove the question either way, which story do you prefer? Which is the better story, the story with animals or the story without animals?" (*Life* 352)

The animals, whether allegorical in intent or not, do, according to Martel, represent human traits: "the zebra, the hyena and the orang-utan . . . arose naturally, each one a function of a human trait I wanted to embody, the hyena cowardliness, the orang-utan maternal instincts and the zebra exoticism" ("How"). One can, if one wishes, subscribe to the view that the zebra is the Taiwanese sailor, the orang-utan is Pi's mother, and the cannibalistic cook is the hyena, but that is just one way of reading the story, and not, in Pi's view, the better story.

Although they agree that the story with animals is the better story, the last word is given to the other, worse story, minus the animals except for the incontrovertible Bengal tiger. The leap of faith, in Martel's estimation, requires that we choose the

Stevens 6

better story, select the one more aesthetically pleasing, perhaps the one easier to live with. This view of reality accords with something that Martel explains in one of his interviews: "To me a belief is something you cling to and faith is a letting go. Not only in religious terms—when you love someone, you let go, you trust them. When you love a system or anything, you let go—that's faith. When you have a belief you cling" ("Ask"). So Martel brings the reader round to the kind of faith that involves letting go, but to no particular system of belief. For him, as he explains in the same interview, each religious perspective is a kind of cuisine, any of which can sustain life, but all of which are very different.

In some respects, Martel's *Life of Pi* is the quintessence of Canadian fiction, if one sees Canada, as Martel does, as a mosaic rather than a melting pot, the image typically used of America. As Martel comments, "Canada is very open to other voices. . . . the world is in Canada. It's a country with two official languages but no official culture. So people from all over the world are welcome to come and tell their own stories" ("Ask"). His study of the boy in the lifeboat demonstrates that all creatures from all cultures, everywhere, are in the same boat and use their imaginations to leap beyond the ordinary to tell their own stories of life, with luck, as imaginatively and courageously as Martel's does.

Stevens 7

Works Cited

"Ask Booker Prize Winner Yann Martel." *BBC News* 24 Oct. 2002. Web. 28 June

    2011.

Defoe, Daniel. *Robinson Crusoe*. Ed. Michael Shinagel. New York: Norton, 1975.

    Print.

Hopkins, Gerard Manley. "The Wreck of the Deutschland." *A Little Treasury of*

    Modern Poetry: English and American. 3rd ed. Ed. Oscar Williams. New York:

    Scribner's, 1970. Print.

"Joyful Martel Wins Booker." *BBC News* 23 Oct. 2002. Web. 30 June 2011.

"Martel's Quirky Path." *BBC News* 23 Oct. 2002. Web. 30 June 2011.

Martel, Yann. *Life of Pi*. Toronto: Vintage Canada, 2002. Print.

–––"How I Wrote Life of Pi." *Powell's Books*. Web. 29 June 2011.

Walsh, Bryan. "Castaway with Karma." Rev. of *Life of Pi*, by Yann Martel. *Time Asia*

    2 Sept. 2002. Web. 29 June 2011.

"Yann Martel Relishes Booker Boost." *BBC News* 24 Oct. 2002. Web. 30 June

    2011.

List only works cited or used in the essay. Note that the title of this page is not underlined or italicized.

Abbreviate publication information without sacrificing clarity.

List works cited in alphabetical order.

If you use two entries by the same author, use three hyphens in place of the name.

Include date that websites were accessed.

Use hanging indents for bibliographical entries, with subsequent lines indented 1.3 cm or five spaces.

CHAPTER 21
The Book Review

Having been unpopular in high school is not just cause for book publication.
—FRAN LEBOWITZ

In this chapter:

- How to write a book review
- How to critique a book or article

Most of the book reviews you will be asked to write have a more specific purpose than the kind you see in newspapers and magazines. You will be asked not only to report on the content of a book and to evaluate it, but also to analyze it in terms of its contribution to the discipline. A book review gives you a chance to examine one potential source in a given area, often as a prelude to writing a research essay. Like any other essay, it demands a thesis statement that clarifies your reaction to the book.

If you are asked to review a book as part of a course requirement, select a book with a subject matter that appeals to you and with which you feel comfortable. Proceed according to the following stages:

1. Describe or summarize the contents of the book.
2. Describe and evaluate its tactics.
3. Consider its contribution.
4. Illustrate your argument.
5. Maintain your critical balance.

To write a focused book review, remember your role as a fair-minded and helpful critic.

The Role of the Book Review

Do not be misled by the words "book review." Often in post-secondary learning, you may encounter assignments that ask you to critique a book or a shorter piece, such as an essay. When you critique something, you are not writing a simple book report; you are analyzing the contents of the reading and determining why it is important to your area of study. You are explaining to the reader what the work is, how it is put together, how convincing or effective you find it, and what it contributes to its area of study. These four elements are at the heart of a critique. You need to explain these in turn:

- What is the point of this work? (its thesis)
- How does it make its point? (its methodology)
- How well does it make its point? (your assessment of its arguments)
- So what? (its significance in a broader context)

Like other essays, the book review's form is determined by its readers and its function.

AUDIENCE: someone who has not read the book, but who is interested in its subject matter and has some background in the discipline

PURPOSE: to summarize, analyze, and evaluate a book, and to show your critical acumen in so doing; then, to recommend, to criticize, or to dismiss the book according to careful judgment

Describe the Book

1. Determine the thesis of the book (if it is a critical text), the theme (or general meaning) of the book (if it is not), and the audience for whom the book is intended.
2. Summarize the book's contents briefly, without giving the show away.
3. Use the book's preface, introduction, and table of contents as a rough guide for your discussion of the work.
4. Discuss the general purpose of the book, without getting caught up in too much detail.

Neil Postman, in his book *Teaching as a Conserving Activity* (1979), argues that the **Example** function of formal education should be to counteract the biases of the culture, rather than to reinforce them. To illustrate this point, he focuses on the pervasive influence of television and other media and recommends that education teach society to be more critical of the media. Postman intends this book to be a modification of his earlier work, *Teaching as a Subversive Activity* (1969), in which he advocated innovation. In this book, his argument is that education must work against the unthinking forces of change that prevail in the culture as a whole.

Describe and Evaluate the Book's Tactics

1. If the book is a critical text, describe its method of argument. If it is not a critical text, describe the techniques by which the material is presented.
2. Note how well the book does what it sets out to do.
3. Note what else might have been done or what might have been done differently.
4. Note why you liked (or disliked) the book.

The book sets out to show how television has affected our way of seeing the world. **Example** It argues that television has made us less conscious of the past, that it has lowered our attention span, and that it has made us more susceptible to "quick-fix" solutions to problems—as a consequence of too much exposure to television commercials, which reduce life to shallow and easily remedied problems.

Postman insists that the way to counter this problem is to teach people about the media and about how the media alter our perceptions of things. He argues that the development of strong critical-thinking skills will put a stop to the passivity and superficiality of the cultural attitudes provoked by television viewing.

The chief flaw in Postman's approach is his own lack of sources. Given that he advocates critical appraisal of the means by which information is conveyed, the onus is on him to show that some of the effects of television that he lists are, in fact, present.

Consider the Book's Contribution

1. Compare the book to others you have read with a similar thesis or theme.
2. Ask yourself what you learned from the book.

Example   *Teaching as a Conserving Activity* seems to present a useful corrective to the problems of value in education today. Postman points to some real dangers created by the commercialization of the media and emphasizes the role that education must play in maintaining old values in society as well as espousing new ones.

Illustrate Your Argument

1. At every step of the way, use snippets from the book to back up your position and to give the reader a taste of the work.
2. Include both positive and negative illustrations, unless, of course, your review is entirely positive or negative (rarely the case).
3. Be sure to integrate your illustrations from the book as part of your argument, and not simply as decoration.

Example   Although some of the charges Postman makes about the negative effects of television are justified—such as its invasion of privacy and its stress on seeing things from the outside, superficially rather than analytically—some of his charges are exaggerated. When he claims that television is not analytic because it is "picture-centered," he argues that we cannot prove a picture true or false the way we can a proposition. But Postman here is comparing apples and oranges. Words are not always used to create propositions either; sometimes they tell stories, just as pictures do, and these stories cannot be categorized as being true or false either. The fault, if there is one, does not lie with the medium, but instead, perhaps, with the use to which it is put. In other words, television in itself does not automatically lead to a deterioration in critical-thinking skills.

Maintain Your Critical Balance

1. Don't be intimidated by ideas just because they are in print. Your object is to assess the merits of the book in question.
2. Don't be too harsh in your judgments. Remember that the author deserves mercy as well as justice.

Ultimately, Postman's position that education should move to counteract some of the biases of the culture is a valid one; some of his arguments for it, however, need more support and closer critical scrutiny than he has given them.

Example

Writing a Critique of an Article as a Research Summary

In post-secondary education, students are often asked to write a critique as one of their first assignments. Professors assign critiques because they get to the heart of the matter: they allow students to engage with the material. Critiques may also provide the fundamental background to a course. The articles or books that you critique in a course are almost certainly central to an understanding of the language and the methodology of the course. Professors chose these books or articles because they are landmarks in their subject area.

When you read an article to critique it, ask the following questions:

- What? What is the point of the article?
- How? What methodology is used in the study?
- How well? How convincing did you find the argument of the article?
- So what? What have you learned from the article?

This approach, by the way, is also a great way to accumulate information for an essay that you are going to write or for an exam that you must take. The process of writing a critique, in its own right, allows you to clarify your own thinking in an abbreviated way. A critique need not be a formal assignment; it may be just an approach to reading your materials critically for your own writing purposes.

CHAPTER 21 EXERCISES

Read the following book review and analyze its structure, using the questions that follow.

Moonbeam on a Cat's Ear by Canadian author/illustrator Marie-Louise Gay is a highly recommended addition to any collection of children's literature. In 1987, it was awarded a well-deserved Amelia Frances-Howard Gibbon Medal from the Canadian Library Association. Aimed at the preschool audience, the text is sparse and characterized by slight rhyme, and the illustrations are rounded, colourful, lively, and detailed. Specifically, *Moonbeam on a Cat's Ear* is the ideal bedtime book for children, and the illustrations and text are integrated with this purpose in mind.

Like the large-bodied, broad-faced, tiny-limbed characters in her other books (*Lizzy's Lion, Rainy Day Magic, Angel and the Polar Bear*) who embark on amazing journeys before returning to reality, Rosie and Toby Toby awake from their beds and journey through the sea and sky on the moon with a cat and a mouse before they return to their beds and sleep.

All of the action in the story is carried by the illustrations. The pictures show a strong substory not necessarily indicated by the text. The story begins by describing the illustrated scenes of the sleeping cat, then switches as Toby Toby enters Rosie's room and entreats her to go on an adventure. As Toby Toby begins musing about their plans with increasing excitement, the pictures show the characters actually doing the things he describes. This process escalates to the point of the characters being in the sky surrounded by lightning bolts, when Rosie says, "Oh Toby Toby it's so frightening!" The next page shows them both asleep on the bed. At this point, the text asks a direct question of the child:

Was it a dream

or did they really try

to steal the moon right out of the sky?

As the illustrations *show* a stronger story than the text (just as the imagination is sometimes stronger than reality), the question posed is answered for the child by the final illustration of the cat and mouse still seated on the moon in the sky. Flipping back to the previous page confirms the animals' absence from the bedroom.

Through her use of such ambiguities, Gay reveals great insight into the minds of children. She omits adults from the story and focuses directly on the problems facing a child being put to bed. Children's bodies are relatively still (like the text), but their imaginations are alive and travelling (like the pictures). When the characters return to earth and are shown sleeping, a sense of calm is produced, but the last picture and teasing question allow something for children to think about as they fall asleep.

The author uses colours and techniques conducive to sleep. Blue is the predominant colour in *Moonbeam on a Cat's Ear*. This colour, combined with a margin of white space surrounding each page, creates, even in the most active scenes, a quiet mood appropriate for bedtime. Marie-Louise Gay, in an interview with Marie Davis, speaks of the story as a "moon book": "The quietness, the serenity in *Moonbeam* is also due to the contrast between the bluish light and the stark white light. Everything seems to float in space." She speaks of other ways in which she invokes this mood: "I had tiny little borders, but they're not too intrusive. They have little things happening in them, but they're much calmer, like little paintings" (Davis 81). In painting the scenes, Gay has used a somewhat unusual technique that, while still using bright colours and distinct lines, produces a soft, dreamlike quality. By putting a white paint mixture on the gesso board and letting it dry with brush strokes in it, Gay achieves a ridge-like texture when she adds ink and watercolour on top.

The amount of detail in the text serves many functions. It creates a sense of immediacy or realism. Examples from *Moonbeam on a Cat's Ear* include the shadows of moonlight, the messy state of the toys, scarves, coats, and shoes, and the open scissors beside bits of paper on the table top. Detail also helps create a sense of movement. In Gay's story, movement is always present, whether in the slight blowing of curtains, the flying of moths or the leaping of fish, the falling off of a slipper, or the streaks of movement behind the lightning bolts or the children as they fall.

The details also enhance the sense of flow and connection in the pictures. The cat and the mouse are present on every page, if one looks hard enough. (So is Toby Toby's frog until it wisely jumps off when they leave the water.) The moon appears on almost all the pages, whether it's in the sky, on Rosie's pyjamas, in the margins, or on the picture hanging on the bedroom wall. Even the mouse, dreamed by the cat, dreams of little cheese moons. Likewise, lightning bolts accompany the knock on the door; they are on the wallpaper, in the margins, and in the sky. The airplanes on Toby Toby's pyjamas are also found in the margins; the bed sheet turns into a sail, then back into the bed sheet again. Detail can enhance the flow of the story in even subtler ways, such as in the repetition of the shape of the cat's ear in the curtains or in the butterfly wings.

The detail in the borders has a more formalized structure. The tiny pictures help the flow of the words and alert the viewer to related details in the bigger illustration. When Toby Toby is high in the tree, there are images of rockets and kites in the margin. When the moon-boat leaves the sea for the sky, fish are shown leaping amongst clouds. The borders reinforce, but they also foreshadow. On the first page, the sequence of the phases of the moon is shown in the border. Apples are shown on the border of the page before the apple tree is shown. The cat and the mouse peek around the picture in the border of the page before they are shown sleeping on the moon on the last page.

This examination of *Moonbeam on a Cat's Ear* suggests some criteria for deciding a book's place in a collection of children's literature. One may want to consider Canadian content or medals awarded. One may also want to ponder intended audience, purpose, or message, and how well that purpose is achieved. The colour and quality of illustrations are important. As well, the integration between a text and its illustrations is vital to the coherence of a story intended for children. Here, technical issues like detail, style, innovation, consistency of scale, arrangement of text and pictures, flow, length, and readability come into play. The author's understanding of children and their interests is crucial if a picture book is to reach its intended audience.

1. How does the essay show the integration of text and illustrations?

2. What kinds of support does the essay writer use?

3. Analyze the strengths of the introduction and conclusion.

Part Six

DOCUMENTING AND DELIVERING YOUR PAPER

CHAPTER 22

Planning Your Paper's Layout

An expert is a person who has made all the mistakes that can be made in a very narrow field.
—NIELS BOHR

In this chapter:

- How to lay out an essay in MLA style
- How to lay out an essay in APA style
- How to lay out an essay in Chicago style

When you organize your final printed manuscript for submission to an instructor, you need to be careful to meet the specifications demanded for the paper's presentation. The paper should be easy to read, neat, and presented in a style consistent with a standard form of documentation. The specifications you follow depend, in large part, on whether you are using the MLA, APA, or University of Chicago style of documentation. Each of these styles requires certain things of the manuscript. For the sake of consistency, follow these guidelines as closely as you can.

The Layout of a Paper in MLA Style

You will likely follow MLA guidelines if you study English, philosophy, classics, or visual arts.

1. Use letter-quality white bond paper, 22 cm × 28 cm (8 1/2" × 11").
2. Make sure the print quality is sharp, and the font is commonly accepted, such as Times New Roman in 12-point font. Do not use decorative fonts.
3. Double space everything, including quotations, notes, and Works Cited, and use one side of the page only.
4. Leave 2.5-cm (1") margins. Do not justify the right margin. Indent paragraphs 1.3 cm (1/2") or five spaces. Indent long quotations an additional 1.3 cm (1/2") or five spaces with a normal right margin.
5. Place page numbers in the upper right-hand corner beside your last name (without a page abbreviation or a comma).
6. On the first page, place your name, your instructor's name, the course name, and the date in the upper left corner. Double space between the date and the title, centre the paper's title without underlining, bolding, italicizing, or quotation marks. Note that a title page is not required.

MLA Works Cited List

Work Cited

Bernard, Louise. "Countermemory and Return: Reclamation of the (Post-modern) Self in Jamaica Kincaid's *The Autobiography of My Mother and My Brother*." *Modern Fiction Studies* 48.1 (2002): 113–138. Web. 19 May 2011.

Gilmore, Leigh. *The Limits of Autobiography.* Ithaca: Cornell UP, 2001. Print.

Kincaid, Jamaica. *My Brother*. New York: Farrar, Straus and Giroux, 1998. Print.

Page, Kezia. "'What If He Did Not Have a Sister [Who Lived in the United States]?': Jamaica Kincaid's *My Brother* as Remittance Text." *Jamaica Kincaid*. Ed. Harold Bloom. New York: Infobase Publishing, 2008. 189–206. Print.

Smith, Deri, and Cliff Beumel. "My Other: Imperialism and Subjectivity in Jamaica Kincaid's *My Brother*." *Jamaica Kincaid and Caribbean Double Crossing*. Ed. Linda Lang-Peralta. Newark, NJ: U of Delaware P, 2006. 96–112. Print.

Wallace, Ann E. "'Look at This, Just Look at This': Melancholic Remains in Jamaica Kincaid's *My Brother*." *Come Weep With Me: Loss and Mourning in the Writings of Caribbean Women Writers*. Ed. Joyce C. Harte. Newcastle upon Tyne: Cambridge Scholars Publishing, 2007. 110–127. Print.

7. Use a paper clip to attach the pages, or staple if your instructor prefers.
8. Keep a copy for your own protcction.
9. Refer to the sample MLA essay on pp. 130–133.

The Layout of a Paper in APA Style

When you use APA style for a manuscript, you are probably preparing a paper in the social sciences, where the date of publication is particularly important. Follow these guidelines for the proper preparation of a paper in APA style:

1. Use letter-quality white bond paper, 22 cm × 28 cm (8 1/2" × 11").
2. Use a clear font or typeface. Times New Roman 12-point is preferred. Use italics to indicate titles of published books within your essay. Keep the right margin unjustified.
3. Double space everything, including quotations and References.
4. Use 2.5-cm (1") margins. Indent paragraphs 1.3 cm (1/2") or five spaces. Indent long quotations an additional 1.3 cm (1/2") or five spaces.
5. Use a shortened version of the paper's title as a header in the upper left-hand corner of each page in full caps. Number pages, starting with the title page, without an abbreviation for page or any punctuation.
6. Make a separate title page. The top line will be the header and the page number. On the title page only, the header should read "Running head:" with the shortened title in full caps. Centre the title and capitalize major words. Titles should be unadorned. Include other identifying information, centred, and then centre the page vertically.
7. Use headings to separate sections of the paper, if desired. Centre main headings, boldface with ordinary capitalization; type the next level of headings flush left, boldface with ordinary capitalization; indent the next level of headings with boldface and only the first word capitalized, and follow these headings with a period, with the text continuing after one space.
8. Use a paper clip to attach the pages, or staple if your instructor prefers.
9. Keep a copy for your own protection.
10. Refer to the sample APA essay on pp. 84–97.

The Layout of a Paper in University of Chicago Style

The University of Chicago style is often used in disciplines like history, where notes are extremely important. There are some major differences between the look of a manuscript in MLA or APA and University of Chicago style. The following list should make the changes clear:

1. Use letter-quality white bond paper, 22 cm × 28 cm (8 1/2" × 11").
2. Use a clear, standard font, like Times New Roman or Palatino. Use no less than 10-point type, but the preference is for 12-point. Use italics for titles of published books in your essay.
3. Double space most of the paper. Footnotes, endnotes, indented quotations, and visual elements are single-spaced, though separated by double spacing. The right margin should be unjustified.

APA Reference List

References

Adelson, N. (2000). Re-imaging aboriginality: An indigenous peoples' response to social suffering. *Transcultural Psychiatry, 37(1)* , 11–34.

Arthur, N., & Collins, S. (2010). *Culture-infused counselling*. Calgary, AB: Counselling Concepts.

Bedi, R. P., Davis, M. D., & Williams, M. (2005). Critical incidents in the formation of the therapeutic alliance from the client's perspective. *Psychotherapy: Theory, Research, Practice, Training, 42(3)*, 311–323. doi: 10.1037/0033–3204. 42.3.311.

Corenblum, B., & Stephan, W. G. (2001). White fears and native apprehensions: An integrated threat theory approach to intergroup attitudes. *Canadian Journal of Behavioural Science, 33(4)*, 251–268. doi: 10.1037/h0087147

Cote, H., & Schissel, W. (2002). Damaged children and broken spirits: A residential school survivor's story. In B. Schissel, & C. Brooks (Eds.) *Marginality and condemnation: An introduction to critical criminology* (pp. 175–192). Black Point, NS: Fernwood Publishing.

Day-Vines, N., Wood, S. M., Grothaus, T., Craigen, L., Holman, A., DotsonBlake, K., et al. (2007). Broaching the subjects of race, ethnicity, and culture during the counselling process. *Journal of Counseling and Development, 85(4)*, 401–409.

Gone, J. P. (2008). 'So I can be like a Whiteman': The cultural psychology of space and place in American Indian mental health. *Culture and Psychology, 13(3)*, 369–399.

Chicago Manual of Style Bibliography

Bibliography

Alia, Valerie. *Uncovering the North*. Vancouver: UNB Press, 1999. Accessed February 11, 2011. *http://site.ebrary.com. libaccess.lib.mcmaster.ca/lib/oculmcmaster/docDetail. action?docID=10210495.*

Edgar, Andrew. *Cultural Theory: The Key Concepts*. London: Routledge, 2006.

Innis, Harold A. "Minerva's Owl." In *Introduction to Communication*, 2nd ed., edited by Alexandre Sévigny, 1–16. Dubuque, IA: Kendall-Hunt Publishing, 2010.

Jackson, John D., and Paul Millen. "English-Language Radio Drama: A Comparison of Central and Regional Production Units." *Canadian Journal of Communication* 15, no. 1. (1990): 1–18. Accessed February 4, 2010. http://www.cjconline.ca/index.php/journal/ issue/view/55/showToc.

Lorimer, Rowland, Mike Gasher, and David Skinner. *Mass Communication in Canada*. Don Mills, ON: Oxford UP, 2008.

McLuhan, Eric, and Frank Zingrone, eds. "Playboy Interview with Marshall McLuhan." In *Introduction to Communication*, edited by Alexandre Sévigny, 17–41. Dubuque, IA: Kendall-Hunt Publishing, 2010.

Minister of Indian Affairs and Northern Development. "Travel in the North-west Territories and Nunavut." *Affaires Indiennes et Du Nord Canada/Indian and Northern Affairs Canada*. Accessed March 3, 2011. http://www.ainc-inac.gc.ca/ach/lr/ks/cr/pubs/ trav-eng/asp.

4. Margins should be set at no less than 2.5 cm (1"). On the first page, the top margin must be 5 cm (2"); subsequent pages must be 2.5 cm (1").
5. Number pages at the top-right corner of the first page of text.
6. Make a separate title page, centred vertically and horizontally. Do not count the title page in your numbering.
7. If a title page is not required, centre the title of your paper 5 cm (2") from the top of the next page. Leave three line spaces and begin the text.
8. If you use headings, make the first-level head centred, boldface or italic with headline-style capitalization; the next level should be centred, regular type with headline-style capitalization; the next level should be flush left, boldface or italic with headline-style capitalization.
9. Use a paper clip to attach pages, or staple if your instructor prefers.
10. Keep a copy for your own protection.

CHAPTER 23

Documenting— MLA, APA, and University of Chicago Guidelines

Whatever has been well said by anyone is mine.

—SENECA

In this chapter:

- How to do citations and bibliography in MLA style
- How to do citations and bibliography in APA style
- How to do citations and bibliography in Chicago style

At the end of your research paper, you should provide a list of the works you used to write it. Commonly known as a bibliography, or list of books, your list of sources in a research paper should include books you refer to in the paper, either by mention, by paraphrase, or by specific citation. Any book in which you found an idea that you include should be listed. Three basic styles of documentation will be covered in this section: MLA style, most commonly used in the humanities; APA style, often used in the social sciences; and University of Chicago style, often used in history and other disciplines that prefer a traditional footnote (or endnote) style.

To create entries for a Works Cited page in MLA style, you need to consult the copyright information available on the title page of any book that you used.

Gathering Publication Information from a Book

To find publication information, it is best to check the title page and copyright page of the actual book, rather than a library catalogue or another source. In the case of this book, these are on the first page and its reverse.

To create an entry for this book in a Works Cited page (though usually you don't need to include reference books such as this one), do the following:

Find the author's name on the title page and reverse it.

Example   Buckley, Joanne.

Follow it with the title and a colon with the subtitle, if there is one, after it. These should be italicized in MLA style.

Buckley, Joanne. *Fit to Print: The Canadian Student's Guide to Essay Writing.*

Follow this with the edition number that appears on the title page.

Buckley, Joanne. *Fit to Print: The Canadian Student's Guide to Essay Writing*. 8th ed.

Then follow that with the place of publication as listed on the copyright page (usually the reverse of the title page) and a shortened version of the publisher's name along with the date of publication. Lastly, indicate the medium of publication.

Buckley, Joanne. *Fit to Print: The Canadian Student's Guide to Essay Writing*. 8th ed. Toronto: Nelson Education, 2013. Print.

If this book also had an editor, you would include that information, found on the book's title page, which would appear in your entry after the book's title and edition. Normally, you would list the book under the author's name on your Works Cited page, unless you used the book primarily because of the contributions made by the editor (a foreword or notes, perhaps). A translator would also appear in the same form as that shown for the editor.

Buckley, Joanne. *Fit to Print: The Canadian Student's Guide to Essay Writing*. 8th ed. Ed. Sandy Matos. Toronto: Nelson Education, 2013. Print.

Use the first place of publication that is listed on the title page, if there is more than one office listed for publication. If the publisher has an imprint, such as Anchor Books for Doubleday or Vintage Books for Random House, use a shortened version of the imprint, followed by a hyphen, and then the publisher's shortened name.

McEwan, Ian. *Atonement*. Toronto: Vintage-Random, 2001. Print.

Use the most recent date, except where a work has been republished in a different version. For example, for a work like *Anne of Green Gables,* you would use the original date first after the title, and then the publication information with the most recent date of publication. Indicate the medium of publication.

Montgomery, Lucy Maud. *Anne of Green Gables*. 1908. Toronto: McGraw-Hill, 2003. Print.

Sample Bibliographical Entries in MLA Style

The examples that follow show how certain entries would appear in a bibliography, if you follow the guidelines of the Modern Language Association. These entries should serve as models when you prepare your own bibliography page. In MLA style, this page is called "Works Cited." If you need further information, consult the *MLA Handbook for Writers of Research Papers,* 7th ed. (New York: Modern Language Association, 2009).

Books
ONE AUTHOR:

Frazer, James George. *The Golden Bough: A Study in Magic and Religion*. New York: Macmillan, 1922. Print.

Use a shortened version of the publisher's name (in this case, Macmillan Publishing Company), making sure that your label for the company is still recognizable. Include complete subtitles in bibliographical entries, and italicize the title and subtitle.

TWO AUTHORS AND EDITION (IF NOT THE FIRST EDITION):

Strunk, William, Jr., and E. B. White. *The Elements of Style*. 4th ed. New York: Pearson Allyn & Bacon, 2000. Print.

THREE AUTHORS:

Jardine, David W., Patricia Clifford, and Sharon Friesen. *Back to the Basics of Teaching and Learning: Thinking the World Together*. Mahweh, NJ: Erlbaum, 2003. Print.

MORE THAN THREE AUTHORS:

Bonsanti, Georgio, et al. *La Basilica di San Francesco ad Assisi*. Modena: Panini, 2002. Print.

CORPORATE AUTHOR:

Imperial Oil Limited. *The Review*. Toronto: Imperial Oil, Spring 2003. Print.

EDITOR:

Chong, Woei Lien, ed. *China's Great Proletarian Cultural Revolution: Master Narratives and Post-Mao Counternarratives*. Lanham, MD: Rowman & Littlefield, 2002. Print.

GOVERNMENT PUBLICATION:

Canada. Minister of Supply and Services Canada. *Canada Year Book 2002*. Ottawa: Statistics Canada, 2003. Print.

STORY OR ARTICLE FROM AN ANTHOLOGY:

Davies, Robertson. "Stratford Forty Years Ago." *The Harbrace Reader for Canadians*. Ed. Joanne Buckley. Toronto: Harcourt, 2001. 28–32. Print.

TRANSLATION:

Ringuet. *Thirty Acres*. Trans. Felix Walker and Dorothea Walker. Toronto: McClelland & Stewart, 1960. Print.

REPRINT:

Montgomery, L. M. *Anne of Green Gables*. 1908. Toronto: McGraw-Hill, 2003. Print.

The original hardcover edition was published in 1908. The paperback version appeared in 2003.

A WORK IN MORE THAN ONE VOLUME:

Rollins, Hyder Edward, ed. *The Letters of John Keats: 1814–1821*. 2 vols. Cambridge: Harvard UP, 1958. Print.

A WORK IN A SERIES:

Woodman, Ross. *James Reaney*. Toronto: McClelland & Stewart, 1971. Print. Canadian Writers New Canadian Library 12.

The series number is given in Arabic numerals and without the abbreviation *vol.* Note that if you are using only one volume in the series, you may omit the series names.

Magazines, Newspapers, and Journals

UNSIGNED ARTICLE:

"Terminator Set to Run for Governor in California." *Globe and Mail* 7 Aug. 2003, natl. ed.: A1. Print.

The names of months other than May, June, and July are usually abbreviated. "A1" refers to the section and page number of the newspaper.

DAILY NEWSPAPERS:

Martin, Don. "World's Longest Undecided Border." *National Post* 5 Aug. 2003, natl. ed.: A1+. Print.

When not part of the newspaper's name, the city's name should be given in brackets after the title, except in the case of a national edition. The + indicates that the article continues on non-consecutive pages.

WEEKLY MAGAZINE OR NEWSPAPER:

Gatehouse, Jonathon. "Iraq: The Price of Victory." *Maclean's* 28 July 2003: 20–22. Print.

MONTHLY OR BI-MONTHLY MAGAZINE:

Simon, Barry, Dr. "Weighty Issues." *Canadian Living* May–Sept. 2003: 52–55. Print.

JOURNAL—CONTINUOUS PAGINATION THROUGH THE YEAR:

Campbell, Jane. "'Competing Towers of Babel': Some Patterns of Language in *Hard Times*." *English Studies in Canada* 10 (1984): 416–35. Print.

When the pages of a journal are numbered consecutively through the year, the issue number and month are not included in your entry.

JOURNAL—SEPARATE PAGINATION FOR EACH ISSUE:

Davis, Marie. "Parable, Parody, or 'Blip in the Canadian Literary Landscape': Tom King on *A Coyote Christmas Story*." *Canadian Children's Literature* 84.4 (1996): 24–36. Print.

When the pages of a journal are numbered separately for each issue, an issue number ("4" in this case) follows the volume number "84." They are separated by a period.

EDITORIAL:

Robinson, Svend. "When It Comes to Immorality, Look Who's Talking!" Editorial. *Globe and Mail* 7 Aug. 2003: A13. Print.

BOOK REVIEW:

Miller, J. R. Rev. of *The Man from Halifax: Sir John Thompson, Prime Minister*, by P. B. Waite. *Queen's Quarterly* 93 (1986): 646–48. Print.

Encyclopedia

SIGNED WITH NAME OR INITIALS:

So[utham], B[rian] C. "Austen, Jane." *Encyclopaedia Britannica: Macropaedia*. 1974 ed. Print.

This article appears with the initials "B.C. So." appended to it. To identify it, you need only check the index of the encyclopedia and enclose the added information in brackets.

UNSIGNED ARTICLE:

"Literature." *The Cambridge Encyclopedia*. 1994 ed. Print.

Government Publications

Canada. Royal Commission on Aboriginal Peoples. *Restructuring the Relationship*. Public Policy and Aboriginal People 1985–1992 Volume 2. Ottawa: Ministry of Supply and Services, Canada, 1996. Print.

- - -. Standing Committee on Aboriginal Affairs. *Minutes of Proceedings and Evidence of the Standing Committee on Aboriginal Affairs*. 19 March 1990, Issue No. 22. Ottawa: Queen's Printer, 1990. 14–15. Print.

The government agency is considered the author, unless the name of the author is given.

PAMPHLETS, BULLETINS, AND REPORTS:

Canada. Employment and Immigration Canada. *Aboriginal Employment and Training Working Group*. Ottawa: Government of Canada, 1991. Print.

Unpublished Dissertations

DuBroy, Michael Thomas. "The Tale of the Folk: Revolution and the Late Prose Romances of William Morris." Diss. U of Western Ontario, 1982. Print.

Micropublications

Books or periodicals in microprint form are documented as they would be in their original form. Indicate the medium, whether CD, DVD, Radio, Film, Television, or whatever is relevant.

Non-Print Sources

TELEVISION OR RADIO PROGRAM:

"Killing Time." *Cold Squad*. CTV. CKCO-TV, Kitchener, ON. 12 Aug. 2003. Television.

TELEVISION INTERVIEW:

Gowdy, Barbara. Interview with Vicki Gabereau. *Vicki Gabereau*. CTV. CFTO, Toronto. 5 Aug. 2003. Television.

FILM:

Atanarjuat: The Fast Runner. Dir. Zacharias Kunick. National Film Board, 2002. Film.

VIDEO:

It's a Wonderful Life. Dir. Frank Capra. 1946. Republic, 1993. Videocassette.

Include the title, director, distributor, and year. Note that the original year is included before the distribution information. Include other information such as writer or performers, if relevant.

PERFORMANCE OF STAGE PLAY:

Troilus and Cressida. By William Shakespeare. Dir. Richard Monette. Perf. David Snelgrove, Claire Jullien. Tom Patterson Theatre, Stratford. 30 July 2003. Performance.

RECORDING:

The Tragically Hip. *Music@Work*. Universal Music, 2000. CD.

SONG:

The Tragically Hip. "Putting Down." *Music@Work*. Universal Music, 2000. CD.

LECTURE:

Gedalof, Allan. "Mystery Writing." U.W.O. Senior Alumni Series. Wesanne McKellar Room, U of Western Ontario, London, Ontario. 14 Apr. 1987. Lecture.

INTERVIEW:

Wiseman, Adele. Personal Interview. 15 Apr. 1987.

Electronic Sources

Collect as much of the following information as possible from your Web sources:

- Last name of author or editor, followed by first name, if authorship is given
- Title of article or short work in website, if given
- Title of website or book in italics
- Any information about the version, including volumes, issues, or dates
- Publication information, including date
- Any page numbers, if given
- Medium of publication; in this case, Web
- Date you accessed the material

SCHOLARLY JOURNALS IN ELECTRONIC FORMAT ONLY:

Pettitt, Claire. "Peggotty's Work-Box: Victorian Souvenirs and Material Memory." *Romanticism on the Net 53* (2009): n. pag. Web. 24 Oct. 2009.

Note that page numbers may be missing in this form, and are indicated by n. pag.

The medium appears before the date of access.

SCHOLARLY JOURNALS IN AN ONLINE DATABASE:

If you use the Web to find something that also appears in print, because there may be differences between them, acknowledge your use of the Web and your date of access.

Schilling, Oliver. "Development of Life Satisfaction in Old Age: Another View on the "Paradox"." *Social Indicators Research 75* (2006): 241–271. Web. 24 Oct. 2009.

SCHOLARLY PROJECT:

Orlando Project: An Integrated History of Women's Writing in the British Isles. 25 May 2000. U of Alberta. Web. 1 Aug. 2009.

PROFESSIONAL WEBSITE:

COCH/COSH: Consortium for Computers in the Humanities/Consortium pour Ordinateurs en Sciences Humaines. Web. 1 Aug. 2009.

BOOK:

Braddon, M[ary] E[lizabeth]. *Lady Audley's Secret.* Vol. 1. London, 1862. *Victorian Women Writers Project.* Ed. Perry Willett. 20 June 2000. Indiana U. Web. 1 Aug. 2009.

POEM:

Johnson, Emily Pauline. "The Song My Paddle Sings." *Flint and Feather*. Toronto, 1912. *The Pauline Johnson Archive*. Sept. 1996. McMaster U. Web. 1 Aug. 2009.

ARTICLE IN A REFERENCE DATABASE:

"McLuhan, [Herbert] Marshall." *Britannica Online*. Encyclopaedia Britannica Intermediate Version 1.0, 2000. Web. 1 Aug. 2009.

ARTICLE IN A JOURNAL:

Brown, Susan, and Patricia Clements. "Tag Team: Computing, Collaborators, and the History of Women's Writing in the British Isles." *Technologising the Humanities/Humanitising the Technologies*. Special issue of *Computing in the Humanities Working Papers*. Eds. R. G. Siemens and William Winder. *Text Technology* 8 (1998): 37–52. Web. 1 Aug. 2009.

ARTICLE IN AN ELECTRONIC JOURNAL:

Miles, Adrian, et al. "I Link Therefore I Am." *Kairos* 8.1 (2003). Web. 7 Aug. 2009.

ARTICLE IN A MAGAZINE:

Joy, Bill. "Why the Future Doesn't Need Us." *Wired*. Web. 8 Apr. 2009.

ARTICLE IN A NEWSPAPER:

Lawlor, Allison. "Halifax Blast Forces 400 Residents to Flee." *Globe and Mail*. 7 Aug. 2003. Web. 7 Aug. 2009.

WORK FROM A SUBSCRIPTION SERVICE:

"Marimba." *Compton's Encyclopaedia Online*. Vers. 3.0, 1999. AOL. 12 July 2000. Keyword: Compton's.

POSTING TO A DISCUSSION LIST:

Scaife, Ross. "Trajan's Column." Online posting. 2 Aug. 2000. Humanist Discussion Group, Vol. 14, No. 144. Centre for Computing in the Humanities, King's College London. Web. 3 Aug. 2000.

ELECTRONIC MAIL:

Rockwell, Geoffrey. "Re: Humanities Computing." Message to the author. E-mail. 11 Aug. 2003.

ELECTRONIC SITES, INCLUDING BLOGS, PODCASTS, AND WIKIS:

Treat these the same way as any other electronic website. Include the author, if known, the title of the posting in quotation marks, the name of the website in italics. Then list the publisher, if known, and the date the piece was posted. If you do not know the publisher's name, use n.p. in its place. Remember to include the date that you accessed the material as well.

Goldman, Lisa. "Soldiers Planted Flowers in Tahrir Square." *Lisa Goldman.* n.p. 25 Apr. 2011. Web. 23 May 2011.

Citing Sources in MLA Style

Whenever you refer to material from another source, whether book, journal article, motion picture, or recording, you must acknowledge your source. Citing your sources no longer necessitates footnotes or endnotes. Instead, citations of sources are placed in the body of the essay in parentheses. A footnote or endnote is necessary only if you have supplementary material to add that does not properly belong in the text of the essay itself.

Simple Citation

Include in parentheses after the citation only what is essential to guide the reader to the correct entry in the "Works Cited." Often, all that will be needed is the last name of the author followed by a page number. For example, if you were quoting from Margaret Laurence's *The Diviners,* the citation in the text would look like this:

Example   Morag's collection of photographs gives the reader insight into her own hidden past. As she says, "I keep the snapshots not for what they show but for what is hidden in them" (Laurence 6).

This citation refers the reader to the following entry on the "Works Cited" page:

Example   Laurence, Margaret. *The Diviners*. Toronto: Bantam, 2003.

If this is the only entry listed under Laurence, there is no confusion, and the reader knows that the quotation can be found on page 6 of the listed text.

Citation of More Than One Work by the Same Author

If, on the other hand, there are references to two works by the same author, a more specific notation is required. Say that you referred in the same essay to Margaret Laurence's earlier novel, *A Jest of God*. You might, perhaps, make the following reference:

Example   Rachel discovers her own capacity to hide the truth from herself. As she explains, "There is room enough in anyone's bonehouse for too much duplicity (Laurence *Jest* 182).

This reference makes it clear that more than one book by Laurence is listed in the "Works Cited."

Citation of a Work in More Than One Volume

If, in an essay about Keats's poetry, you decide to quote from the two-volume collection of Keats's letters, the citation would read as follows:

> Keats, in the composition of the odes, dedicates himself to the search for "the true voice of feeling" (*Letters* 2: 167).

Example

Here the Arabic numeral 2 refers to the second volume of the letters. A colon is used to separate the volume number from the page number.

Similar adjustments must be made to clarify abbreviated citations. Always remember to ask yourself what the reader needs to know in order to find the reference easily.

Citation of Poetry and of Long or Short Quotations

Avoid redundant citations. If the body of your essay already explains the source adequately, do not restate the information in parentheses. For example, you might write the following analysis of Keats's poetry:

> The poet speaks of the lure of death in "Ode to a Nightingale":
>
> *Darkling I listen; and, for many a time*
>   *I have been half in love with easeful Death,*
>
> *Call'd him soft names in many a mused rhyme,*
>   *To take into the air my quiet breath. (51–54)*

Example

Here only the line numbers are listed in parentheses, since the title of the poem is given in the body of the essay itself. Note, too, that a long quotation is double-spaced, indented, and written without quotation marks. Because the quoted matter is poetry, the lines are given as they are in the text. If the quotation were fewer than four lines, it would be written in the body of the essay in the following way, using quotation marks:

> The poet speaks of the lure of death in "Ode to a Nightingale": "Darkling I listen; and, for many a time/I have been half in love with easeful Death" (51–52).

Example

Citation of Poetic Drama

A reference to a play must refer to act, scene, and line numbers, as in the following case:

> In Shakespeare's *A Midsummer Night's Dream*, Titania, enchanted with Bottom, sees the world around her with romantic eyes. As she says, "The moon methinks looks with a watery eye; /And when she weeps, weeps every little flower, /Lamenting some enforced chastity" (3.1.202–04).

Example

Note that as many as three lines of poetry may be cited without indentation; four lines or more, however, do require indentation.

Citation of a Website

Identify the author or the website's title in a sentence that introduces the quotation. To make finding the citation in the source material easier for your reader, use any Web page text divisions as substitutes for page numbers.

Example   Miles writes in "I Link Therefore I Am" that

> [I]n a screen-literate world where print and the page are no longer exemplars for the expression of knowledge, we remain hesitantly standing at the cusp of new academic genres. Hence, to use these works you need to be an active reader, at times you must do things with the text or digital artifacts for anything to happen, yet at other times the work will insistently run of its own accord. (Introduction)

Punctuation of Citations

Note that for citations within the text, punctuation appears *after* the parentheses. In quotations set off from the text, citations *follow* the final punctuation. To make citations as unobtrusive as possible, try to place them at the end, rather than in the middle, of sentences.

For more detail, see Joseph Gibaldi, *MLA Handbook for Writers of Research Papers,* 7th ed. (New York: Modern Language Association, 2009), or consult the Web at < www. mla.org/ > .

Sample Bibliographic Entries in APA Style

The following entries are arranged according to the style of the *Publication Manual of the American Psychological Association.* In this case, the bibliography is given the heading "References." The APA uses an author–date system of citation. Here are some guidelines to citations in the reference pages. See also the References page of the APA model essay on pp. 94 and 95, and for more details consult this text: American Psychological Association. (2010). *Publication Manual of the American Psychological Association.* 6th ed. Washington, DC: Author, or on the Web at < www.apa.org/ > .

Information Needed for APA References

1. Use hanging indents for each entry. The first line of each reference should be indented one-half inch from the left margin.
2. List authors alphabetically last name first, followed by initials. List all authors this way unless the work has more than six. If there are more than six authors, use the abbreviation et al. after the sixth author's name.
3. When a work is co-authored, use an ampersand (&) to add the final name.
4. If there is more than one entry by the same author, list in order of publication, starting with the earliest.
5. Capitalize all the main words in a journal title, but capitalize only the first letter of the title and subtitle of a book article or Web page.

6. Italicize titles of books and journals, but do not italicize, underline, or put quotations around article or essay titles.
7. Italicize volume numbers, but not issue numbers.
8. Abbreviate names of commercial publishers by using only the main elements of the name. Cite names of university publishers in full, but do not repeat the location of the publisher if it is included in the university name.
9. Separate sections of entries with periods, even words in parentheses. But separate the place of publication from the publisher's name by a colon and one space.
10. Use only one space between items in APA references and citations.
11. For articles, give the complete page range (e.g., 211–214).
12. The examples shown below are single-spaced to save paper. When you submit your paper, all entries should be double-spaced.

APA Format in References

1. For "unpolished" manuscripts, that is, work not intended for publication, indent the first line five to seven spaces (the default tab setting on your word processor is acceptable). For finished manuscripts, "hanging indents" are used, as illustrated in the following examples. The latter format is recommended. However, the APA guidelines defer to your professor's style preference; you should clarify this before submitting your paper.
2. List authors by last names and initials. If a work is co-authored, invert the names of all the authors and use an ampersand ($\&$) to join the final name.
3. For books, capitalize the first word of the title and the subtitle as well as proper names; everything else is lower case. For periodicals, use both upper and lower case as usual, a comma, and a volume number. Italicize titles and volume numbers.
4. Abbreviate names of commercial publishers by using only the main elements of the name. Cite names of university publishers in full.
5. Separate sections of entries with periods, even the words in parentheses. But separate the place of publication from the publisher's name by a colon and one space.
6. Use only one space between items in APA citations.
7. For articles, list the complete page range (211–214).
8. The examples shown below are single-spaced to save paper. When you submit your paper, all entries should be double-spaced.

Books

ONE AUTHOR:

Selye, H. (1956). *The stress of life.* New York: McGraw-Hill.

TWO AUTHORS:

Klug, B. J., & Whitfield, P. T. (2003). *Widening the circle: Culturally relevant pedagogy for American Indian children*. New York: RoutledgeFalmer.

A CHAPTER IN AN EDITED BOOK:

Lam, D. C. K. (2005). Depression. In S. M. Freeman & A. Freeman (Eds.), *Cognitive behavior therapy in nursing practice* (pp. 45–81). New York: Springer.

Journals

ONE AUTHOR:

Turner, J. (1981). Social support as a contingency in psychological well-being. *Journal of Health and Social Behavior, 22,* 357–367.

MULTIPLE AUTHORS IN A JOURNAL WITH SEPARATE PAGING:

Blanton, S., Robin, B., & Kinzie, M. (1991). Repurposing a feature film for interactive multi-media. *Educational Technology, 31*(12), 7–12.

NEWSPAPER ARTICLE:

Fowlie, J. (2003, August 16). People short of breath hard hit. *The Globe and Mail,* National Edition, p. A13.

A Review

Johnson, B. D. (2003, June 16). Whales of a time [Review of the film *Whale Rider*]. *Maclean's,* 85–86.

A Film

Egoyan, A. (Director). (2002). *Ararat* [Film]. Toronto: Alliance Atlantis.

Electronic Publications

ONLINE ARTICLES:
Online articles follow the same APA guidelines as articles in print. You do, however, have to indicate where you found the material online so that the reader may access it.

ONLINE SCHOLARLY ARTICLE:
Since URLs may change, APA asks that you provide a Digital Object Identifier (DOI) when it is available, rather than a URL.

Kowatch, R. A., & DelBello, M. P. (2006). Pediatric bipolar disorder: Emerging diagnostic and treatment approaches. *Child and Adolescent Psychiatric Clinics of North America, 15,* 73–108. doi:10.1016/j.chc.2005.08.013

ONLINE SCHOLARLY ARTICLE WITHOUT A DOI:
If there is no DOI, give the URL.

Pawlik-Kienlen, L. (2009, September 30). The top 10 qualities of good psychologists: Important personality traits of therapists working in psychology. Retrieved from http://counseling.suite101.com/article.cfm/ the_top_10_qualities_of_good_psychologists

If there is no DOI but there is also a print version available, indicate that you are using the electronic version.

Jennings, L., & Skovholt, T. M. (1999). The cognitive, emotional, and relational characteristics of master therapists. [Electronic Version]. *Journal of Counseling Psychology 46*(1), 3–11.

ARTICLE FROM A DATABASE:

You can treat an article from a database as if it were an ordinary print source, unless it would be difficult to find. You do not need retrieval dates unless the source (a Wiki, for example) might be subject to change.

Buckley, J. (1997). The invisible audience and the disembodied voice: Online teaching and the loss of body image. *Computers and Composition, 14*(2), 179–188.

ELECTRONIC RESOURCES SUCH AS BLOGS, PODCASTS, AND WIKIS:

Roth, J. D. (2011, May 26). How to run a profitable garage sale. [Web log comment]. Retrieved from http://www.getrichslowly.org/blog/

Include the title of the piece (not in italics) and the URL from which you retrieved it.

Coupland, D. (The 2010 CBC Massey Lectures). Player One: What is to become of us? CBC Radio Podcast. Podcast retrieved from http://www.cbc.ca/ideas/episodes/massey-lectures/2010/11/08/massey-lectures-2010-player-one-what-is-to-become-of-us/

Leonard Cohen: Hallelujah. (n.d.) Retrieved May 27, 2011 from LyricWiki: http://lyrics.wikia.com/Leonard_Cohen:Hallelujah

In all cases, include the title of the piece (not in italics) and the URL from which you retrieved it.

Citing Sources in APA Style

As with the MLA style of documentation, you may cite your sources in parentheses in APA style. In APA style, however, the year of publication is given with the author's last name; hence, the title of a work is not usually needed. Note details in the following examples:

SHORT QUOTATION: **Example**

Social support is defined as "those relationships among people that provide not only material help and emotional assurance, but also the sense that one is a continuing object of concern on the part of other people" (Pilsuk, 1982, p. 20).

BLOCK QUOTATION (MORE THAN FORTY WORDS):

Seligman (1975) argues that helplessness may lead to depression:

> *Those people who are particularly susceptible to depression may have had lives relatively devoid of mastery; their lives may have been full of situations in which they were helpless to influence the sources of suffering and relief. (p. 104)*

Note that, in this passage, the author's last name and the date of publication are not included in parentheses because they are already given in the body of the essay. This use of a signal phrase provides acknowledgment even though page numbers are not necessary in this case.

Example   PARAPHRASE:

> Cobb (1976) insists that stress, not social support, is the key to understanding changes in health. Social support only acts as a buffer.

Following these basic guidelines should help you assemble your notes and your bibliography with relative ease. Remember these guidelines as you prepare the documentation for your essay:

1. Be consistent.
2. Give your reader all the information needed to find a reference.
3. Check the sample research essay on pp. 84–97 for a model of APA format.
4. Check the appropriate style guide for further details.

For more detail, see the *Publication Manual of the American Psychological Association*, 6th ed., and consult the World Wide Web: < http://www.apastyle. org/electref.html >. The Web version supersedes the text for online sources.

Web Citations in Text

For specific parts of a document on the Web, cite the chapter, figure, table, or appropriate section. For quotations, give page numbers or paragraph numbers where available (using the abbreviation "para." for "paragraph"). Omit them if they are not available.

For Materials You Publish on the Web

Be aware of copyright permission requirements, and seek permission where necessary. Permission is not necessary for extracts in papers submitted to an instructor.

References may appear in block style rather than with hanging indents, to accommodate browser limitations. Italics may be used instead of underlining, if they are used consistently. References may be single-spaced to allow for limitations of browsers.

Sample Bibliographic Entries in University of Chicago Style

Some disciplines, in particular history and political science, prefer a traditional footnoting style. The best sources of information about this style are Kate Turabian's *A Manual for Writers* and *The Chicago Manual of Style*.

If your instructor advises you to use this traditional style, rather than the parenthetical forms just outlined, refer to this section.

Since bibliographic listings can be complex, try to include as much information as possible in each entry. Remember that you are trying to help your reader locate the sources.

Books

ONE AUTHOR:

Miller, J. S. *Skyscrapers Hide the Heavens: A History of Indian–White Relations in Canada*. Toronto: University of Toronto Press, 1989.

TWO AUTHORS AND COMPONENT PART IN A LARGER WORK:

Rogers, E. S., and Flora Tobobondung. "Parry Sound Farmers: A Period of Change in the Way of Life of the Algonkians of Southern Ontario." In *Contributions to Canadian Ethnology*, edited by David Brez Carlisle. Ottawa: National Museums of Canada, 1975.

MORE THAN THREE AUTHORS:

Martin, Nancy, Pat D'Arcy, Bryan Newton, and Robert Parker. *Writing and Learning Across the Curriculum 11–16.* Upper Montclair, N.J.: Boynton/Cook, 1976.

Note that it would be permissible to shorten the note form of this entry to read:

1. Nancy Martin and others, *Writing and Learning Across the Curriculum 11–16* (Upper Montclair, N.J.: Boynton/Cook, 1976), 50.

EDITION AFTER THE FIRST:

Barker, Larry L. *Communication.* 4th ed. Englewood Cliffs, N.J.: Prentice-Hall, 1987.

ASSOCIATION AUTHOR AND REPRINT:

Nin.Da.Waab.Jig. *Minishenhying Anishnaabe-aki Walpole Island: The Soul of Indian Territory*. Windsor: Commercial Associates/Ross Roy Ltd., 1987; reprint, 1989.

This book is by a Native community, and the title is in Ojibwa. The name of the community is listed first.

It is important to list information about a reprint, in case changes have been made to the pagination.

EDITOR:

Storr, Anthony, ed. *The Essential Jung.* Selected and introduced by Anthony Storr. Princeton, N.J.: Princeton University Press, 1983.

TRANSLATION:

Pushkin, Alexander. *Eugene Onegin.* Translation by Charles Johnston with an Introduction by John Bayley. Harmondsworth, Middlesex: Penguin, 1977.

A WORK IN MORE THAN ONE VOLUME:

Campbell, Joseph. *The Masks of God.* 4 vols. New York: Viking Press, 1960–68.

A WORK IN A SERIES:

Stanley, George F. G. *The War of 1812: Land Operations.* Canadian War Museum Historical Publication No. 18. Toronto: Macmillan, 1983.

COMPONENT PART BY ONE AUTHOR IN A WORK BY ANOTHER:

Purvis, Jane. "The Experience of Schooling for Working-Class Boys and Girls in Nineteenth Century England." In *Defining the Curriculum: Histories and Ethnographies,* edited by Ivor F. Goodson and Stephen J. Ball, 89–115. London: Falmer Press, 1984.

Magazines, Newspapers, and Journals

ARTICLE IN A POPULAR MAGAZINE:

Mohr, Merilyn. "The Evolutionary Image." *Equinox,* March/April 1989, 80–93.

ARTICLE IN A SCHOLARLY JOURNAL:

Creighton, D. G. "The Economic Background of the Rebellions of 1867." *The Canadian Journal of Economics and Political Science* 4 (1937): 322–34.

NEWSPAPER:

"Feminists Demand Legal System Review." *London Free Press,* 10 February 1990, D1.

BOOK REVIEW:

Rugoff, Milton. "The Feminine Mystic." Review of Spiritualism and Women's Rights in Nineteenth Century America by Ann Braude. *The New York Times Book Review,* 14 January 1990, 19.

Non-print Sources

MOTION PICTURE:

Phillips, Robin. Dir. *The Wars.* Toronto: Spectra Films, 1983.

TELEVISION OR RADIO PROGRAM:

CBC. "The Nature of Things." 7 February 1990. "Thirty Years of Discovery." David Suzuki, narrator.

PUBLISHED INTERVIEW:

Davies, Robertson. "Interview with Robertson Davies: The Bizarre and Passionate Life of the Canadian People." Interview by Silver Donald Cameron (9 November 1971). *Conversations with Canadian Novelists.* Toronto: Colbert Agency, Inc., 1973.

UNPUBLISHED INTERVIEW:

Beedle, Merle Assance. Interview by author, March 1989.

Special Forms

UNPUBLISHED MATERIALS:

Crown Attorney's Case Book for Cases Prosecuted Under the Liquor Control Act (1927) in Middlesex County. Regional Room, D. B. Weldon Library, University of Western Ontario, London.

DISSERTATIONS:

Rockwell, Geoffrey. "A Unity of Voices, A Definition of Philosophical Dialogue." PhD diss., University of Toronto, 1995.

Government Publications

Here are some basic rules to follow when citing government documents:

1. List name of country, province, state, city, or district first in bibliographies. In notes, however, this information may be left out because it will be obvious from the text.
2. Next, list the name of the legislative body, department, or board. Use the name of the office rather than the name of the officer.
3. Follow with the name of the division or commission, if any.
4. Give the title of the document, underlined or italicized.
5. Include any additional information needed to find the document.

Use the following bibliographical format for a government publication:

Issuing Body. *Title*. Personal Author. (Report number; medium). Edition. Place: Publisher, Date. (Series title, number).

Ontario. Commission on Planning and Development Reform in Ontario. *New Planning for Ontario: Final Report*. John Sewell. (Chair). Toronto: Queen's Printer for Ontario, 1993.

CANADIAN DOCUMENTS:

List Canadian documents according to the executive department that issued them. Identify them by calendar year. The note would also include the chapter number.

Canada. House of Commons. *Order Paper and Notices*. 16 February 1972.

The note form would be:

1. House of Commons, *Order Paper and Notices,* 16 February 1972, 6.

AMERICAN DOCUMENTS:

U.S. Congress. Senate. Committee on Foreign Relations. *Aid Programs to Developing Countries.* Washington, D.C.: GPO, 1989.

Here "GPO" stands for Government Printing Office. The note form would be:

1. U.S. Congress, Senate, Committee on Foreign Relations, *Aid Programs to Developing Countries* (Washington, D.C.: GPO, 1989), 7.

BRITISH DOCUMENTS:

U.K. Board of Education. Report of the Committee on the Position of Natural Science in the Educational System of Great Britain. London: HMSO, 1918.

Here "HMSO" stands for Her (His) Majesty's Stationery Office. The note form would be:

1. Board of Education, Report of the Committee on the Position of Natural Science in the Educational System of Great Britain (London: HMSO, 1918), 6.

Listing Electronic Sources

The Chicago Manual of Style has recently published its 16th edition and presented detailed information on how to document electronic sources. It recommends either the system suggested by MLA or the author–date system suggested by APA, and its accompanying rules on electronic documents.

ON THE WEB:

Modern Language Association

<http://www.apastyle.org/index.aspx> American Psychological Association

CITING ELECTRONIC SOURCES:

Hacker, Diane, and Barbara Fister. *Research and Documentation Online*. 5th ed. New York: Bedford Books, 2010.

Hacker, Diane, and Barbara Fister. Research and Documentation *Online*. 5th ed.

*Or check its more current website at <http://bcs.bedfordstmartins.com/resdoc5e/>.

Citing Sources in University of Chicago Style

Although notes can be used both for commentary and for reference, this section will concentrate on their use in making reference to particular works. Remember, though, that a note is often a good place to include supplementary commentary that does not belong in your paper proper, but that needs to be included.

In the University of Chicago style of documentation, you include notes compiled at the bottom of pages (footnotes) or in a list compiled at the end of the paper (endnotes). Each entry in your notes should correspond to a number in the text of your paper. The note numbers should appear a half line above your text at the end of the passage you are quoting or paraphrasing. The first line of each note is indented eight spaces from the left margin.

When you use this traditional style of documentation, always single-space your notes, and leave a space between each one.

The first note should contain complete information about the location of the source. Be sure to include everything that your reader will need to find it. Take your information from the title page of the work in question. The order of information for the first note follows this format:

For a First Complete Note, in this Case a Book

Note number, followed by a period

Name of author(s), editor(s), or organization(s) in normal order

Title and subtitle, if any, underlined or italicized

Name of editor or translator, if listed on title page

Name or number of edition, if not the first

Total of volume numbers (if multivolume work) or individual volume, if applicable

Series title and volume number if series is numbered

Facts of publication, enclosed in parentheses: (place of publication: name of publisher, date of publication)

Page number

URL for Internet sources or an indication of the medium (CD-ROM, DVD, etc.)

Sometimes some of these things will not apply to the text you are citing. Occasionally, too, some of the facts of publication may be missing. These may be supplied in square brackets, if you know them, or they may be indicated by these abbreviations:

n.p. meaning "no place" or "no publisher" or both

n.d. meaning "no date"

A first full reference to a book would look like this:

6. Northrop Frye, *The Great Code: The Bible and Literature* (New York: Harcourt Brace Jovanovich, 1982), 117.

For a First Complete Note, in this Case an Article

Follow this order for an article in a magazine or periodical:

Note number, followed by a period

Name of author(s)

Title of article in quotation marks

Name of periodical underlined or italicized

Volume number or issue

Publication date in parentheses

Page numbers, inclusive (These normally are not preceded by "p." for page or "pp." for pages, unless confusion is possible.)

A first full reference to an article would look like this:

3. Peter Elbow, "Embracing Contraries in the Writing Process," *College Composition and Communication* 35 (1984): 161.

Note that long quoted passages in University of Chicago style are single-spaced and indented five spaces.

Note too that there are some significant differences between the format of notes and that of bibliographic entries:

1. Notes are listed consecutively by number; bibliographic entries are listed alphabetically by last name of author. Hence, authors' names are not inverted in notes, though they are in bibliographies.
2. In notes, items are usually separated with commas; in bibliographic entries, items are separated with periods.
3. Notes include facts of publication in parentheses; bibliographic entries do not enclose this information in parentheses.
4. Notes include the specific page references of the citation; bibliographic entries do not, though they do include the page range of journal articles, inclusive.

Notes After the First Full Reference to a Work

The best way to cite something after the first full reference is to include the following:

Author's last name

Shortened title of the work, maintaining key words without changing word order

Page number

Note that the use of Latin abbreviations such as *Ibid.* is now discouraged. The second references to the book and article listed above would look like these:

7. Frye, *Code,* 133.

8. Elbow, "Embracing Contraries," 163.

Some instructors may allow you to dispense with a shortened version of the title and use just the author's last name and the page number. This method is used only if you are citing no more than one work by an author. In any case, check with your instructor first.

Part Seven

FIT, FORM, AND FUNCTION

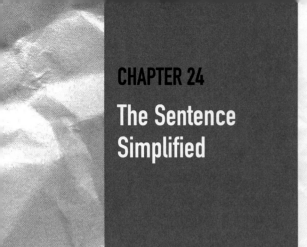

CHAPTER 24

The Sentence Simplified

Any fool can make a rule and every fool will mind it.
—HENRY DAVID THOREAU

In this chapter:

- How to identify parts of speech
- How to identify parts of the sentence

Parts of Speech

A knowledge of the roles parts of speech play will help you understand how your sentences are constructed.

Nouns

Nouns name something: a person, place, or thing. They may be abstract or concrete. As a general rule, something may be classified as a noun if you can put an article ("a," "an," or "the") or a possessive pronoun ("my," "her") in front of it.

Example   advertising   corset

philosophy   computer

doctor   giraffe

Pronouns

Pronouns stand in the place of nouns. There are many kinds of pronouns.

PERSONAL: I, you, he, she, we, they (subjective); me, you, him, her, us, them (objective); my, your, his, her, our, their (possessive); mine, yours, his, hers, ours, theirs (absolute possessive)

Example   I never should have lent **her my** notes from yesterday's class.

REFLEXIVE OR INTENSIVE: himself, myself, yourself, and so on

> Frankenstein's creature was shocked when he looked at **himself** in the mirror. (reflexive)
>
> I did it all by **myself**. (intensive)

Example

RELATIVE: who, which, that, whose, whoever, whomever, whichever, and so on

> The best friends are those **who** remain loyal to the end.

Example

These pronouns connect subordinate clauses to main clauses.

INTERROGATIVE: who, whom, which, what

> **Who** do you think you are?

Example

These pronouns begin questions.

DEMONSTRATIVE: this, that, these, those, such

> **Such** is life.

Example

These pronouns point to someone or something.

INDEFINITE: any, some, each, every, few, everyone, everybody, someone, somebody

> **Everybody** loves **somebody** sometime.

Example

These pronouns stand for an indefinite number of people or things.

RECIPROCAL: each other, one another

> Scott and Zelda loved and hated **each other** intensely.

Example

These pronouns express a reciprocal relationship.

Verbs

A verb is an action word or a word that describes a state of being. It may have many forms and tenses. In other words, verbs are the parts of speech that change to indicate a change in time. Verbs also may be composed of an auxiliary, or helping, verb and a main verb. Verbs may be transitive or intransitive (some verbs may be either), or linking.

A transitive verb needs an object to be complete.

> Winston **shut** his mouth.

Example

An intransitive verb is complete without an object.

Example   Hayden **sneezed.**

A linking verb connects the subject to a state of being.

Example   Anne **is** pregnant.

Adjectives

Adjectives describe or modify nouns and often appear in front of a noun.

Example
delicious	wooden
handsome	abstract
devilish	superstitious

Jitterbug was a **beautiful, exotic, shorthaired** cat.

Adverbs

Adverbs describe or modify verbs, adjectives, and other adverbs. They often end in "ly." Adverbs are often the hardest words to categorize. As a general rule, if you can't figure out what part of speech something is, it is probably an adverb.

Example
soon	too
devilishly	now
often	generally

We have **seldom** seen such wisdom in one **so** young.

Prepositions

The preposition is a linking word that is always followed by a noun or a pronoun (and its modifiers, if any).

Example
on the wagon	**according to** her
in your mind	**by** all accounts
to the lifeboats	**from** me **to** you

Prepositions are used to link objects to verbs or nouns and to form a phrase that shows place, time, position, or manner. These phrases usually function as adjectives or adverbs in a sentence.

Example   I'll get back **to her** as soon as possible.

Two players **on my team** were taken **to hospital.**

Conjunctions

Conjunctions are used to join two words, phrases, or clauses. Conjunctions can be coordinating conjunctions (and, or, for, nor, but, yet, so) or subordinating. Coordinating conjunctions join two equal sentence structures (independent clauses); subordinating conjunctions (like "which," "although," "because") join an independent or main clause to a dependent or subordinate clause. Adding a subordinate conjunction makes the clause unable to stand by itself.

Peter was exhausted. (independent clause)

Example

Because Peter was exhausted (dependent clause)

The office sent invoices to those **who** owed money **and** greeting cards to those **who** did not.

Example

After the war was over, Ashley returned to Melanie.

Love is **as** strong **as** death.

Interjections

Interjections are exclamatory words or phrases that interrupt a sentence.

No, I don't want to go to the dentist.

Example

My word! I simply don't believe what you say.

Parts of the Sentence

In addition to parts of speech, there are some definitions you need to keep in mind as you read the next chapter.

Phrase

A phrase is a group of related words that lacks a subject and a verb.

playing doctor

Example

in the tree house

Clause

A clause is a group of related words with a subject and a verb.

We were playing doctor in the tree house.

Example

Some fundamental understanding of the way a sentence is put together will help you analyze your style, eliminate grammatical errors, and punctuate more accurately. First, learn to differentiate the parts of a sentence. When analyzing a sentence, always find the verb first. The verb is the part of the sentence that describes the action or the state of being. Next, find the subject: ask who performed the action or what is being described. Note that, usually, the subject appears before the verb.

Example   The German shepherd chased the raccoon.

What is the verb? (chased—an action)
What is the subject? Who or what chased the raccoon? (the German shepherd)

Example   Her sunglasses look sophisticated, like something out of *The Matrix* movies.

What is the verb? (look—a state of being)
What is the subject? Who or what looks sophisticated? (her sunglasses)

The most common English sentence is made up of a subject, a verb, and an object, usually in that order.

Example   Sweetiepie, the chimpanzee, refused to eat the banana.

         S   V   O

It threw its food on the floor of the cage.

         S   V   O

It gave the zookeeper a nasty look.

         S   V   O

Even chimpanzees lose their temper.

         S   V   O

In each of these cases, the first noun or pronoun in the sentence is the subject, which performs the action. What follows the subject is the predicate, made up of the verb, which describes the action, and the object, which receives the action.

Another common simple sentence pattern is subject, verb, and complement, sometimes called a "subjective completion." Here, the verb must be a linking verb that describes a state of being, rather than an action.

Example   Vladimir is a brilliant Web designer.

         S   V   C

His work seems elegant and contemporary.

         S   V   C

Knowing how to use all the latest software is the key.

         S   V   C

Some people are gifted that way.

              S   V   C

A sentence is a grammatical unit that can stand alone. It must be composed of a subject and a verb and is usually accompanied by an object or a complement.

CHAPTER 24 PARTS OF SPEECH EXERCISES

Answers begin on p. 279.

A. Circle all the nouns in the following sentences:
   1. Carol gave up eating meat after she saw a documentary detailing what happened during the production of food.
   2. Ethel celebrated her seventeenth birthday by going to the park, not knowing that she would lock her keys in the car accidentally and have to walk four kilometres to get home.
   3. Drinking more than two drinks a day is considered unhealthy.
   4. London, Ontario is purportedly the thunderstorm capital of North America.
   5. Grow old along with me; the best is yet to be.

B. Circle all the adverbs in the following sentences:
   1. His manner was jolly, but she did not find his friendly demeanor remotely convincing.
   2. Unfortunately, we are not able to offer you a position now.
   3. My boss wanted to give me a very substantial raise; however, untoward financial circumstances prevented her from doing so.
   4. I will never reveal my secret recipe for making peanut brittle.
   5. Henceforward, you will be expressly forbidden to answer the phone.

C. Circle all the prepositions in the following sentences:
   1. After all we have been through, you do not need to ask my permission to keep a pet in your room.
   2. Emma had a plan for her retirement: she hoped to find wealthy friends who were in the habit of paying their companions' bill, or if that did not work out, she hoped to cash in on the lottery.
   3. Never again will I offer to go in to work on a Saturday; during the weekends I need to catch up on my sleep.
   4. In my opinion, you are within your rights to file a complaint about their behaviour yesterday.
   5. Between you and me, Michael regularly made appointments, but at the last moment he often reconsidered and stayed at home in bed.

D. Circle all the verbs in the following sentences:
   1. Whatever do you mean, Mr. Johnson?
   2. The tornado wreaked havoc in the small rural community.
   3. Underline all the parts of speech that you can find in the sentence.
   4. Be still my beating heart!
   5. You are smiling, so things must have worked out well.

E. Circle all the pronouns in the following sentences:
   1. Anyone who had a heart would be sympathetic to that cause.
   2. This suitcase must be ours; it matches our other bags, even if the porter didn't notice their similarity.

3. Nothing would make me happier than having you accompany me to lunch.
4. Somebody had better call the police; did you hear the cry for help?
5. Who is knocking at my door?

F. Circle all the conjunctions, whether subordinate or coordinate, in the following sentences:
1. Despite my best intentions, I am unable to complete the work on time, and I must request an extension.
2. Because I stayed up all night, I was unable to wake up when the alarm rang this morning.
3. Until you came into my life, I was lost and confused.
4. After the ball, Cinderella returned to her humble cottage just before her coach turned into a pumpkin.
5. Either you pay your dues, or you are out of the union.

G. Identify all subordinate clauses in the following sentences:
1. Dudley Doright is a man you can trust.
2. Whatever you want for dinner is fine with me.
3. Who have you been talking to on the phone all this time?
4. Unless you ask me to do so, I will not breathe a word of this to anyone.
5. She is the woman whom I love.

H. Identify all subordinate clauses in the following sentences:
1. Be all that you can be.
2. You can call on us whenever you are in need.
3. However you explain verb tenses, I will never understand them.
4. The book that won the Governor General's Award for fiction this year was Diane Warren's *Cool Water.*
5. No matter what the temperature outside is, I will not use the air conditioner.

What is written without effort is in general
read without pleasure.
—SAMUEL JOHNSON

In this chapter:

- How to identify and correct fragments, run-ons, comma splices
- Problems with modifiers
- Problems with pronouns
- Problems with subject and verb agreement
- Problems with punctuation
- Problems with the apostrophe

A well-structured sentence tells its readers where to start and where to stop. The sentence, if it is correctly formed, constitutes a complete thought. It contains a main subject and a main verb connected to the subject.

Sentence Structure: Fragments, Run-Ons, Comma Splices

Avoid Fragments

A sentence fragment lacks either a subject or a main verb. Or, sometimes, it ignores the connection between them.

> ✗ Ramona did not follow the cheesecake recipe. But added cheddar instead of cream cheese. (missing subject: she)   **Example**

> ✓ Ramona did not follow the cheesecake recipe. She added cheddar instead of cream cheese.

> ✗ Wilhelm enjoyed many forms of relaxation. Practising tai chi, doing origami, and baking cookies. (no connection to the subject: he)

> ✓ Wilhelm enjoyed many forms of relaxation: practising tai chi, doing origami, and baking cookies.

✗ Norrie didn't bring his homework. Because Fido ate it. (dependent clause fragment)

✓ Norrie didn't bring his homework because Fido ate it.

Note: A fragment may, on rare occasions, be used for rhetorical effect. Deliberate fragments must, however, be used sparingly. It is also a wise idea to use a dash (two hyphens in typing) before a deliberate sentence fragment to indicate its purpose to your reader.

Example   Should colleges and universities have the right to charge foreign students higher tuition than Canadian students?—Under no circumstances.

Avoid Run-on Sentences

A run-on sentence is two sentences that run together without any punctuation to indicate where one ends and the next begins.

Example   ✗ Hedda couldn't sleep on the new waterbed she always felt seasick.
✓ Hedda couldn't sleep on the new waterbed. She always felt seasick.

Avoid Comma Splices

A comma splice is similar to a run-on sentence. It occurs when two main clauses are "spliced," or incorrectly joined, by a comma. The comma splice fails to show the relationship between two clauses.

Example   ✗ Graeme had too much to drink, he got the hiccups.
✗ His mother was the designated driver, she took him home.

A comma splice, like a visible seam, is a sign of faulty workmanship. There are several methods by which it may be corrected. Run-ons may also be treated the same way:

1. JOIN THE TWO IDEAS WITH ONE OF THE FOLLOWING COORDINATING CONJUNCTIONS: "AND," "OR," "NOR," "FOR," "BUT," "YET," "SO."

Example   ✓ Graeme had too much to drink, and he got the hiccups.
✓ His mother was the designated driver, so she took him home.

2. JOIN THE TWO IDEAS WITH A SUBORDINATING CONJUNCTION.

Example   ✓ Because Graeme had too much to drink, he got the hiccups.
✓ Since his mother was the designated driver, she took him home.

3. FORM TWO SEPARATE SENTENCES.

✓ Graeme had too much to drink. He got the hiccups.
✓ His mother was the designated driver. She took him home.

Example

4. JOIN THE TWO IDEAS WITH A SEMICOLON.

Use this method of correction only if the two ideas in question are logically connected. Note that sometimes a word may be used as a conjunctive adverb to join two sentences with a semicolon. Such words as "however," "therefore," and "hence" frequently serve this function. For more information, see p. 239.

✓ Graeme had too much to drink; he got the hiccups.
✓ His mother was the designated driver; she took him home.

Example

CHAPTER 25 SENTENCE STRUCTURE EXERCISE A

Correct the comma splices, run-ons, and fragments in these sentences. Some may be fine as they are. Answers begin on p. 280.

1. For most people playing cards is more than a hobby, it is a social activity and a way to gamble without stigma.
2. While bridge is, for the most part, a civilized game, it depends on partnership and can lead to arguments.
3. Thomas bought a new computer, the other one he planned to sell on eBay.
4. Weather disturbances are on the rise, however, not everyone believes that they are real.
5. Doing yoga at lunch every day, Aileen and Mei Ling had fun still they did not lose weight.
6. On medical shows patients never have chronic illnesses nevertheless the reality is that chronic illnesses account for the majority of health care costs.
7. These days baby boomer audiences do not want to travel far in search of entertainment. Which is why the Metropolitan Opera and England's National Theatre are now broadcast in local movie theatres.
8. The coffee shop sued the newspaper food critic after she criticized the poor service and the mediocre food, even though the reviewer won, she boycotted the shop thereafter.
9. Last year Poppy and Jane stayed in northern California in Bodega Bay. Near where Alfred Hitchcock filmed *The Birds*.
10. In Lake Tahoe they went on a cruise it afforded a view of the mansion where *The Godfather II* was filmed.

CHAPTER 25 SENTENCE STRUCTURE EXERCISE B

1. Consultants always seem overpaid and underworked because I lack ambition but have expensive shopping habits, I would like to become a consultant.
2. In Michel Tremblay's *Les Belles-Soeurs* the characters—all female—showing how their lives were affected by men.

3. Shy when company comes, my cats ignoring activities in the living room in favour of their beds.

4. Canada is the home of many famous chefs. A list which includes Susur Lee, Mark McEwan, and Michael Smith.

5. The city of Winnipeg has experienced many floods, it is difficult, if not impossible, to get flood insurance there.

6. This place has everything I want in a house, a hot tub, a swimming pool, and a huge, two-tiered deck.

7. I am impressed, however, I do not have enough to make a down payment.

8. The National Ballet's artistic director is Karen Kain, she was a world-class dancer who retired at age forty-four.

9. There are many national parks in Canada. Which include Banff, Point Pelee, and Algonquin.

10. Musicians who cannot get paying jobs may busk, that way they can practise their art and perform for appreciative audiences.

Modifiers

Modifiers are descriptive words or phrases. A modifier may be a simple adverb or an adjective, or a more complex adverbial phrase or adjectival phrase. A modifier should describe clearly and unambiguously. To do so, it must be as near in the sentence as possible to the thing described.

Avoid Misplaced Modifiers

A modifier, whether a word or a phrase, should be placed next to the word it describes.

Example   ✗ Rotting on the vine, the farmers could not sell the grapes to wineries.

✓ The farmers could not sell the grapes rotting on the vine to wineries.

✗ Licking each other fondly, the children admired the kittens.

✓ Licking each other fondly, the kittens were admired by the children.

Watch the Position of Limiting Modifiers

A limiting modifier is a word that qualifies part or all of the statement. Consider carefully the placement of the following modifiers (and others): "only," "just," "nearly," "almost," "hardly."

Example   Only Gilbert brought a case of beer. (No one else brought one.)

Gilbert only brought a case of beer. (He didn't do anything else.)

Gilbert brought only a case of beer. (He brought only one case.)

Gilbert brought a case of beer only. (He didn't bring a case of wine.)

Avoid Squinting Modifiers

A squinting modifier is ambiguously placed in the sentence, so that the writer's intention is unclear.

   ✗ The suspect confessed that he had served time **later**.   **Example**

   ✓ The suspect confessed **later** that he had served time.

Avoid Dangling Modifiers

A modifier dangles when what it is meant to describe is accidentally left out of the sentence. To figure out what it does describe, ask who or what is being described.

   ✗ After vacuuming the living-room rug, the cat tracked mud all over it.   **Example**

   ✓ After vacuuming the living-room rug, I saw that the cat had tracked mud all over it.

or

   ✓ After I vacuumed the living-room rug, the cat tracked mud all over it.

Dangling modifiers that end in "ing" are usually easy to spot. Remember, however, that a dangling modifier may also involve a prepositional phrase or an infinitive form. A dangling modifier may also occur at the end of a sentence.

   ✗ As a weightlifter, my muscles are in tremendous shape.   **Example**

   ✓ As a weightlifter, I believe that my muscles are in tremendous shape.

Here the prepositional phrase "as a weightlifter" needs to be closer to the word it describes. Note that a prepositional phrase begins with a preposition followed by a noun or a pronoun.

   ✗ To get a high-paying job, education is essential.

   ✓ To get a high-paying job, you need education.

Here the infinitive phrase, "To get a high-paying job," needs to be more closely connected to the subject. Note that infinitives are the form of the verb that begins with "to."

✗ Fernando's travel bills were expensive, being used to flying first class.

✓ Being used to flying first class, Fernando had expensive travel bills.

or

✓ Since Fernando was used to flying first class, his travel bills were expensive.

Note that modifiers may occur at the beginning, middle, or end of the sentence. Wherever they occur, you need to place the word they modify as close as possible to the modifiers used.

Note that some modifiers apply to the entire sentence rather than to any one word or phrase within it. These constructions, called "absolute modifiers," include phrases such as "To make a long story short" and "All things considered."

CHAPTER 25 MODIFIERS EXERCISE A

Correct problems with modifiers in the following sentences. Some may be correct as they stand. Check your answers on p. 281.

1. Unless they are Siamese, most cat owners do not tolerate obstreperous behaviour.
2. When kayaking, cold water temperatures are a threat to amateurs.
3. As a teacher, complaints about low grades are annoying.
4. Theresa heard on Monday that she was expected to perform at the violin recital.
5. The tax bill nearly cost $6000.
6. Driving home in the dark, chocolate chip cookies and the radio will keep me awake.
7. I just heard there was going to be a storm on the radio.
8. I dislike parties where desserts are served to people on a diet with lots of whipped cream and syrups.
9. Asleep on the job, the manager had no choice but to fire the unproductive employee.
10. After inspecting the house from top to bottom, Amy's real estate contract was signed.

CHAPTER 25 MODIFIERS EXERCISE B

1. Smothered in gravy, the diners feasted on the poutine.
2. When plowed, the farmer prepares fields to get them ready for planting.
3. Lemon in tea is good for you if drunk in the morning.
4. After spending all that money, my TV remote froze the first time I used it.
5. Wine at dinner can be expensive if corked.
6. Large paintings may be difficult to hang on office walls, if plastered.
7. Veena discovered there was a huge increase in the world's population on the Internet.
8. Juiced and grated, the chef added lemon to the mayonnaise.
9. Yowling angrily, the owner carried the cat to the vet to be vaccinated.
10. Sleeping late in the morning, my doctor suspected that I had a thyroid condition.

Pronoun Reference and Agreement

A pronoun, as the name suggests, acts for a noun or in the place of a noun. A pronoun should almost always refer to a specific noun in the sentence itself. The noun to which it refers is called an "antecedent." When a pronoun does not refer clearly to its antecedent, confusing or ambiguous writing is the result.

A Guide to Proper Pronoun Usage

Make sure your pronoun matches its antecedent. A pronoun must agree in gender: it may be masculine (he, him, his), feminine (she, her, hers), or neuter (it, it, its). A pronoun must also agree in number: it may be singular or plural.

In Gender

Nancy named **her** dachshund Simon.   **Example**

Nancy named **him** Simon.

In the second sentence, "her dachshund" has been replaced by the masculine pronoun "him."

In the past, the masculine pronouns ("he," "his," "him") were used to refer generally to nouns that were not specifically feminine.

The reader must make up **his** own mind.   **Example**

Although the masculine pronoun is still, strictly speaking, grammatically correct, many people now find its general use inappropriate because it is not inclusive. It is now more common to find such cases phrased as

The reader makes up **his or her** own mind.   **Example**

For those who find the use of "his or her" cumbersome, the best solution is to use the plural pronoun, and an accompanying plural noun, of course.

Readers make up **their** own minds.   **Example**

The determination of gender in English does not pose much of a problem, apart from this dispute. Problems do arise, however, with the number of pronouns.

In Number

1. BE SURE TO LOCATE THE CORRECT ANTECEDENT FOR THE PRONOUN IN QUESTION.

Chloë is one of those students **who** skip their classes regularly.   **Example**

"Students" is the antecedent of the relative pronoun **who**. Both the verb "skip" and the pronoun "their" are plural. Note that "one of those" takes the plural, but "one of these" is singular, as in "One of these gloves, which I bought last week, is lost." "One of those that" (or who) is restrictive and takes a plural verb because the antecedent refers to the entire group; "one of these, which" (or who) is non-restrictive and takes a singular verb since the antecedent refers to the singular "one."

2. BE ESPECIALLY CAREFUL WITH COLLECTIVE NOUNS AND THEIR PRONOUN REPLACEMENTS.

When a collective noun is considered as a unit, the pronoun that stands for it is singular.

Example   The jury has reached its decision.

Here the jury acts as a unit.

When the component parts of a collective noun are considered individually, the pronoun that stands for it is plural.

Example   The jury have expressed their differences of opinion.

Here the jury acts individually; each member has his or her own opinion.

3. BE CAREFUL OF IMPRECISE USE OF SOME INDEFINITE PRONOUNS.

"Anyone," "anybody," "someone," "somebody," "everyone," "everybody," "each," "either," "neither," "nobody," and "no one" are indefinite pronouns, all of which generally take singular verbs.

Example   Nobody wore his or her bathing suit.

Ideally, "his or her" should allow an indefinite pronoun, if the construction is to avoid charges of sexism. In conversation, many people would get around this problem by saying,

Example   Nobody wore their bathing suits.

This form, despite its regular occurrence in spoken English, is still considered grammatically imprecise. It should properly be replaced by the following:

Example   None of us wore our bathing suits.

The best approach is to use the plural form.

In Case

Pronouns, besides being masculine or feminine, singular or plural, also have different forms, depending on their case. They may be used as subjects ("he," "she," "they"), objects ("him," "her," "them"), or possessives ("his," "her," "their").

1. USE THE SUBJECTIVE FORM IF THE PRONOUN IS THE SUBJECT OF A VERB (STATED OR IMPLIED).

The police officer stated that it was **she** who had reported the theft of the painting. **Example**

"She" is used here because a verb is implied.

It was **they** who had masterminded the heist. **Example**

"They" and not "them" is used here because it functions as the subject of the verb "had masterminded."

This precision is essential in writing English, but in informal speech, by contrast, "It's me" or "It was her" is considered acceptable.

2. MAKE SURE TO USE THE OBJECTIVE FORM OF THE PRONOUN IF IT IS THE OBJECT OF A VERB.

The poodle gave his master fleas. **Example**

The poodle gave **him them**.

In the second version, the objective forms for both pronouns—objects of the verb "gave"—have been substituted.

The poodle gave **his master and me** fleas. **Example**

Although you might be tempted to write "The poodle gave his master and I fleas," it becomes obvious that the objective pronoun "me" is correct when you remove the words "his master and." When the pronoun case is a problem, try taking out part of a compound subject and reading the sentence. The correct pronoun should then be obvious.

3. MAKE SURE TO USE THE OBJECTIVE FORM OF THE PRONOUN AFTER A PREPOSITION.

Between **you** and **me**, I think you should use deodorant. **Example**

It's important for **you** and **me** to wear clean underwear every day.

4. AFTER "THAN" OR "AS," USE THE FORM OF THE PRONOUN THAT WOULD BE REQUIRED IN THE COMPLETE IMPLIED CLAUSE.

A sloth is harder working than **he** [is]. **Example**

A monkey can communicate as well as **she** [can].

Note the difference in meaning in the following examples:

Example   I love you as much as **he** [does].

I love you as much as [I love] **him**.

Pronoun Problems in Essay Writing

Use Personal Pronouns with Discretion

Too few personal references in an essay may be as awkward as too many. Few instructors disallow the use of "I" entirely. Its occasional use should prevent needless circumlocution and impersonality. Never stoop to cold and formal constructions like "It is the opinion of this writer," or the overly polite "myself." "We" is sometimes acceptable, though its overuse may sound pompous. "One" may serve as an alternative, though it runs the risk of sounding too distanced and impersonal.

You are writing your paper: its words and thoughts are yours. Avoid "I" and "in my opinion" only when a personal perspective might make your point seem weak or merely a matter of personal idiosyncrasy.

Check to See that Your Pronoun References are Present and Accounted for.

Example   UNCLEAR: In small towns, they do not lock their cars.

CLEARER: Residents of small towns do not lock their cars.

UNCLEAR: Esther changed the baby's diaper, and it screamed.

CLEARER: When Esther changed its diaper, the baby screamed.

UNCLEAR: Robert hates studying floristry, but he intends to become one anyway.

CLEARER: Robert hates studying floristry, but he intends to become a florist anyway.

Avoid Broad Pronoun References

A broad pronoun reference occurs when "this," "which," or "that" is used to refer to an idea rather than to a specific word in the sentence. Some broad references may be tolerated, if the meaning is generally clear. Be careful, however, of raising unanswered questions in the reader's mind.

Example   UNCLEAR: Dexter stays up all night watching reruns of "Leave It to Beaver," which is why he falls asleep on the job so often.

CLEARER: Dexter stays up all night watching reruns of "Leave It to Beaver," a habit which causes him to fall asleep on the job so often.

"Which" does not clearly refer to any specific noun in the preceding sentence. Add a noun before "which" to clarify the point.

"This" too is a broad reference. Although its usage is gaining ground, many instructors still do not find it is precise enough. Look at the following example:

UNCLEAR: Using vague pronouns makes reading difficult. This should not be accepted.

CLEARER: Using vague pronouns makes reading difficult. This practice should not be accepted.

Example

"This" is best accompanied by a noun that makes its reference clear. It should refer to a specific, easily identifiable noun.

CHAPTER 25 PRONOUNS EXERCISE A

Find and correct problems with pronouns in the following sentences. Some may be correct as they are. Check your answers on p. 281.

1. Who do you hope to meet in that chat room?
2. Everyone needs to be on their best behaviour.
3. When the weather changed suddenly, it meant that many of the tourists were caught without umbrellas.
4. He wore old blue jeans to the party, which was disgusting.
5. People like you and I are happy to be in the workforce.
6. Daphne wants to be a funeral director, though she has never studied it formally.
7. In the newspaper, it suggests that Canada's economy has been positively affected by natural resources, immigration, and a restrained national temperament.
8. In her home, Romula has many beautiful photographs because it is her passion.
9. When the trainer removed the dog's harness, it barked loudly.
10. I answered the phone, which meant that I interrupted my dinner while they tried to sell me insurance on my credit card.

CHAPTER 25 PRONOUNS EXERCISE B

1. Each of us has their own axe to grind, and they must behave themselves even when angry.
2. They say that Canada is one of the happiest countries in the world.
3. Whom do you think is the highest paid performer in Canada?
4. After working for a year in the hospital, I no longer find them disturbing.
5. No one can do the job like me.
6. Like I always say, you live and learn.
7. When I released the dog from the chain, it yelped at me.
8. In this book, it says that there is no way to escape the judgment to come.
9. I almost drank a whole case of sparkling water.
10. We asked to speak to the owner, but they did not take our complaint seriously.

Subject and Verb Agreement

The subject and verb in a sentence are closely connected. In order for the sentence to express itself clearly, the subject and the verb must agree.

Most problems with agreement between subject and verb result from difficulties in locating the subject of a verb. Solve these problems by locating the verb in each clause. Remember, first, that a verb describes either an action or a state of being. Next, ask **who** or **what** is performing that action or is being described. The answer to the question **who** or **what** is the subject of the verb. Having located the subject and verb, you may then check to see that they match.

Example   Big Brother is watching you.

Who is watching?

—Big Brother (the subject of the verb "is watching")

How to Match Subjects and Verbs Correctly

Check to see that verbs agree in number with their subjects. In other words, singular subjects take singular verbs; plural subjects take plural verbs.

Problems to watch for:

1. THE NOUN THAT IMMEDIATELY PRECEDES THE VERB MAY NOT BE THE SUBJECT.

Example   Not one of these science-fiction writers has ever seen an extraterrestrial creature.

The correct subject is "one." Another way to arrive at the correct answer is to remember that words after a preposition are always the object of the preposition and thus never the subject. So the prepositional phrase "of these science-fiction writers" indicates that the subject is the word in front of it, rather than "writers."

2. SUBJECTS JOINED BY "AND" ARE USUALLY, BUT NOT ALWAYS, PLURAL.

Example   My friend and guardian angel has come to my rescue.

"My friend and guardian angel" refers to one person.

3. SINGULAR SUBJECTS THAT ARE JOINED BY A PHRASE OTHER THAN "AND" ARE NOT MADE PLURAL. SUCH PHRASES AS "AS WELL AS," "IN ADDITION TO," AND "ALONG WITH" HAVE NO EFFECT ON THE AGREEMENT OF THE VERB SINCE THEY ARE NOT PART OF THE SUBJECT.

Example   A hamburger, along with French fries, is Dee's typical dinner.

"Along with French fries" is not part of the subject.

4. SUBJECTS JOINED BY "OR" OR "NOR" ARE EACH CONSIDERED SEPARATELY. THE VERB AGREES WITH THE SUBJECT CLOSEST TO IT.

Neither tears nor litigation moves Scrooge to act fairly toward his employees. **Example**

"Tears" and "litigation" are each considered separately; since "litigation" is closer, the verb is singular.

5. THE FOLLOWING SUBJECTS ALWAYS TAKE SINGULAR VERBS: "EACH," "EITHER," "NEITHER," "ONE," AND WORDS ENDING IN "BODY" OR "ONE."

Neither of the twins eats turnip. **Example**

6. SUBJECTS LIKE "SOME," "ALL," "MOST," "ANY," OR "NONE" MAY TAKE SINGULAR OR PLURAL VERBS, DEPENDING ON THE NOUN TO WHICH THEY REFER.

Some of the guests refuse to eat parsnip. **Example**

All of us enjoy caviar. (plural verb)

All of the caviar is gone. (singular verb)

7. A COLLECTIVE NOUN, USED TO REFER TO A GROUP OF PEOPLE OR THINGS, TAKES A SINGULAR VERB WHEN THE COLLECTIVE IS CONSIDERED AS A UNIT, AND A PLURAL VERB WHEN EACH MEMBER IS CONSIDERED INDIVIDUALLY.

Singular: The union is planning a strike. (considered a unit) **Example**

Plural: The union are voting on the new benefits package. (considered as individuals within the group)

8. A LINKING VERB (A VERB DESCRIBING A STATE OF BEING) AGREES WITH ITS SUBJECT AND NOT WITH ITS PREDICATE.

The only thing Myrna ever buys is cigarettes. **Example**

"Thing" is the subject; hence, "is" is the appropriate verb.

or

Cigarettes are the only thing Myrna ever buys.

In this example, "cigarettes" is the subject; hence, the plural verb is correct.

9. A VERB STILL AGREES WITH ITS SUBJECT, EVEN WHEN THEIR ORDER IS INVERTED. THE SUBJECT FOLLOWS "THERE IS" OR "THERE ARE," "HERE IS" OR "HERE ARE," AND THE VERB IS SINGULAR OR PLURAL ACCORDINGLY.

Example   Here are the pizzas you ordered.

"Pizzas" is the subject; hence, the correct verb is "are."

10. RELATIVE PRONOUNS ("WHO," "WHICH," "THAT"), ACTING AS SUBJECTS, TAKE SINGULAR OR PLURAL VERBS, DEPENDING ON THE WORDS TO WHICH THEY REFER (THEIR ANTECEDENTS).

Example   Harry is one of those people who cheat at Scrabble.

"People," the antecedent of "who," is plural; hence, the verb "cheat" is also plural.

But note:

Harry is the only one of us who spells badly.

"One" is the antecedent in this case; hence, the verb "spells" is singular.

11. SOME NOUNS MAY LOOK PLURAL, THOUGH THEY ARE ACTUALLY SINGULAR. EXAMPLES INCLUDE "PHYSICS," "ECONOMICS," "ETHICS," AND "NEWS." CHECK DOUBTFUL USAGE IN A DICTIONARY.

Example   News is big business on television today.

12. UNITS OF TIME, MASS, LENGTH, AND DISTANCE ARE SINGULAR IN MEANING AND REQUIRE SINGULAR VERBS.

Example   Twenty dollars is not a lot to pay for a textbook.

Seven kilometres was not far to walk to the nearest gas station.

CHAPTER 25 SUBJECT AND VERB AGREEMENT EXERCISE A

Correct the agreement problems in the following sentences. Some sentences may be fine as they are. Check your answers on p. 282.

1. Pauline, together with Harjeet, spend time writing letters, talking to clients, and shopping for new clothes.
2. Neither the manager nor the president were in favour of Adele's new get-rich-quick scheme.
3. The cost of the tummy tuck and the facelift were prohibitive, so Penny decided to accept herself the way she was.

4. Increasing online subscriptions and promoting interest in the magazine is my job in public relations.

5. There is a number of reasons to avoid getting into the real estate market now: the price of houses have skyrocketed, and mortgage rates are likely to go higher.

6. The price of hotels in London, England are high, so the group are planning to stay with relatives.

7. Every single one of the reasons I had for working have vanished since my job description changed.

8. At the bottom of Carmen's suitcase underneath her swimsuit was two bottles of wine and a corkscrew.

9. In Alvin's will was a bequest to his sister and a trust fund arrangement for the charities he supported.

10. The calorie count of this meal, along with its fat content, are not healthy for someone with heart disease.

CHAPTER 25 SUBJECT AND VERB AGREEMENT EXERCISE B

1. The only thing that Cameron works at are forming social networks and sending out résumés for other jobs.

2. A series of consumer reports have been published about those contractors.

3. Either Tim or Desmond produce the party favours for the children's birthday celebrations.

4. Gilbert, with his new truck and his camper, enjoy going on hiking expeditions.

5. Economics have always been part of the suggested business curriculum.

6. Neither Marion nor Anna are available to come to your aid.

7. The lack of funds, along with an increase in my credit card debt, have led me to declare bankruptcy.

8. Nail polish remover, along with many other cosmetics, are considered toxic substances.

9. Exchange programs at distant universities is an excellent way to travel inexpensively.

10. My sedentary lifestyle and my smoking was to blame for my high blood pressure.

End Punctuation

1. USE A PERIOD AFTER A STATEMENT, AN INDIRECT QUESTION, OR A COMMAND.

I have something to tell you. (statement)   **Example**

Penny asked me when I got my nose fixed. (indirect question)

Don't look now. (command)

2. USE A PERIOD AFTER MOST ABBREVIATIONS, UNLESS THEY ARE EASILY RECOGNIZED. Note that some formal abbreviations, such as Mr., Mrs., and Dr., always end with a period in common usage.

Example

Mr.	CBC
Mrs.	DVD
Dr.	CD player

3. USE A QUESTION MARK AFTER A DIRECT QUESTION.

Example   Who's been eating my porridge?

Whatever is the matter?

What's for supper?

4. USE EXCLAMATION MARKS SPARINGLY TO EXPRESS EMPHASIS IN AN INFORMAL ESSAY. USE THEM IN A FORMAL ESSAY AT YOUR OWN RISK.

Example   ✗ Hugo did his homework!

✓ Amazingly, Hugo did his homework.

The Colon

The colon (:) is used to introduce something. Remember the following rules for colon usage:

1. USE A COLON ONLY AFTER A COMPLETE SENTENCE (THAT IS, AFTER A GROUP OF WORDS WITH A SUBJECT AND VERB THAT STANDS BY ITSELF AND FORMS A COMPLETE THOUGHT—IN OTHER WORDS, AN INDEPENDENT CLAUSE).

Example   ✗ Delores loved: foreign vacations, fur coats, and cold cash.

✓ Delores loved three things: foreign vacations, fur coats, and cold cash.

2. USE A COLON AFTER A COMPLETE SENTENCE TO INTRODUCE IDEAS, LISTS, OR QUOTATIONS.

Example   This report can mean only one thing: we are going to be parents.

Dorothy Parker makes this claim: "The two most beautiful words in the English language are 'Cheque enclosed.'"

3. USE A COLON TO INDICATE AMPLIFICATION OR FURTHER DEVELOPMENT OF AN IDEA.

Thanatology is a branch of psychology: it deals with the subject of death and dying.   **Example**

The Semicolon

A semicolon (;) is a heavier punctuation mark than a comma, but lighter than a period. Use a semicolon generally only where you might use a period instead.

Semicolons are especially useful in the following cases:

1. USE A SEMICOLON TO JOIN TWO CLOSELY RELATED MAIN CLAUSES.

The use of a semicolon instead of a coordinating conjunction shows a close connection (or a sharp antithesis) between two ideas.

Man proposes; God disposes.   **Example**

2. USE A SEMICOLON WITH A TRANSITIONAL WORD OR PHRASE WHEN IT IS USED TO JOIN TWO MAIN CLAUSES.

Transitional words or phrases such as "however," "moreover," "furthermore," "hence," "as a result," and "consequently" may be used in this way.

I won't accept charity; however, I will take cash or travellers' cheques.   **Example**

The semicolon takes the place of a period in this sentence.

But note:

I will not, however, accept charity.

In this case, "however" is not used to join two main clauses. Since the transitional word interrupts one main clause, commas are adequate punctuation.

3. USE A SEMICOLON TO SEPARATE ITEMS LISTED IN A SERIES IF COMMAS ARE ALREADY USED AS INTERNAL PUNCTUATION.

Maxwell always did three things before he went to bed: one, he put on his pyjamas;   **Example**
two, he drank warm milk; three, he fell asleep in the armchair in front of the TV set.

CHAPTER 25 COLON AND SEMICOLON EXERCISE A

Add or remove colons and semicolons where appropriate. Some may be correct as they stand. Answers are on p. 283.

1. According to his partner, Nick is: lazy, sloppy, and irresponsible, however, the partner, if truth be told, is rigid and lacking in sympathy.

2. Having heard of your recent inheritance, I would like to request one thing: can I see the spreadsheet?

3. Buying a condominium in a large city like Vancouver or Toronto is costly, hence, I am planning to live in a cardboard box over a hot air vent.

4. There are only ninety-eight days left till my birthday, that's plenty of time for you to save up to buy me a two-week vacation in Milan.

5. The bestselling fiction writers in Canada in the past few years are; Margaret Atwood, Yann Martel, Alice Munro, and Carol Shields.

6. Summer movies are highly entertaining but not very deep, they replace sophisticated plot, character, and setting with car chases, sexy actors, and unbelievable stunts nevertheless, they succeed at the box office.

7. Two things are bothering me; my computer has a virus, and my hard drive needs defragmenting.

8. Your online business can be saved only if you marry money or inherit a fortune from a long-lost relative.

9. The incumbent politician had a goal in mind, to win back the shaken confidence of his constituents after the scandal.

10. Rico's dream was: to be a bronco buster at the Calgary Stampede.

CHAPTER 25 COLON AND SEMICOLON EXERCISE B

1. Kerry told Malo that it would be all right after five or six years presumably, everyone would forget what the quarrel had been about by then anyway.

2. Here is what I learned today from watching The Food Network; how to finish a dessert, using a blow torch, how to set fire to the kitchen curtains, using the same blow torch, and how to scare off my dinner guests, even before dinner is over.

3. The new parents considered these names for the twins, Ben and Jerry, Mick and Keith, or Mutt and Jeff.

4. If you have high blood pressure, you should avoid eating salt, gaining weight, and drinking alcohol.

5. Banff is a glorious tourist town it has beautiful mountain scenery it also has the highest rate of sexually transmitted disease in Canada, according to some sources.

6. The German shepherd was afraid of thunderstorms, his owner always drove home to keep him company during any weather disturbance.

7. Green vegetables are good for you, why can't we get lettuce on our sandwiches in this cafeteria?

8. The shih tzu next door would benefit from obedience school, he bites his owners' ankles every chance he gets.

9. Buying coffee in a Tim's outlet is the number one Canadian pastime there are more doughnut shops than there are houses, it seems.

10. Anya disliked her new living room furniture, hence, she decided to spend more time in the family room.

The Comma

A comma (,) is a light mark of punctuation. Some basic rules that govern its use are listed below. When in doubt about a particular usage, let ease in reading be your guide.

1. USE A COMMA BEFORE "AND," "OR," "NOR," "FOR," "BUT," "YET," "SO" IF ANY OF THESE WORDS ARE USED TO JOIN TWO INDEPENDENT CLAUSES.

Gunther doesn't normally snore, but tonight his dog needs earplugs.   **Example**

But note:

A comma is not needed if a complete independent clause does not follow.

Ivor hates school but loves recess.   **Example**

In this case, "but" actually joins a compound verb, rather than two independent clauses.

2. YOU MAY USE A COMMA AFTER ANY MATERIAL (A WORD, A PHRASE, OR A CLAUSE) THAT COMES BEFORE THE MAIN CLAUSE. THE COMMA IS ESSENTIAL IF THE SENTENCE WOULD BE CONFUSING WITHOUT IT.

Bracing himself, Rocky applied for a job as a snake charmer. Because he had never   **Example**
seen a snake before, Rocky was different from the other candidates. Alas, the snake
did not find him charming enough.

3. USE A COMMA AFTER A WORD OR PHRASE THAT MODIFIES AN ENTIRE SENTENCE. TO FIND OUT WHETHER SOMETHING IS A SENTENCE MODIFIER, TEST TO SEE IF IT CAN BE MOVED ELSEWHERE IN THE SENTENCE WITHOUT CHANGING THE MEANING.

However, he did find work cleaning cages at the zoo.   **Example**

"However" can be shifted in the sentence; hence, it is a sentence modifier:

He did, however, find work cleaning cages at the zoo.

4. USE A COMMA IF YOU WOULD LIKE TO EMPHASIZE CONTRAST.

Tracy attended school for the social life, not for the good of her mind.   **Example**

Pee-Wee wanted precious antiques, but found worthless junk.

5. USE COMMAS TO SEPARATE ELEMENTS IN A SERIES OF THREE OR MORE ITEMS. NOTE THAT THE COMMA BEFORE THE WORD "AND" IS OPTIONAL IN THIS CASE.

Cinderella invited Flora, Fauna, and Merryweather to her coming-out party.   **Example**

A comma before "and" at the end of the list is usually advisable to prevent confusion.

Example   Ogden tells us that his old age begins, and middle age ends, and now his descendants outnumber his friends.

Here a comma is used to separate a series of independent clauses. Note, however, that two independent clauses together must normally be separated by a semicolon.

6. PUT COMMAS AROUND WORDS, PHRASES, OR CLAUSES THAT INDICATE DIRECT ADDRESS. COMMAS MAY BE USED AROUND A WORD OR A GROUP OF WORDS IF THAT PART OF THE SENTENCE MIGHT BE REMOVED AND STILL LEAVE A SUBJECT AND PREDICATE.

Example   Frankly, my dear, I am indifferent.

Yes, Virginia, there is a Santa Claus.

7. PUT COMMAS BETWEEN COORDINATE ADJECTIVES.
Adjectives that can change their order without changing the meaning of the sentence, or coordinate adjectives, need commas between them. If you find you cannot change the order of the adjectives without changing the meaning, do not use commas.

Alex was a smart, creative web designer.

Her grandmother lived in a little old red brick house.

8. PUT COMMAS AROUND INTERRUPTING PHRASES OR CLAUSES THAT ARE NON-RESTRICTIVE IN MEANING.

Example   My grandmother, who lives in Halifax, is getting a divorce.

Here the clause "who lives in Halifax" is non-restrictive, and it implies that the author has one grandmother; some incidental information about her is enclosed in commas. But note:

My grandmother who lives in Halifax is getting a divorce.

Here the clause "who lives in Halifax" is restrictive and lacks commas. It implies that the author has two grandmothers and uses the clause to identify which one.
  Note that you also put commas around appositives, words that rename those that precede. These are also non-restrictive phrases.

Example   Jethro and Elly May, Melissa's pet gerbils, are on the loose again.

Madame de Pompadour said that Canada, then a colony of France, was useful only to provide her with furs.

9. COMMAS SHOULD NOT ENCLOSE MATERIAL THAT IS RESTRICTIVE, THAT IS, ESSENTIAL TO THE SENTENCE'S MEANING.

✗ People, who live in glass houses, shouldn't throw stones.   **Example**

This sentence, because of the way it is punctuated, says that all people shouldn't throw stones.

✓ People who live in glass houses shouldn't throw stones.

This statement identifies those people who shouldn't throw stones. The modifier, because it performs the necessary function of identification or limitation, cannot be surrounded by commas.

10. COMMAS SHOULD NOT SEPARATE MAIN SENTENCE ELEMENTS. DO NOT USE A COMMA BETWEEN A SUBJECT AND VERB OR BETWEEN A VERB AND AN OBJECT OR COMPLEMENT.

✗ Everything Zsa Zsa does, gets on my nerves.   **Example**

✓ Everything Zsa Zsa does gets on my nerves.

Punctuation Checklist

Use a comma

when you begin a sentence with a subordinate clause

when you begin a sentence with a long phrase

when you want to set off interrupting words

when you are indicating a non-restrictive phrase or clause

when you divide two main clauses with coordinating conjunctions

when not to do so would make the meaning unclear

Use a semicolon

when you separate main clauses with a conjunctive adverb like "however" or "therefore" used to connect two main clauses logically

between items that have commas in them

when you connect two main clauses without a conjunction

Use a colon

when you introduce a word, a phrase, or a clause

when you wish to amplify the meaning of something

after a complete sentence *only*

CHAPTER 25 PUNCTUATION EXERCISE A

Correct errors in comma usage in the following sentences, by adding or removing punctuation as necessary. Some sentences may be correct as they are. Check your answers on p. 284.

1. Karina thought therefore that the most important thing in the world was work not play.
2. I studied English French psychology and history but the thing I enjoyed doing most in my post-secondary years was collecting antiques from which my business was created.
3. A kind generous person Jake was tolerant of his sister Emily even after that incident which he could never forget that took place over ten years ago.
4. Although he was not finished school working as an intern all winter in a renowned company did not intimidate him nor did he find the work overwhelming.
5. My mother who is a wonderful cook made coq au vin and afterwards she offered us a choice of desserts.
6. The root of all evil if you ask me is: sloth.
7. Honestly sir I do not know where the key to the classroom is nor do I know what you assigned for homework last night, I was asleep during our last class.
8. Homeowners who want every amenity will suffer from enormous debt unless they practise discipline, and stay within their budgets.
9. This apartment which is located in beautiful Vancouver has a great view of the city and it is affordable.
10. Michael Ignatieff Michael Ondaatje and Sylvia Fraser have all explored their lives in memoirs but then most authors do in fact draw on their lives for subject matter.

CHAPTER 25 PUNCTUATION EXERCISE B

1. My pets Crusty and Flathead are great examples of beauty: if not brains.
2. Pierre Berton reportedly said "A Canadian is someone, who knows how to make love in a canoe."
3. Those people whom we met yesterday at the conference said they were planning to start a wiki for participants in the field.
4. For their anniversary Mildred and Henry got these gifts, from their daughter, a gluten-free cake, from their son, a trip to Myrtle Beach and from us, a card and some yellow roses.
5. When exploring tourist attractions people demand affordable events, however, many will pay exorbitant amounts so they can experience the best.
6. Expensive candy often comes in elegant small shiny packages, nevertheless, high-priced chocolate despite its exotic origins and glamorous appearance is just as fattening as cheaper candy.
7. Leila's dream was to write a sensational novel, and win international acclaim.
8. The postal service is on strike, however, most of our business is conducted by telephone and mail.
9. My secret method for dealing with anxiety is eating six meals a day sleeping ten hours each night and watching lots of relaxing television.
10. Knowledge comes, wisdom lingers.

The Dash

Type a dash using two hyphens, with no spaces before or after.

> I won't drink—I want to know when I'm having a good time.   **Example**

1. USE A DASH FOR EMPHASIS AROUND PARENTHETICAL EXPRESSIONS.

> The show—though a huge success with the public—was panned by the critics.   **Example**

Note: Commas are also correct in this sentence, but less emphatic.

2. USE A DASH TO INTRODUCE SOMETHING WITH EXTRA EMPHASIS.

> Rob loved birthday cards—whether cheques were enclosed or not.   **Example**

Note: A colon is also correct in this sentence but less emphatic.

3. RESERVE THE DASH FOR SPECIAL OCCASIONS. USE IT SPARINGLY, ESPECIALLY IN FORMAL WRITING.

Parentheses

Parentheses are used to enclose incidental material. They (that is, the words they enclose) serve the same function as an aside in a theatrical production. Though they get the reader's attention, the material they enclose is presented as "inside information."

1. USE PARENTHESES IN FORMAL WRITING TO ENCLOSE THE NECESSARY DEFINITION OF A TERM AT ITS FIRST APPEARANCE.

> The NFB (National Film Board of Canada) has won several Academy Awards for its productions.   **Example**

2. USE PARENTHESES TO ENCLOSE ANY PART OF A SENTENCE THAT MIGHT BE ENCLOSED BY COMMAS OR DASHES, IF THE READER HAS ONLY PASSING INTEREST IN IT.

> In the next episode of "Rick Mercer Report" (tonight at eight), Rick goes to a snowmobile race in Kincardine.   **Example**

3. USE PARENTHESES SPARINGLY. TOO MANY MAKE THE WRITING SELF-CONSCIOUS AND HARD TO FOLLOW.

> ✗ In this report (which is the product of months of arduous research), I will discuss various methods of sleep-teaching.   **Example**

The Apostrophe

Apostrophes are used after nouns and indefinite pronouns (e.g., "anyone," "somebody") to indicate possession. Note these general rules:

1. ADD "'S" TO FORM THE POSSESSIVE CASE IF THE OWNER IS SINGULAR.

Example   monkey's uncle—the uncle of the monkey

horse's mouth—the mouth of the horse

pig's eye—the eye of the pig

Note that even when the word ends in "s," the ending is usually " 's," since that is how we pronounce it.

Example   James's novels—the novels of James

Stevens's poetry—the poetry of Stevens

2. ADD "S'" TO THE FORM OF THE POSSESSIVE CASE IF THE OWNERS ARE PLURAL.

Example   workers' coalition—the coalition of workers

boys' team—the team of boys

But note that words that do not form the plural with "s" are made possessive by the addition of "'s."

Example   women's rights—the rights of women

people's court—the court of people

men's washroom—the washroom of men

3. DO NOT USE AN APOSTROPHE WITH POSSESSIVE PRONOUNS.

Example   The villa is his, the Mercedes is hers, and the Swiss bank account is theirs.

Note that "its" (another possessive pronoun) also does not have an apostrophe. Do not confuse the possessive pronoun "its" with the contraction "it's" for "it is."

Apostrophes are, of course, used in contractions, that is, in constructions where a letter is left out, such as "don't" for "do not" or "can't" for "cannot." Note, however, that contractions are usually not acceptable in formal essay writing.

It's time to take you home. (it is time)

Its diaper wet, the baby fussed noisily. (possessive case)

CHAPTER 25 APOSTROPHE EXERCISE A

Correct the possessives in the following sentences. Some may be fine as they are. Turn to p. 285 for answers.

1. The theatre goers went to Elton Johns *Billy Elliot* and to Shakespeares *A Midsummer Nights Dream* as well as to Judith Thompsons *White Biting Dog* and Michel Tremblays *Hoseanna.*

2. The president compared the companys efforts to those of Starbucks and Wendys to capture a large expanding market.

3. The candidates in 2010 for the Man Booker Prize were Peter Careys *Parrot and Olivier in America,* Emma Donoghues *Room,* Damon Galguts *In a Strange Room,* Andrea Levys *The Long Song,* and Tom McCarthys *C.*

4. Theas father knew that he couldn't make a silk purse out of a sows ear, but he tried to complete the old houses renovations anyway.

5. Jasons pets were a dog named Molly and another smaller mixed-breed dog named Pico: Picos fear of storms made her unable to go outside for much of the year; Mollys advanced age and mobility issues made her housebound too.

6. Senyos office was just a stones throw from Carries, but their approaches were worlds apart.

7. Can you buy me fifty dollars worth of gas, so I can go in and do a decent days work?

8. Philip Roths works were recognized by the International Man Booker Award; in the past the same organization has honoured Canadas Alice Munro and Nigerias Chinua Achebe.

9. The Rolling Stones longevity can be witnessed in Martin Scorceses film *Shine a Light.*

10. All the students complaints in that course were justified because of its focus on the instructors eccentric interests in the field.

CHAPTER 25 APOSTROPHE EXERCISE B

1. Its muscles strengthened, my body recovered after a months regime of yoga and six months of running every morning.

2. Christie Blatchfords column in *The Globe and Mail* has its charms: she often describes the courts seamy side and presents Canadas most controversial issues in a brash and humourous way.

3. Denys Arcands *The Decline of the American Empire,* Atom Egoyans *Exotica,* Norman Jewisons *Moonstruck,* not to mention James Camerons *Avatar* and *The Titanic* give some idea of the contributions Canadian directors have made to the film industry.

4. Canadas reputation in the entertainment industry has long been upheld by comedians: Martin Shorts work is known on Broadway and in films, Lorne Michaels involvement in *Saturday Night Live* is well known, as are John Candys films.

5. Even in the early days of film, Canadas actresses played a major role: Mary Pickfords work dates back to 1909, Fay Wrays work in *King Kong* takes place in 1933, and modern examples of Canadas film actresses include Neve Campbell and Carrie Ann Moss.

6. Michael J. Foxs early work was in television; despite Parkinsons disease, he has continued to work in films and on television; in addition, his three books have been on the bestsellers list.

7. This prime minister has none of Trudeaus charm, Mackenzie Kings wisdom, or Pearsons diplomacy.

8. Its obvious that the Hendersons house is empty; the lights are off and the neighbours attempts to rouse them have gone unanswered.

9. The copyright bill poses a danger to citizens; they oppose its use of digital locks that effectively trump others rights.

10. Womens clothing is on the second floor, and boys clothing is on the first floor.

CHAPTER 26

Elements of Style: Structuring the Sentences

Look and you will find it—what is unsought will go undetected.
—SOPHOCLES

In this chapter:

- How to vary your sentence structure
- How to use parallelism
- How to use active and passive voice appropriately

Variety in your sentence structure will ensure that your reader pays attention, not only to what you say, but also to the way you say it. Try to develop an awareness of the subtle changes in emphasis and reading pace that occur when you modify the structure of a sentence. Such consciousness will enhance your style and impress your reader.

Sentence Variation

1. VARY YOUR SENTENCE STRUCTURE.
The following are examples of different types of sentences.

Simple Sentence: one independent clause

> Catherine and Michael agreed to split their assets equitably in the prenuptial agreement.   **Example**

Compound Sentence: two independent clauses joined by one of the coordinating conjunctions ("and," "or," "nor," "for," "but," "yet," "so")

> Donald kept his business empire, and Ivana kept her wardrobe and her cosmetics.   **Example**

Complex Sentence: one independent clause joined to one dependent clause

> Marriage is a lottery in which couples stake their happiness and their worldly goods.   **Example**

Note: Dependent clauses begin with a subordinating conjunction, such as one of the following.

after	because	however	that
although	before	if	though
as	how	since	

Subordinate, or dependent, clauses also begin with words starting with a "wh"—"when," "where," "why," "which," "who," "while," "whereas," "what"—except where these words introduce questions.

Compound–Complex Sentence: a compound sentence joined to a complex sentence

Example
> They knew that a lot of people didn't expect their marriage to last, so they celebrated their first anniversary six months early.

2. PRACTISE SUBORDINATION BY CONVERTING GROUPS OF SIMPLE OR COMPOUND SENTENCES YOU FIND IN YOUR WRITING INTO COMPLEX SENTENCES.

Example
> Joanne hated school. She quit and found a job behind a counter. Later, she returned to college in a different program. This time, the program was more suited to her talents and goals.
>
> REVISED: Because Joanne hated school, she quit and found a job behind a counter. Later, when she returned to college, she entered a different program, which was more suited to her talents and goals.

3. PRACTISE JOINING SIMPLE SENTENCES TOGETHER USING VERBAL PHRASES RATHER THAN SUBORDINATORS. START BY CHANGING THE VERB INTO A PARTICIPLE (USUALLY ENDING IN "ING" OR "ED"). THEN REMOVE ITS SUBJECT, AND CONNECT IT TO THE APPROPRIATE WORD IN THE FOLLOWING SENTENCE.

Example
> Joshua makes extra money. He plays piano in a restaurant downtown.
>
> REVISED: By playing piano in a restaurant downtown, Joshua makes extra money.

4. PRACTISE CUTTING TANGLED CONSTRUCTIONS DOWN TO SIZE BY CREATING SIMPLE SENTENCES WHERE THE READER MIGHT HAVE DIFFICULTY IN UNDERSTANDING OR WHERE YOU WISH TO PLACE MORE EMPHASIS.

Example
> A factory job is superior to a job requiring postsecondary education. Some would argue the opposite. Still, the advantages of a factory job are numerous. Here are some of these advantages. A factory worker makes more money at an earlier age than a college student. Thus, he can live on his own earlier. A factory worker also has more spare time to pursue other goals. There is also less stress placed on a factory worker. He is more likely to be happy and healthy.
>
> REVISED: Although some would argue the opposite, a factory job is superior to a job requiring postsecondary education. Because a factory worker makes more

money at an earlier age than a college student, he is able to live on his own earlier. In addition, a factory worker has more time to pursue other goals and faces less stress than someone in a white-collar job. Hence, he is more likely to be happy and healthy.

5. TRY CONVERTING SOME OF THE PHRASES AND DEPENDENT CLAUSES IN YOUR WRITING INTO ABSOLUTES (PHRASES WITH CONNECTING WORDS REMOVED). KEEP THE SUBJECT OF THE CLAUSE AND ITS ACCOMPANYING PARTICIPLE; REMOVE OTHER WORDS.

Because his sports car was wrecked and his hopes of winning races gone, Mario decided to become a gas-station attendant.   **Example**

REVISED: His sports car wrecked and his hopes of winning races gone, Mario decided to become a gas-station attendant.

6. VARY YOUR SENTENCES BY MAKING THEM MORE SUSPENSEFUL. THE TYPICAL ENGLISH SENTENCE MOVES DIRECTLY FROM SUBJECT TO VERB TO OBJECT OR COMPLEMENT, A STRUCTURE OFTEN CALLED "LOOSE." IN OTHER LANGUAGES, THE WORD ORDER IS OFTEN NOT SO DIRECT, PLACING SUBJECT OR VERB NEAR THE END OF THE SENTENCE. THIS STRUCTURE IS CALLED "PERIODIC." TRY MAKING YOUR OWN SENTENCES PERIODIC OCCASIONALLY, SO THAT THE IMPACT OF THE THOUGHT IS DELAYED.

LOOSE: Desmond gave Molly a diamond ring.   **Example**

PERIODIC: Shyly, anxiously, and with tears in his eyes, Desmond gave Molly a diamond ring.

CHAPTER 26 SENTENCE VARIATION EXERCISE

1. Join these sentences, using verbal phrases. Answers are on p. 286.
    a. Muhammed wanted to buy a computer tablet. He checked the advertisements on the Internet every day, but a new tablet seemed too expensive. He settled on an older model. He found it easily on eBay.
    b. Timothy castigated the employees for being too careless about vacation days. He called in a consultant to investigate their morale. The mood of the workplace sometimes improved mysteriously when he was on holidays.
    c. The best instructor in this institution is a marvel. He entertains his class. He teaches them at the same time. He gives challenging homework. He manages to motivate students into doing their best. He is a model of pleasant behaviour and a good teacher.
2. Rewrite these sentences using absolutes, rather than dependent clauses or simple sentences.
    a. As she bared her teeth, the tiger leaped at the trainer.
    b. This class on how to write an essay was a waste of time. I need more examples of how to begin and less abstract discussion about things I already know.
    c. When the party was over, we cleaned up the room and washed the dishes.

3. Rewrite these simple sentences to form complex sentences. Use verbal phrases and absolutes where appropriate.

   Charles Dickens's work seems to come from a well-educated man. He did not receive much formal school. He worked first in a boot-blacking factory. Then he worked as a clerk in a law office. He learned a great deal of the material that would appear in his novels. He became a prolific writer. He was also a famous man. He edited a well-known magazine. He went on speaking tours to America. He was also the father of ten children. Dickens was a very productive and brilliant author. Altogether he wrote fifteen serial novels and some shorter works.

4. Take the following loose sentences and make them periodic. Make the subject or the verb more complicated, or change the word order to delay the impact of the sentence.
   a. The missing key was on the floor of the car under the blanket on the passenger side.
   b. Although chocolate was high in calories, Harriet couldn't resist it.
   c. Increasingly in restaurants across North America, French fries are a significant part of the restaurant menu.

5. Analyze an essay written by one of your classmates to determine what sentence patterns he or she uses most commonly. Make suggestions on how to rewrite some of the sentences, and examine the changes in emphasis that such revision creates.

6. Analyze some writing in a current newspaper or magazine you enjoy. Try to model some sentences on the structure of those you find.

Parallelism

Parallelism is one of the basic components of good writing style. The repetitive rhythm of parallel structure allows the reader to anticipate what comes next and to keep the overall construction in mind. Consider the following sentences:

Example   NOT PARALLEL: Dawn finished her essay by staying up all night, working without a break, and finally, she asked her mother to type the paper for her.

　　　　　　　PARALLEL:　　　Dawn finished her essay by staying up all night, working without a break, and finally, asking her mother to type the paper for her.

Making sentences that are logical, powerful, and easy to understand requires a developed sense of parallel construction. To sharpen this sense, you need to become aware of certain basic requirements of balanced sentence structure.

1. MAKE SURE GRAMMATICAL ELEMENTS MATCH.
To form a parallel construction, join nouns with nouns, verbs with verbs, participles with participles, adjectives with adjectives, and so on. Connecting words like "and," "or," "but," and "yet" are often signals of the need for a parallel construction.

Example   NOT PARALLEL: The actor was handsome, articulate, and he loved to look at himself in a mirror.

　　　　　　　PARALLEL:　　　The actor was handsome, articulate, and vain, loving to look at himself in a mirror.

Since the first two items are adjectives ("handsome" and "articulate"), the last item in the series should be an adjective too.

> NOT PARALLEL: People who are in debt should give up credit cards, borrowing money, eating out in expensive restaurants, and living above their means.

> PARALLEL: People who are in debt should give up using credit cards, borrowing money, eating out in expensive restaurants, and living above their means.

Example

The parallelism is improved when each of the nouns in question is preceded by an "ing" form.

> NOT PARALLEL: They divorced because the husband thought that no one should read while he was talking, and the wife thought that while she was reading, no one should talk.

> PARALLEL: They divorced because the husband thought that no one should read while he was talking, and the wife thought that no one should talk while she was reading.

Example

The balance is improved by maintaining the same word order in each clause.

2. USE PARALLEL CONSTRUCTIONS AFTER "THAN" OR "AS."

> NOT PARALLEL: It is better to light a candle than curse the darkness.

> PARALLEL: It is better to light a candle than to curse the darkness.

Example

What follows "than" should be parallel with what precedes this word. Hence, the word "to" should be repeated.

> NOT PARALLEL: My grades are just as good as Stephanie.

> PARALLEL: My grades are just as good as Stephanie's grades.

Example

or

> My grades are just as good as Stephanie's.

The grades are being compared, not the grades and Stephanie.

3. BALANCE SENTENCE ELEMENTS CONNECTED BY CORRELATIVES.
Correlatives come in pairs. They include "not only . . . but also," "both . . . and," "either . . . or," "neither . . . nor," and "whether . . . or."

The grammatical constructions that follow the first coordinator should also follow the second.

> NOT PARALLEL: Derek didn't only apologize to her and admit that he had been wrong, he gave her a red rose and asked her forgiveness.

Example

PARALLEL: Not only did Derek apologize to her and admit that he had been wrong, but he also gave her a red rose and asked her forgiveness.

Correlative conjunctions are used here to join two clauses.

Example   NOT PARALLEL: Whether you take the bus or if you go by plane, two days is not long enough for a trip to Disneyland.

PARALLEL: Whether you take the bus or you go by plane, two days is not long enough for a trip to Disneyland.

Correlatives are used here to join two main clauses. Note the revisions in the following sentences:

Example   NOT PARALLEL: Arnold was sound both mentally and in body.

PARALLEL: Arnold was sound both in mind and in body.

What follows "both" should be grammatically parallel to what follows "and."

Example   NOT PARALLEL: You either give Jason his toy back, or I'll tell your mother.

PARALLEL: Either you give Jason his toy back, or I'll tell your mother.

What follows "either" must be grammatically parallel to what follows "or." In this case, a subject and verb follow both items.

4. PARALLEL CONSTRUCTIONS MAY ALSO BE INDICATED BY TRANSITIONAL SIGNPOSTS SUCH AS "FIRST," "SECOND," AND "THIRD."

Example   NOT PARALLEL: The sales clerk quit his job: first, the customers were rude; second, he was tired of minimum wage; and third, annoyed at having to work on Saturday nights.

PARALLEL: The sales clerk quit his job: first, the customers were rude; second, he was tired of minimum wage; and third, he was annoyed at having to work on Saturday nights.

Lists need to be parallel for ease of reading and comprehension.

5. MAKE SURE THAT ITEMS IN A LIST ARE GRAMMATICALLY PARALLEL.

Example   NOT PARALLEL: This report makes four recommendations:

1. divers should be certified by an accredited school
2. they should wear appropriate equipment at all times
3. they should work in pairs
4. regular health checkups

PARALLEL: This report makes four recommendations:

1. divers should be certified by an accredited school
2. they should wear appropriate equipment at all times

3. they should work in pairs

4. they should get regular health checkups

In this case, the items listed have been changed so that they are all main clauses; in the incorrect example, the fourth item is a phrase.

Remember that parallel construction need not be confined to words and phrases; it may extend to subordinate clauses and to sentences. Effective use of parallel structure will enhance your writing by making it clear, balanced, and carefully structured.

NOT PARALLEL: Every one of these buildings, public and private, restored or dilapidated, will share a similar fate: bought by a developer, or if the city expands, they will be destroyed.

Example

PARALLEL: Every one of these buildings, public and private, restored or dilapidated, will share a similar fate: if a developer buys them, or if the city expands, they will be destroyed.

"Or" in the corrected sentence joins two subordinate clauses, both in the active voice.

CHAPTER 26 PARALLELISM EXERCISE A

Improve the instances of faulty parallelism in the following sentences. Some may be fine as they are. Check your answers on p. 287.

1. Not only did Sheila check the house for pests but also the garage and the backyard.

2. Either I buy that new pair of shoes, or go barefoot to the wedding.

3. Thrills, having the chance to be seen on national television, and a big cash prize are the reasons I plan to try out for that reality show.

4. April is neither working nor is she collecting her pay.

5. Check that all educational consultants are industrious, articulate, and that they have graduated from university.

6. Steve Jobs's notion of computer development is more innovative than Bill Gates.

7. Carol believes and is an advocate of vegetarianism.

8. The increase in early retirement is due to a lack of good jobs for those over the age of fifty, excellent packages for those leaving their positions, and there is a trend toward increased leisure and recreation.

9. The real estate agent asked if I wanted either to buy a condo or a mobile home.

10. You can write your memoirs by making notes on your significant memories, by formulating your philosophy of life, and with an eye to future television appearances.

CHAPTER 26 PARALLELISM EXERCISE B

1. Slugger is an adorable Sheltie although he has a matted coat, a bad temper, and he fights with other dogs in the neighbourhood.

2. Being wealthy is not only a guarantee of security, but it can help you to make new friends.

3. I went shopping for a gift with cachet, beauty, and with a low price.

4. Being a successful volunteer means working long hours, serving others with a sense of self-sacrifice, and you have to pass the police check.

5. Leslie Nielsen movies, like *Airplane*, show the strengths of the Canadian comedian: they are silly, nonsensical, and they parody conventional American spy films.

6. The doctor asked the patient to remove his clothes and that he should step on the scales.

7. Lorne not only catches trout, but he hunts moose as well.

8. Florida not only has alligators, but it is overrun with turkey vultures.

9. I will either be a lawyer or a con artist after I graduate.

10. My royalties for this book are smaller than J. K. Rowling.

CHAPTER 26 PARALLELISM EXERCISE C

Edit the following paragraph to improve its parallelism.

The research on the Canadian public's perception of media concentration shows an increased awareness of the consolidation of media companies, a strong preference for Canadian characteristics in news media, and also sheds light on the premature role of the Internet as a significant source of news. However, critics have also drawn attention to the lack of ethnic diversity in news coverage and raise concerns about the limited number of foreign correspondents based abroad to report comprehensively on international news. The potency of the Internet as a tool that allows criticism of the media to take place and the issue of journalist education moving to a corporate model elicit mixed feelings about the future of the media. In the midst of these controversies, where does the Canadian government stand when performing its role to protect the integrity of the news? The main question remains: to what extent is the government actively protecting news writing and distribution from turning into an arena for business rather than becoming a school to cultivate critical minds? While the research may show that Canadians have confidence in the CBC, the government may need to take on a more active and immediate role to continue safeguarding the quality of news media from profit-seeking media vultures.[*]

Active and Passive Voice

The voice of a verb tells you whether the subject acts or is acted upon. There are two voices: active and passive. In the active voice, the sentence takes this form: actor, verb, receiver. In the passive voice, the form is inverted: receiver, verb, actor, and the verb always includes some form of "to be." In an active sentence, the subject is the actor:

Example   The zookeeper fed the lion raw meat.

In a passive sentence, the subject is acted upon:

Example   The raw meat was fed to the lion by the zookeeper.

---

[*] Courtesy of Alyssa Lai

Keep these points in mind when you decide which voice is more appropriate in a given context:

1. THE ACTIVE VOICE IS MORE FORTHRIGHT AND USUALLY MORE CONCISE.

2. THE ACTIVE VOICE EMPHASIZES THE ACTOR; THE PASSIVE VOICE EMPHASIZES THE RECEIVER OF AN ACTION. IN THE EXAMPLE ABOVE, THE ZOOKEEPER IS THE SUBJECT IN THE ACTIVE SAMPLE; THE RAW MEAT IS THE SUBJECT IN THE PASSIVE SAMPLE.

3. THE ACTIVE VOICE EMPHASIZES ACTION; THE PASSIVE VOICE IS BEST USED TO DESCRIBE STASIS.

> ACTIVE: The chihuahua bit the mail carrier.   **Example**
>
> PASSIVE: The mail carrier was bitten by the chihuahua.

4. THE PASSIVE VOICE IS AWKWARD WHEN IT IS USED TO AVOID DIRECT PHRASING OR WHEN IT RESULTS IN UNCLEAR, LENGTHY CONSTRUCTIONS.

> ACTIVE: Amos, the shifty used car dealer, sold 50 lemons last month. (direct)   **Example**
>
> PASSIVE: Last month, 50 lemons were sold. (indirect: This rather dishonest use of the passive voice is typical of writers who wish to avoid responsibility for something or who wish to keep things impersonal.)
>
> ACTIVE: At Hallowe'en, Harry played a prank on his mother. (clear)
>
> PASSIVE: At Hallowe'en, a prank was played on his mother by Harry. (unclear and lengthy)

5. THE PASSIVE VOICE IS OCCASIONALLY USEFUL TO AVOID OVERUSE OF THE PRONOUN "I." BE WARY OF OVERUSING THE PASSIVE VOICE, HOWEVER.

> ACTIVE: I based this study on interviews with computer operators across the country.   **Example**
>
> PASSIVE: This study is based on interviews with computer operators across the country.

6. EMPHASIZE THE RECEIVER OF THE ACTION, RATHER THAN THE PERFORMER.

> ACTIVE: The spectators could see the fireworks from a great distance.   **Example**
>
> PASSIVE: The fireworks could be seen from a great distance.

Since it is unimportant who could see the fireworks, the passive is preferable here.

7. THE PASSIVE VOICE IS ALSO THE BEST CHOICE WHEN YOU WISH TO AVOID BEING TOO PERSONAL.

> ACTIVE: You must obey this summons immediately.   **Example**
>
> PASSIVE: This summons must be obeyed immediately.

Since the summons is meant to be formal and impersonal, the passive is preferable here.

In general, instructors do object to the overuse of the passive voice when the active is more lively and more colourful. So beware of overusing "to be" verbs that are static and dull, when a stronger word can be found.

CHAPTER 26 ACTIVE AND PASSIVE EXERCISE A

Identify the voice of all the verbs in the following sentences as active or passive. Discuss which you would change and why. Answers are on p. 288.

1. Work can be overwhelming when employees are unable to complete tasks that have been assigned to them by unreasonable managers.
2. I chose this college because I believed that I would be successful here and my dreams would be realized.
3. Carol expected that her dog Pico would be delighted that the cats were moving out with her daughter Vanessa.
4. It has been shown that students prefer studying those things that are already known to them.
5. Henriette injured her knee when she was hit by a car at a crosswalk.
6. The hotel kitchen was infested by cockroaches, and a lizard was found under a chair.
7. No one really knows where Joy has gone, though she has left her job.
8. You are being watched by closed circuit television.
9. Never has my mother been so embarrassed as the time she was caught with her teeth in the glass by the bed.
10. The Olympics was held in Vancouver in 2010.

CHAPTER 26 ACTIVE AND PASSIVE EXERCISE B

1. Flamingoes can be seen in Everglades National Park in southwestern Florida.
2. Roger's father Fred was stunned when his car overturned on the road, smashing the presents he had purchased for his son.
3. The stars were shining brightly as we began our fireworks display on Canada Day.
4. The marathon was funded by friends and family of Ryan, who had been paralyzed in a diving accident.
5. When the remote was broken, the television was turned on manually by anyone in the family who was willing to get off the couch.
6. The retirement planning session was taught by an elderly gentleman whose new book was given to audience members.
7. The schools were closed when the news of a snowstorm that was coming was released by the media.
8. The key lime pie was topped with whipped cream and garnished with coconut by the pastry chef.

9. My father joked that the emerald ring he had purchased for me would be delivered in an armoured car.

10. The trip on the Greyhound bus, which was arranged for the family, was postponed by my cousin, who could not take time off work.

CHAPTER 26 ACTIVE AND PASSIVE EXERCISE C

1. Edit the following paragraph to remove passive voice. What difference does the voice make to the writing?

The issue of the Mackenzie River Valley has been the cause of great debate in a variety of fields, varying from economics to ecology to politics. All of these groups have come together and fought for what they believed in, whether it was based upon finances or conservation efforts. It was found that the pipeline would be economically advantageous for most parties involved, providing employment for native populations and allowing the continental United States access to gas which they need. Native populations were satisfied with the economics of the project, but always had concerns about the impact the project would have environmentally. These ecological consequences are profound and cannot be dismissed when looking into this project. Oil consumption, for the sake of the planet and for the reserves, needs to be moderated in order to maintain current function. Although the prospects for the project look gloomy from a biological standpoint, the pipeline's commencement may be a success if the right steps are taken from start to finish.

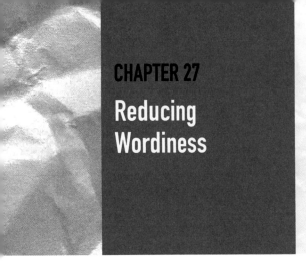

CHAPTER 27

Reducing Wordiness

It is my ambition to say in ten sentences what other men say in whole books — what other men do not say in whole books.
—FRIEDRICH NIETZSCHE

In this chapter:

- How to reduce redundancy
- How to reduce empty words
- How to improve clarity

A wordy essay does not necessarily transgress the word limit of the assignment. Rather, it contains extraneous words that contribute nothing to the meaning and drain force from the essay's argument.

Wordy writing is often characteristic of a first draft. It is close to idle chat: though spontaneous and sometimes even fascinating, it lacks direction. It wanders, perhaps arriving eventually at meaning; it does not set out in orderly pursuit of it. A wordy essay is often a sign of poorly revised and overdressed thought.

Make every word fit. If you can make your writing more succinct, your work will be clearer, and your reader will be more attentive. A few suggestions for improving the conciseness of your writing are listed below.

A Perfect Fit

Avoid Visible Seams

When talking, we commonly join ideas together randomly. Speed is the goal, not beautiful construction. Writing allows us time to reflect and to elaborate, and it benefits from editing that shows reflection. Consider the following example:

Example   Emilio bought the book.

You decide to add a further detail:

Example   Emilio bought the book, which was reputed to be steamy and sensational.

Your new thought shows an obvious seam. "Which" and "that" can often be removed to produce a more graceful line.

Emilio bought the book, reputed to be steamy and sensational. **Example**

Avoid Frills

Often, a speaker describes something by using words accompanied by adverbs meant to accentuate their effect. Here are some examples:

✗ quite elegant   ✗ extremely upset   **Example**
✗ very angry   ✗ altogether pleased
✗ rather uneasy   ✗ not true

Replace these with stronger, less wordy, expressions:

✓ splendid   ✓ distraught
✓ irate   ✓ ecstatic
✓ anxious   ✓ false

In writing, the search for impact is better served by a stronger word, rather than a modified word. And, in writing, there is time to search for it. Use that time to dress your thoughts appropriately.

The same advice holds true for redundant wording. Avoid phrases like these:

✗ past history   ✓ history   **Example**
✗ triangular in shape   ✓ triangular
✗ the city of Saskatoon ✓ Saskatoon
✗ personal opinion   ✓ opinion
✗ refer back   ✓ refer
✗ exactly identical   ✓ identical

In each case, the omitted words added nothing to the meaning.

Avoid Baggy Constructions

A baggy sentence often contains vague words intended to conceal vague thoughts. Such sentences invariably include the following all-too-common words and phrases. Some of these can be excised. Most can be replaced by a single word.

✗ due to the fact that   ✓ because   **Example**
✗ during the time that   ✓ when
✗ with regard to   ✓ about
✗ being   ✓ (omit)
✗ previous to   ✓ before
✗ at which time   ✓ when
✗ in the very near future   ✓ soon
✗ in the event that   ✓ if

Tentative language and unnecessary compound verbs are another frequent cause of bagginess. Avoid phrases like the following and replace them with simple words:

Example

✗ make assumptions about	✓ assume
✗ come to the conclusion	✓ conclude
✗ exhibit a tendency to	✓ tend
✗ be in a position to	✓ can
✗ make a recommendation	✓ recommend
✗ take action on	✓ act

Avoid the "Grand Style"

Writing in the "grand style" uses pompous phrasing to clothe humble ideas. Pompous introductions are a common source of the problem:

Example

✗ It is this theory which needs . . .

✓ This theory needs . . .

✗ It was his view that . . .

✓ He thought that . . .

Avoid Excessive Formality

Just as you wouldn't wear evening dress to compete in a bowling tournament, so you should not use static language to describe active thoughts.

Where possible, keep sentences in their typical order—use the active voice, and move from subject to verb to object. "The Prime Minister gave the order" is a much more direct statement than the passive construction "The order was given by the Prime Minister."

Example

✗ A decision was made by the committee to conduct further studies.

✓ The committee decided to conduct further studies.

While the passive mode has its uses, it is less forceful, and generally harder to understand. It is all talk and no action. When revising, keep a watchful eye on the number of times you resort to the static passive voice. It can occasionally serve as a tactful way of avoiding direct confrontation.

Example

PASSIVE: This amount is owed. (what the bill says)

ACTIVE: You owe us this amount. (what the bill means)

Wordiness Analyzed

The preceding examples illustrate that wordiness is most often caused by speech habits not entirely abandoned in writing. To analyze the causes of your own wordiness, note especially any words you use to *warm up* as you begin to write, to *cover up* your insecurities and uncertainties as you proceed, or to *spruce up* a thought better left unadorned.

Preventive Measures

When editing, check to see that your sentences are designed for simplicity, concreteness, action, grace, and impact.

CHAPTER 27 WORDINESS EXERCISE A

Improve the following sentences by removing or changing redundant words or phrases. Answers are on p. 290.

1. Amelia had not the tiniest bit of experience as a teacher of composition; for that reason, it was difficult to make a recommendation for her to use to apply for that position.

2. In the event that there is a thunderstorm, you should turn off your computer; we are not in a position to replace any of the equipment, so we have made the decision to be very careful.

3. Students who exhibit a tendency to work hard receive excellent grades according to my past experience.

4. In his opinion, it would not be wise for Gio and Carmen to collaborate together on the project; whenever they are in close proximity to each other, they do not accomplish much, due to the fact that they both have bad tempers.

5. One factor in my making the assumption that I will need to find a new job is that I received a pink slip.

6. Martin made a study of the basic fundamentals of the art of kung fu fighting, but his future plans for an action movie career were completely wiped out by his failure to work out on a regular basis.

7. In the view of the court, we owed the sum total of $2000 for refusing to pay the fine in a timely way; we reached the conclusion that tickets are not to be taken lightly.

8. Behaviour of a rude nature will not be tolerated by anyone in contemporary society today.

9. Another reason that taxes have been raised higher is that the government needs to find revenues to support the new programs before its term in office has finally ended.

10. Drivers who are inclined to talk on cell phones while driving are encouraged to remember that those who are paying close attention to one task are less likely to have to make calls to their insurance companies.

CHAPTER 27 WORDINESS EXERCISE B

1. The department store offered free complimentary gift wrapping at no charge for all customers, and it is interesting to note that sales have increased dramatically since that decision was made.

2. My suggestion is that we hire a new director in the event of your suddenly having the need to quit your job.

3. We should make an effort to respond positively to all complaints that our customers make in the future.

4. If Christy makes an attempt to escape out of the backyard, Teagan will do the very same thing.

5. The main thing I want to make clear is that there is nothing in my past history that would suggest a physical problem due to the fact that my medical condition is exceptional.

6. Donna's main field of study was the basics of social work, but her plans were destroyed by her refusal to adapt to changes in the field.

7. Various and sundry suggestions have been considered by the committee, but it has come to the conclusion that the accused is someone with an untrustworthy nature.

8. In today's world, it is essential that we plan ahead to avoid problems of an extreme degree in the future.

9. It is a fact that men who are married have a tendency to live longer than men who are not married.

10. Aaron's dentist made the recommendation that he take a trip to Mexico to visit a dentist who would be less expensive in order to get his teeth fixed in the aftermath of the accident that led to his breaking his jaw.

Some Writing and Grammar Advice for ELL Writers

A man who speaks three languages is trilingual.
A man who speaks two languages is bilingual.
A man who speaks only one language is English.
—CLAUDE GAGNIÈRE

In this chapter:

- How to use articles in English correctly
- How to distinguish verb tenses in English
- How to use infinitives and gerunds after verbs

Writing an essay may pose some unique problems for those whose first language is not English. This chapter isolates some areas of grammar and composition and provides lessons and practice to help non-native speakers of English.

Articles

Although the articles in English come naturally to native speakers, they are not entirely logical and may be a challenge to use correctly. *A* and *an* are the indefinite articles; *the* is the definite article.

Use *a* or *an* when all of these conditions apply:

- when a noun is singular, not plural, like "an elephant" but not with "elephants"
- when it can be counted, like "cups of tea," but not with "tea"
- when it is a common noun and not a proper name, like "a man," but not with "Sanga"
- when it is used for the first time or its specific identity is not known, like "a cat" (just spotted) but not "the cat" (the one we have at home)

Note that noncount nouns like "soup" or "snow" do not take *a* or *an*, and can be modified only with other determiners:

some soup	a little bread
any rain	more snow
much effort (noncount) BUT	many rewards (count)
an amount of food BUT	a number of dishes
less energy BUT	fewer calories

Use *a* when the noun begins with a consonant and use *an* when the noun begins with a vowel. Bear in mind, however, that *h* and *u* may take either *a* or *an* depending on the sounds they make.

an honour	an unknown woman
BUT	
a house	a horror film

Remember that some collective nouns are always plural, like *police*, *military*, and *clergy*. To refer to one member of the group, you would say "a police officer" rather than "a police."

Use *the*

- when the noun has been mentioned already (A cat was rescued from a rooftop yesterday. The cat was returned to its owners.)
- when a modifying word identifies the noun (The first thing to remember is where you parked your car.)
- when it is used with the superlative form, that is, the "est" form of an adjective (The funniest thing happened on my way to school today.)
- when it is one of a kind (The moon is full on Friday.)
- when you know the specific identity of the noun (Pick up the children when you get home from work.)
- when using this pattern of words *the . . . of . . .* (The government of Canada)
- when using plural proper nouns (the Edmonton Oilers)
- when using collective proper nouns (the National Ballet of Canada)
- when using some proper names of geographical features (the Atlantic Ocean, the Rockies)

Don't use *the*

- with most proper nouns
- with plural nouns that refer to something in general (Cats can be finicky.)

Verbs

Using main verbs with auxiliary or helping verbs

All verbs in English use these five forms to create different tenses:

Base (simple form): play, catch

Past Tense: played, caught

Past Participle: played, caught

Present Participle: playing, catching

-s form: plays, catches

Play is a regular verb; *catch* is an irregular verb, which uses an irregular form in its past participle.

Auxiliary Verbs

These verbs (also called helping verbs) come before the main verb. Some auxiliary verbs are used to conjugate the verbs into their various tenses. These auxiliary verbs, which also change form, are *be, do, have*.

Forms of *Be*: be, am, is, are, was, were, being, been

Forms of *Do*: do, does, did (to form questions or for emphasis)

Forms of *Have*: have, has, had

Review of Tenses

Present Tense: Action is in the present or may be habitual

you	run
he/she/it	runs
we	run
you	run
they	run

Present Progressive Tense: Action continues in the present

I	am running
you	are running
he/she/it	is running
we	are running
you	are running
they	are running

Past Progressive Tense: Action began in the past and ended before the present

I	was running
you	were running
he/she/it	was running
we	were running
you	were running
they	were running

Present Perfect Tense: Action took place in the past but implies that it may have taken place more than once and may take place again

I	have run
you	have run
he/she/it	has run
we	have run
you	have run
they	have run

Past Perfect Tense: Action took place in the past before another action or during a particular period of time

I	had run
you	had run
he/she/it	had run
we	had run
you	had run
they	had run

Present Perfect Progressive Tense: Continuing action began in the past, continues in the present

I	have been running
you	have been running
he/she/it	has been running
we	have been running
you	have been running
they	have been running

Past Perfect Progressive Tense: Continuing action begun in the past and ended in the past

I	had been running
you	had been running
he/she/it	had been running
we	had been running
you	had been running
they	had been running

Verbs Followed by Infinitives or Gerunds

1. Memorize which words take the infinitive, which take the gerund, and which take both.

Infinitives are the base or unconjugated form of the verb that begins with "to."

My dog likes to eat red meat.

When do you plan to cook dinner?

Gerunds are forms of the verb that end in "ing" and are used as nouns.

The researcher spent his life looking for a cure for cancer.

Eli put off doing his homework.

2. Note that some verbs take an infinitive only, but need a noun or pronoun in between.

The professor encouraged him to give his speech.

I urge you to vote for this candidate today!

3. Note that some "sense verbs" take a noun or a pronoun with an unmarked infinitive, that is, without the word "to."

His mother made him go to school.

She watched the sun set in the distance.

CHAPTER 28 ARTICLES EXERCISE

Underline the correct article or articles in each sentence or pair of sentences. If no article is needed, cross out the parenthesized articles. (See answers on pp. 291–292.)

1. Clark could not remember the names of (blank, the) cats he was taking care of while he was house-sitting, so he called them Crusty and Fluffyhead.
2. Amanda bought a new dress. (A, An, The) dress was made of silk.
3. I bought a plate of sushi for lunch. It was (a, an, the) plate with eight small pieces of (a, an, the, blank) rice and (a, an, the, blank) salmon.
4. (A, An, The) work of art was considered a masterpiece and it attracted (a, an, the) number of prospective buyers when it was put on auction.
5. It is frustrating to be (a, an, the) only person in (a, an, the) room who cannot participate in (a, an, the) discussion.
6. I received (a, an, the) book I purchased last week in (a, an, the) mail.
7. I have been in (a, an, the, blank) school for most of my life.
8. Mary-Jane wanted (a, an, the) new job because it was more exciting than working at (a, an, the) university as she had been doing, and it was better than joining (a, an, the, blank) army.
9. Banff is (a, an, the, blank) Canadian treasure.
10. If you believe (a, an, the) latest *Globe and Mail*, there is not (a, an, the) more successful songwriter in (a, an, the) country than Leonard Cohen.
11. I work part-time in (a, an, the) local coffee shop downtown for (a, an, the) money to pay my tuition.
12. (A, An, The, blank) deer are mammals.

CHAPTER 28 VERB FORM EXERCISE

1. The following paragraph has some errors in subject and verb agreement and in verb form. Correct the errors:

Many students has believe that residence are cheaper to live in than apartments. They have discover that paying rent is only one cost to having an apartment. There is also groceries that needs to be payed for, and appliances that has to be rent or bought. Many young people have been move out of their apartments because the cost of heat and light have increasing too much.

2. Rewrite the sentence fragments in the dialogue given to make them into complete sentences. Use appropriate auxiliaries.

Beenish: "Dinner?"

Faisal: "Love to."

Beenish: "Our usual place?"

Faisal: "Looking forward to it."

Beenish: "When?"

Faisal: "Six o'clock. Finish your essay?"

Beenish. "Almost."

Faisal: "Great. See you."

CHAPTER 28 GERUND OR INFINITIVE EXERCISE

Choose the gerund or infinitive form, as appropriate in the following sentences:

1. The trainer wanted to discuss (exercising, to exercise) with his clients.
2. Fred really missed (driving, to drive) when he had his knee surgery.
3. I adored (picking, to pick) vegetables out of my own garden.
4. My shift work required (sleeping, to sleep) late in the mornings.
5. She anticipates (seeing, to see) the wild animals in Zanzibar.
6. My roommate does not enjoy (eating, to eat) meat.
7. When will you finish (working, to work) on your assignment?
8. Dustin has agreed (being, to be) the valedictorian.
9. I expect (spending, to spend) my vacation in Costa Rica.
10. We sometimes have difficulty (thinking, to think) of new ways to approach old problems.

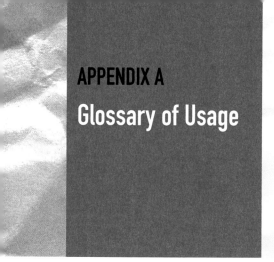

APPENDIX A
Glossary of Usage

I can't write five words but that I change seven.
—DOROTHY PARKER

This glossary lists some words that are a common source of errors, either because they are confused with other words, or because they are not acceptable in standard usage. Check through this list if you are in doubt about a particular usage.

ACCEPT/EXCEPT "Accept" is a verb that means "to consent to"; "except" is a verb or a preposition that means "to exclude."

> I would **accept** your proposition **except** for my husband and six children.

ADVICE/ADVISE "Advice" is a noun; "advise" is a verb.

> I **advise** you to follow your mother's **advice**.

AFFECT/EFFECT "Affect" is usually a verb; "effect" is usually a noun. Note, however, that "effect" may occasionally be a verb, meaning "to bring about."

> His breakup with his girlfriend **affected** his grades.

> A broken heart may have a bad **effect** on scholastic achievement.

> He thought that by writing a tear-stained letter he could perhaps **effect** a reconciliation.

ALL RIGHT/ALRIGHT The *first* word has the correct spelling.

ALL TOGETHER/ALTOGETHER The first means "in a group"; the second means "completely" or "entirely."

> **All together**, the students in the class decided that the teacher was **altogether** incompetent.

ALLUDE/ELUDE "To allude" means "to make indirect reference to"; "to elude" means "to escape."

A lewd reference may **elude** you, but it may perhaps **allude** to another literary source.

ALLUSION/ILLUSION The first word is a veiled or indirect reference; the second word is a deception.

She found the poet's **allusion** to Shakespeare; her belief that the words came from Milton was an **illusion**.

A LOT/ALLOT "A lot" is a colloquialism for "many" or "a great deal"; "to allot" is a verb, meaning "to divide" or "to parcel out." There is no form "alot."

Each of the heirs had been **allotted a lot** of their grandfather's fortune.

AMONG/BETWEEN "Among" involves more than two; "between" involves just two.

Among his peers, he is considered a genius; **between** you and me, I think he is overrated.

AMOUNT OF/NUMBER OF "Amount of" is for quantities that cannot be counted and hence is followed by a singular noun; "a number of" is for quantities that may be counted and takes a plural noun.

A **number** of students drink a large **amount** of alcohol.

AS/BECAUSE "Because" should be used instead of "as" in a sentence meant to show cause and effect, since "as" or "while" may also refer to the passage of time.

✗ **As** he was awaiting trial, he refused to speak to the press. (ambiguous)
✓ **Because** he was awaiting trial, he refused to speak to the press.

ASPECT Avoid this vague word. While not always incorrect, it often contributes to vagueness.

BEING/BEING AS/BEING THAT "Being" can almost always be eliminated. "Being as" or "being that" should be replaced with "because" or "since."

BOTTOM LINE This popular bit of financial jargon has no place in formal writing.

CAN/MAY "Can" implies ability; "may" implies permission or possibility.

I **may** go shopping today since I **can** buy anything I want.

CENTRE ON/REVOLVE AROUND Avoid "centre around," an illogical phrase.

COMPRISES/COMPRISED OF "Comprises" means "consists of." Do *not* use "is comprised of."

✗ Canada is **comprised** of ten provinces and three territories.
✓ Canada **comprises** ten provinces and three territories.

CONSCIOUS/CONSCIENCE "Conscious" is an adjective meaning "aware"; "conscience" is one's inner sense of morality.

The jury became increasingly **conscious** of the criminal's lack of **conscience**.

CONTINUAL/CONTINUOUS "Continual" means "repeated"; "continuous" means "without ceasing."

Her homework was **continually** interrupted by telephone calls from people selling vacuum cleaners.

The air conditioner was used **continuously** throughout the long, hot day.

COULD OF/SHOULD OF/WOULD OF You mean "could have," "should have," "would have."

DATA/CRITERIA/PHENOMENA/MEDIA All of these words are plural. Their singular forms are "datum," "criterion," "phenomenon," and "medium." Check the subject and verb agreement carefully with each word.

Some people think the media **are** responsible for all modern ills.

DISINTERESTED/UNINTERESTED "Disinterested" means "impartial"; "uninterested" means "bored" or "unconcerned."

The ideal referee is **disinterested** in the outcome of the game, but shouldn't be **uninterested** in the actions of the players.

DUE TO "Due to" is acceptable only after some form of the verb "to be." Use "because of" to imply a causal relationship.

The bus is **due to** arrive in fifteen minutes.

Because of his allergies, he had to give up Muffy, his Persian cat.

ELICIT/ILLICIT "To elicit" is a verb meaning "to evoke"; "illicit" is an adjective meaning "illegal."

The questions at the press conference should **elicit** some response to the president's **illicit** behaviour.

ENTHUSE/ENTHUSED Avoid these as verbs. Use the verb "to be enthusiastic" instead.

Shania Twain's fans were **enthusiastic** about her concert tour.

EQUALLY AS Do not use "equally" and "as" together. Instead, use one or the other.

She and her brother are **equally** good at contact sports.

She is **as** good as her brother at contact sports.

ETC. Avoid this abbreviation, which usually means that the author does not know what else to say

THE FACT THAT Avoid this wordy expression.

FACTOR This word generally adds nothing; leave it out.

FARTHER/FURTHER "Farther" refers to actual distance; "further" is abstract.

The **farther** he walked, the more his feet hurt.

She would not stand for any **further** shenanigans.

FEWER/LESS "Fewer" is used with plural nouns; "less" is used with singular nouns.

The **fewer** the guests, the **less** liquor we will need.

FIRSTLY, SECONDLY "First" and "second" are all you really need.

HOPEFULLY Replace this word with "It is hoped that," or more simply, "I (we) hope that."

✗ **Hopefully**, the paper will be finished tomorrow.

This sentence implies that the paper itself is hopeful.

✓ **It is hoped** that the paper will be finished tomorrow.
✓ **I hope that** the paper will be finished tomorrow.

IMPACT ON "Impact" is a noun, not a verb. Replace it with "have an impact on."

The economy will **have an impact on** workers' salaries.

Note, however, that business usage increasingly accepts "impact" as a verb.

IMPLY/INFER "To imply" means "to suggest"; "to infer" means "to conclude."

She **implied** that he was cheap; he **inferred** that he should have offered to pay her bus fare.

INPUT Avoid this word and other computer jargon, except when you are discussing computers.

IN THE CASE OF A wordy construction, best avoided.

✗ **In the case of** your mother-in-law, she means well.
✓ Your mother-in-law means well.

INTO Avoid using this preposition to mean "interested in."

✗ He was **into** macramé.
✓ He was **interested** in macramé.

IRREGARDLESS The correct word is "regardless."

ITS/IT'S "Its" is the possessive form, like "his" or "her." "It's" is a contraction for "it is" or "it has."

> That dog's bark is worse than **its** bite.

> **It's** certainly got big teeth, though.

-IZE Avoid some of the newly created verbs with this ending. They are part of the growing and deplorable tendency to turn nouns into verbs, as in "prioritize." There is usually a simpler form.

> ✗ He **utilized** the facilities.
> ✓ He **used** the facilities.

LAY/LIE "Lay" takes an object; "lie" does not.

> The farmer made the hen **lie** on the nest to **lay** an egg.

LIKE/AS/AS IF "Like" is a preposition and should not be used as a conjunction. Substitute "as" or "as if" if a clause follows.

> ✗ He looks **like** he's going to make it.
> ✓ He looks **as if** he's going to make it.
> ✓ He looks **like** a winner.

MYSELF "Myself" is not a more polite form of "I" or "me." It should be reserved for use as an intensifier or reflexive.

> ✗ The host introduced my wife and **myself** to the guests.
> ✓ The host introduced my wife and **me** to the guests.
> ✓ I, **myself**, solved the problem.
> ✓ I drove **myself** to the airport.

PARAMETERS/PERIMETERS Avoid the use of "parameters" except in its specific application to geometry. Use "perimeters" to mean "boundaries," or to refer to a length or distance.

PARENT Do not use this word as a verb; "parenting" is also suspect. "Parenthood" is a perfectly acceptable substitute.

PRACTICE/PRACTISE "Practice" is the noun; "practise" is the verb. American spelling uses "practice" for both.

> I know **practice** makes perfect, but I hate to **practise**.

PRESENTLY Substitute "currently" or "now." "Presently" actually means "soon," though its usage has widened to include "now."

PRINCIPAL/PRINCIPLE The first means "chief" or "main" as an adjective, the head of a school as a noun; the second means "a basic truth."

His **principal** objection to her comments was that they were based on questionable **principles**.

QUOTE/QUOTATION "Quote" is a verb, *not* a noun—"quotation" is the noun.

✗ This **quote** from Pierre Trudeau makes the point clear.
✓ This **quotation** from Pierre Trudeau makes the point clear.

RELATE TO Use this verb to indicate how one idea is related to another. Do not use it to mean "get along with."

✗ How do you **relate to** your new psychiatrist?
✓ This point **relates** directly to my argument.

SUPPOSE TO Use "supposed to," or better, use "should" or "ought to."

THAN/THEN Use "than" in comparative structures.

Bill Gates makes more money **than** I do.

"Then" is an adverb that makes a reference to time or is used to draw a conclusion.

Then, it follows that I am not in the same tax bracket as he is.

THAT/WHICH Use "that" when what follows restricts the meaning. Use "which" in a non-restrictive case.

Here is the book **that** I told you about. (not just any book, but a specific one)

His fortune, **which** included stock certificates, bonds, and the first penny he had ever earned, was kept in an old shoebox under his bed. (the words surrounded by commas supply incidental, non-restrictive information)

THEIR/THERE/THEY'RE "Their" is possessive; "there" is an adverb or an expletive; "they're" is a contraction of "they are."

There ought to be a law against **their** foolishness. **They're** asking for trouble.

TRY AND Replace this phrase with "try to."

We must **try to** stop meeting like this.

UNIQUE "Unique" means "one of a kind." It cannot be modified.

✗ Her sequined dress was **very unique**.
✓ Her sequined dress was **unique**.

WHO'S/WHOSE "Who's" is a contraction of "who is" or "who has"; "whose" is the possessive form.

Who's been sleeping in my bed?

Whose bed is this, anyway?

-WISE Avoid this suffix.

✗ Timewise, the project is on schedule.
✓ The project is on schedule.

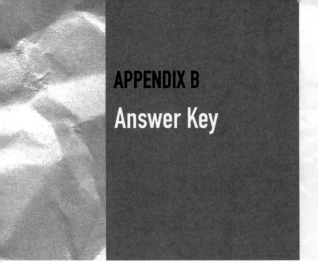

APPENDIX B

Answer Key

CHAPTER 3 EXERCISE 7A

1. Diana Krall and Avril Lavigne are well-known Canadian singers.
2. The perpetrator of the crime was in the country illegally.
3. Because he had polio, Lou used a scooter.
4. People with disabilities need your help.
5. The woman who works on the switchboard must be well-spoken.
6. Call the firefighters if you smell smoke.
7. Margaret Atwood is a celebrated Canadian poet.
8. Human beings cannot live by bread alone.
9. Whenever he went to the variety store, he felt that he was cheated.
10. Lin Song was an Asian student.

CHAPTER 3 EXERCISE 7B

1. Native Canadians often choose to live on the reservation.
2. Because she had West Nile virus, Bette is paralyzed and confined to a wheelchair.
3. There were many men in the office, along with the women at the reception desk.
4. People who are aged and infirm use this transportation system.
5. A man and a woman came in this morning to rent an apartment.
6. People with AIDS take special medications.
7. People with disabilities can apply for supplemental income.
8. Dodi was committed to a reform school for young people.
9. Gentlemen accompanied the ladies to the celebration.
10. May I speak to the head of the house?

CHAPTER 24 PARTS OF SPEECH EXERCISE

A. 1. Carol, eating, meat, documentary, production, food

    2. Ethel, birthday, park, keys, car, kilometres, home

    3. Drinking, drinks, day

    4. London, Ontario, thunderstorm, capital, North America

    5. best

B. 1. remotely

    2. Unfortunately, now

    3. very, however, so

    4. never

    5. Henceforward, expressly

C. 1. through, in

    2. for, in, of, in on

    3. in, on, during, up on

    4. In, within, about

    5. Between, at, at, in

D. 1. do mean

    2. wreaked

    3. Underline, can find

    4. Be

    5. are smiling, must have worked

E. 1. who

    2. ours, it, our, their

    3. Nothing, me, you, me

    4. Somebody, you

    5. Who, my

F. 1. and

    2. Because, when

    3. Until

    4. before

    5. Either, or

G. 1. a man you can trust

    2. Whatever you want for dinner

    3. NONE

    4. Unless you ask me to do so

    5. whom I love

H. 1. that you can be

2. whenever you are in need

3. However you explain verb tenses

4. that won the Governor General's Award for fiction this year

5. No matter what the temperature outside is

CHAPTER 25 SENTENCE STRUCTURE EXERCISE A

These responses are suggestions only. Other corrections may be possible.

1. For most people playing cards is more than a hobby. It is a social activity and a way to gamble without stigma.

2. CORRECT

3. Thomas bought a new computer; the other one he planned to sell on eBay.

4. Weather disturbances are on the rise; however, not everyone believes that they are real.

5. Doing yoga at lunch every day, Aileen and Mei Ling had fun. Still they did not lose weight.

6. On medical shows patients never have chronic illnesses; nevertheless, the reality is that chronic illnesses account for the majority of health care costs.

7. These days baby boomer audiences do not want to travel far in search of entertainment, so the Metropolitan Opera and England's National Theatre are now broadcast in local movie theatres.

8. The coffee shop sued the newspaper food critic after she criticized the poor service and the mediocre food. Even though the reviewer won, she boycotted the shop thereafter.

9. Last year Poppy and Jane stayed in northern California in Bodega Bay, near where Alfred Hitchcock filmed *The Birds.*

10. In Lake Tahoe they went on a cruise. It afforded a view of the mansion where *The Godfather II* was filmed.

CHAPTER 25 SENTENCE STRUCTURE EXERCISE B

1. Consultants always seem overpaid and underworked. Because I lack ambition but have expensive shopping habits, I would like to become a consultant.

2. In Michel Tremblay's *Les Belles-Soeurs* the characters—all female—show how their lives were affected by men.

3. Shy when company comes, my cats ignore activities in the living room in favour of their beds.

4. Canada is the home of many famous chefs, including Susur Lee, Mark McEwan, and Michael Smith.

5. The city of Winnipeg has experienced many floods. It is difficult, if not impossible, to get flood insurance there.

6. This place has everything I want in a house, including a hot tub, a swimming pool, and a huge, two-tiered deck.

7. I am impressed; however, I do not have enough to make a down payment.

8. The National Ballet's artistic director is Karen Kain; she was a world-class dancer who retired at age forty-four.

9. There are many national parks in Canada, which include Banff, Point Pelee, and Algonquin.

10. Musicians who cannot get paying jobs may busk. That way they can practise their art and perform for appreciative audiences.

CHAPTER 25 MODIFIERS EXERCISE A

1. Most cat owners do not tolerate obstreperous behaviour, unless their cats are Siamese.

2. When kayaking, amateurs find cold water temperatures are a threat.

3. As a teacher, I find complaints about low grades annoying.

4. Theresa heard that she was expected to perform at the violin recital on Monday.

5. The tax bill cost nearly $6000.

6. Driving home in the dark, I use chocolate chip cookies and the radio to keep myself awake.

7. I just heard on the radio that there was going to be a storm.

8. I dislike parties where desserts with lots of whipped cream and syrups are served to people on a diet.

9. Because the unproductive employee was asleep on the job, the manager had no choice but to fire him.

10. After inspecting the house from top to bottom, Amy signed her real estate contract.

CHAPTER 25 MODIFIERS EXERCISE B

1. The diners feasted on the poutine smothered in gravy.

2. The farmer prepares the plowed fields to get them ready for planting.

3. Lemon in tea is good for you if you drink it in the morning.

4. After spending all that money, I was amazed that my TV remote froze the first time I used it.

5. Wine at dinner can be expensive if it is corked. [although it is, strictly speaking, correct, as is]

6. Large paintings may be difficult to hang on plastered walls in the office.

7. Veena discovered on the Internet that there was a huge increase in the world's population.

8. Juiced and grated, lemon was added to the mayonnaise by the chef.

9. The owner carried the cat, yowling angrily, to the vet to be vaccinated.

10. Because I was sleeping late in the morning, my doctor suspected that I had a thyroid condition.

CHAPTER 25 PRONOUNS EXERCISE A

1. Whom do you hope to meet in that chat room?

2. Everyone needs to be on his or her best behaviour.

3. When the weather changed suddenly, many of the tourists were caught without umbrellas.

4. He wore old blue jeans to the party, clothing which was disgusting.

5. People like you and me are happy to be in the workforce.

6. Daphne wants to be a funeral director, though she has never studied funeral directing formally.

7. The newspaper suggests that Canada's economy has been positively affected by natural resources, immigration, and a restrained national temperament.

8. In her home, Romula has many beautiful photographs because photography is her passion.

9. When the trainer removed the dog's harness, the dog barked loudly.

10. I answered the phone, an action which meant that I interrupted my dinner while an agent tried to sell me insurance on my credit card.

CHAPTER 25 PRONOUNS EXERCISE B

1. All of us has their own axe to grind, and we must behave ourselves even when angry.

2. Reports say that Canada is one of the happiest countries in the world.

3. Who do you think is the highest paid performer in Canada?

4. After working for a year in the hospital, I no longer find hospitals disturbing.

5. No one can do the job like I can.

6. As I always say, you live and learn.

7. When I released the chains on the dog, it yelped at me.

8. This book says that there is no way to escape the judgment to come.

9. I drank almost a whole case of sparkling water.

10. We asked to speak to the owner, but he did not take our complaint seriously.

CHAPTER 25 SUBJECT AND VERB AGREEMENT EXERCISE A

1. Pauline, together with Harjeet, spends time writing letters, talking to clients, and shopping for new clothes.

2. Neither the manager nor the president was in favour of Adele's new get-rich-quick scheme.

3. The cost of the tummy tuck and the facelift was prohibitive, so Penny decided to accept herself the way she was.

4. Increasing online subscriptions and promoting interest in the magazine are my job in public relations.

5. There are a number of reasons to avoid getting into the real estate market now: the price of houses has skyrocketed, and mortgage rates are likely to go higher.

6. The price of hotels in London, England is high, so the group are planning to stay with relatives.

7. Every single one of the reasons I had for working has vanished since my job description changed.

8. At the bottom of Carmen's suitcase underneath her swimsuit were two bottles of wine and a corkscrew.

9. In Alvin's will were a bequest to his sister and a trust fund arrangement for the charities he supported.

10. The calorie count of this meal, along with its fat content, is not healthy for someone with heart disease.

CHAPTER 25 SUBJECT AND VERB AGREEMENT EXERCISE B

1. The only thing that Cameron works at is forming social networks and sending out résumés for other jobs.

2. A series of consumer reports has been published about those contractors.

3. Either Tim or Desmond produces the party favours for the children's birthday celebrations.

4. Gilbert, with his new truck and his camper, enjoys going on hiking expeditions.

5. Economics has always been part of the suggested business curriculum.

6. Neither Marion nor Anna is available to come to your aid.

7. The lack of funds, along with an increase in my credit card debt, has led me to declare bankruptcy.

8. Nail polish remover and many other cosmetics are considered toxic substances.

9. Exchange programs at distant universities are an excellent way to travel inexpensively.

10. My sedentary lifestyle and my smoking were to blame for my high blood pressure.

CHAPTER 25 COLON AND SEMICOLON EXERCISE A

1. According to his partner, Nick is lazy, sloppy, and irresponsible; however, the partner, if truth be told, is rigid and lacking in sympathy.

2. CORRECT

3. Buying a condominium in a large city like Vancouver or Toronto is costly; hence, I am planning to live in a cardboard box over a hot air vent.

4. There are only ninety-eight days left till my birthday; that's plenty of time for you to save up to buy me a two-week vacation in Milan.

5. The bestselling fiction writers in Canada in the past few years are Margaret Atwood, Yann Martel, Alice Munro, and Carol Shields.

6. Summer movies are highly entertaining but not very deep: they replace sophisticated plot, character, and setting with car chases, sexy actors, and unbelievable stunts; nevertheless, they succeed at the box office.

7. Two things are bothering me: my computer has a virus, and my hard drive needs defragmenting.

8. Your online business can be saved if you marry money or inherit a fortune from a long-lost relative.

9. The incumbent politician had a goal in mind: to win back the shaken confidence of his constituents after the scandal.

10. Rico's dream was to be a bronco buster at the Calgary Stampede.

CHAPTER 25 COLON AND SEMICOLON EXERCISE B

1. Kerry told Malo that it would be all right after five or six years; presumably, everyone would forget what the quarrel had been about by then anyway.

2. Here is what I learned today from watching The Food Network: how to finish a dessert, using a blow torch; how to set fire to the kitchen curtains, using the same blow torch; and how to scare off my dinner guests, even before dinner is over.

3. The new parents considered these names for the twins: Ben and Jerry, Mick and Keith, or Mutt and Jeff.

4. CORRECT

5. Banff is a glorious tourist town: it has beautiful mountain scenery; it also has the highest rate of sexually transmitted disease in Canada, according to some sources.

6. The German shepherd was afraid of thunderstorms: his owner always drove home to keep him company during any weather disturbance.

7. Green vegetables are good for you: why can't we get lettuce on our sandwiches in this cafeteria?

8. The shih tzu next door would benefit from obedience school: he bites his owners' ankles every chance he gets.

9. Buying coffee in a Tim's outlet is the number one Canadian pastime: there are more doughnut shops than there are houses, it seems.

10. Anya disliked her new living room furniture: hence, she decided to spend more time in the family room.

CHAPTER 25 PUNCTUATION EXERCISE A

1. Karina thought, therefore, that the most important thing in the world was work, not play.

2. I studied English, French, psychology, and history, but the thing I enjoyed doing most in my post-secondary years was collecting antiques, from which my business was created.

3. A kind, generous person, Jake was tolerant of his sister Emily even after that incident, which he could never forget, that took place over ten years ago.

4. Although he was not finished school, working as an intern all winter in a renowned company did not intimidate him, nor did he find the work overwhelming.

5. My mother, who is a wonderful cook, made coq au vin, and afterwards she offered us a choice of desserts.

6. The root of all evil, if you ask me, is sloth.

7. Honestly, sir, I do not know where the key to the classroom is, nor do I know what you assigned for homework last night, for I was asleep during our last class.

8. Homeowners who want every amenity will suffer from enormous debt unless they practise discipline and stay within their budgets.

9. This apartment, which is located in beautiful Vancouver, has a great view of the city, and it is affordable.

10. Michael Ignatieff, Michael Ondaatje, and Sylvia Fraser have all explored their lives in memoirs, but then most authors do, in fact, draw on their lives for subject matter.

CHAPTER 25 PUNCTUATION EXERCISE B

1. My pets, Crusty and Flathead, are great examples of beauty, if not brains.

2. Pierre Berton reportedly said, "A Canadian is someone who knows how to make love in a canoe."

3. Those people, whom we met yesterday at the conference, said they were planning to start a wiki for participants in the field.

4. For their anniversary, Mildred and Henry got these gifts: from their daughter, a gluten-free cake; from their son, a trip to Myrtle Beach; and from us, a card and some yellow roses.

5. When exploring tourist attractions, people demand affordable events; however, many will pay exorbitant amounts, so they can experience the best.

6. Expensive candy often comes in elegant, small, shiny packages; nevertheless, high-priced chocolate, despite its exotic origins and glamorous appearance, is just as fattening as cheaper candy.

7. Leila's dream was to write a sensational novel and win international acclaim.

8. The postal service is on strike; however, most of our business is conducted by telephone and mail.

9. My secret method for dealing with anxiety is eating six meals a day, sleeping ten hours each night, and watching lots of relaxing television.

10. Knowledge comes; wisdom lingers.

CHAPTER 25 APOSTROPHE EXERCISE A

1. The theatre goers went to Elton John's *Billy Elliot* and to Shakespeare's *A Midsummer Night's Dream* as well as to Judith Thompson's *White Biting Dog* and Michel Tremblay's *Hoseanna*.

2. The president compared the company's efforts to those of Starbucks and Wendy's to capture a large expanding market.

3. The candidates in 2010 for the Man Booker Prize were Peter Carey's *Parrot and Olivier in America,* Emma Donoghue's *Room,* Damon Galgut's *In a Strange Room*, Andrea Levy's *The Long Song,* and Tom McCarthy's *C.*

4. Thea's father knew that he couldn't make a silk purse out of a sow's ear, but he tried to complete the old house's renovations anyway.

5. Jason's pets were a dog named Molly and another smaller mixed-breed dog named Pico: Pico's fear of storms made her unable to go outside for much of the year; Molly's advanced age and mobility issues made her housebound too.

6. Senyo's office was just a stone's throw from Carrie's, but their approaches were worlds apart.

7. Can you buy me fifty dollars worth of gas, so I can go in and do a decent day's work?

8. Philip Roth's works were recognized by the International Man Booker Award; in the past the same organization has honoured Canada's Alice Munro and Nigeria's Chinua Achebe.

9. The Rolling Stones' longevity can be witnessed in Martin Scorcese's film *Shine a Light*.

10. All the students' complaints in that course were justified because of its focus on the instructor's eccentric interests in the field.

CHAPTER 25 APOSTROPHE EXERCISE B

1. Its muscles strengthened, my body recovered after a month's regime of yoga and six months of running every morning.

2. Christie Blatchford's column in *The Globe and Mail* has its charms: she often describes the court's seamy side and presents Canada's most controversial issues in a brash and humourous way.

3. Denys Arcand's *The Decline of the American Empire,* Atom Egoyan's *Exotica,* Norman Jewison's *Moonstruck,* not to mention James Cameron's *Avatar* and *The Titanic,* give some idea of the contributions Canadian directors have made to the film industry.

4. Canada's reputation in the entertainment industry has long been upheld by comedians: Martin Short's work is known on Broadway and in films, Lorne Michaels' involvement in *Saturday Night Live* is well known, as are John Candy's films.

5. Even in the early days of film, Canada's actresses played a major role: Mary Pickford's work dates back to 1909, Fay Wray's work in *King Kong* takes place in 1933, and modern examples of Canada's film actresses include Neve Campbell and Carrie Ann Moss.

6. Michael J. Fox's early work was in television; despite Parkinson's disease, he has continued to work in films and on television; in addition, his three books have been on the bestsellers' list.

7. This prime minister has none of Trudeau's charm, Mackenzie King's wisdom, or Pearson's diplomacy.

8. It's obvious that the Hendersons' house is empty; the lights are off and the neighbours' attempts to rouse them have gone unanswered.

9. The copyright bill poses a danger to citizens; they oppose its use of digital locks that effectively trump others' rights.

10. Women's clothing is on the second floor, and boys' clothing is on the first floor.

CHAPTER 26 SENTENCE VARIATION EXERCISE

1. a. Because Muhammed wanted to buy a computer tablet, he checked the advertisements on the Internet every day, but a new tablet seemed too expensive. Once he settled on an older model, he found one easily on eBay.

   b. After Timothy castigated the employees for being too careless about vacation days, he called in a consultant to investigate their morale. Whenever he was on holidays, the mood of the workplace sometimes mysteriously improved.

   c. The best instructor in this institution is a marvel, who both entertains and teaches his class. A model of pleasant behaviour and a good teacher, although he gives challenging homework, he manages to motivate students into doing their best.

2. a. Her teeth bared, the tiger leaped at the trainer.

   b. A waste of time, this class on how to write an essay did not provide me with enough examples of how to begin and gave me too much abstract discussion about things I already know.

   c. The party over, we cleaned up the room and washed the dishes.

3. Charles Dickens's work seems to come from a well-educated man, though he did not receive much formal school. Working first in a boot-blacking factory, he then worked as a clerk in a law office, where he learned a great deal of the material that would appear in his novels. He became a prolific writer, a famous man, who edited a well-known magazine and went on speaking tours to America. The father of ten children, Dickens was a very productive and brilliant author who altogether wrote fifteen serial novels and some shorter works.

4. a. On the floor of the car under the blanket on the passenger side was the missing key.

   b. Harriet couldn't resist one food, though it was high in calories: chocolate.

   c. A significant part of the restaurant menu increasingly across North America is French fries.

CHAPTER 26 PARALLELISM EXERCISE A

1. Not only did Sheila check the house for pests but also she checked the garage and the backyard.

2. Either I buy that new pair of shoes, or I go barefoot to the wedding.

3. Experiencing thrills, having the chance to be seen on national television, and winning a big cash prize are the reasons I plan to try out for that reality show.

4. April is neither working nor collecting her pay.

5. Check that all educational consultants are industrious, articulate, and graduated from university.

6. Steve Jobs's notion of computer development is more innovative than Bill Gates'.

7. Carol believes in and is an advocate of vegetarianism.

8. The increase in early retirement is due to a lack of good jobs for those over the age of fifty, excellent packages for those leaving their positions, and a trend toward increased leisure and recreation.

9. The real estate agent asked if I wanted to buy either a condo or a mobile home.

10. You can write your memoirs by making notes on your significant memories, by formulating your philosophy of life, and by speculating about future television appearances.

CHAPTER 26 PARALLELISM EXERCISE B

1. Slugger is an adorable Sheltie although he has a matted coat, he has a bad temper, and he fights with other dogs in the neighbourhood.

2. Not only is being wealthy a guarantee of security, but also it can help you to make new friends.

3. I went shopping for a gift with cachet, beauty, and a low price.

4. Being a successful volunteer means working long hours, serving others with a sense of self-sacrifice, and passing the police check.

5. Leslie Nielsen movies, like *Airplane*, show the strengths of the Canadian comedian: they are silly and nonsensical, as they parody conventional American spy films.

6. The doctor asked the patient to remove his clothes and step on the scales.

7. Not only does Lorne catch trout, but also he hunts moose.

8. Florida has not only alligators, but also turkey vultures.

9. I will be either a lawyer or a con artist after I graduate.

10. My royalties for this book are smaller than J. K. Rowling's.

CHAPTER 26 PARALLELISM EXERCISE C

The research on the Canadian public's perception of media concentration shows an increased awareness of the consolidation of media companies, a strong preference for Canadian characteristics in news media, and the premature role of the Internet as a significant source of news. However, critics also draw attention to the lack of ethnic diversity in news coverage and raise concerns about the limited number of foreign correspondents based abroad to report comprehensively on international news. Both the potency of the Internet as a tool that allows criticism of the media to take place and the issue of journalist education moving to a corporate model elicit mixed feelings about the future of the media. In the midst of these controversies, where does the Canadian government stand when performing its role to protect the integrity of the news? The main question remains: to what extent is the government actively protecting news writing and distribution from turning into an arena for business rather than becoming a school to cultivate critical minds? While the research may show that Canadians have confidence in the CBC, the government may need to take on a more active and immediate role to continue safeguarding the quality of news media from profit-seeking media vultures.

CHAPTER 26 ACTIVE AND PASSIVE EXERCISE A

1. Work can be (ACTIVE) overwhelming when employees are unable to complete (ACTIVE) tasks that have been assigned (PASSIVE) to them by unreasonable managers.

2. I chose (ACTIVE) this college because I believed (ACTIVE) that I would be (ACTIVE) successful here and my dreams would be realized (PASSIVE).

3. Carol expected (ACTIVE) that her dog Pico would be delighted that the cats were moving out (ACTIVE) with her daughter Vanessa.

4. It has been shown (ACTIVE) that students prefer studying (ACTIVE) those things that are already known (PASSIVE) to them.

5. Henriette injured (ACTIVE) her knee when she was hit (PASSIVE) by a car at a crosswalk.

6. The hotel kitchen was infested (PASSIVE) by cockroaches, and a lizard was found (PASSIVE) under a chair.

7. No one really knows (ACTIVE) where Joy has gone (ACTIVE), though she has left (ACTIVE) her job.

8. You are being watched (PASSIVE) by closed circuit television.

9. Never has my mother been so embarrassed (PASSIVE) as the time she was caught (PASSIVE) with her teeth in the glass by the bed.

10. The Olympics was held (PASSIVE) in Vancouver in 2010.

CHAPTER 26 ACTIVE AND PASSIVE EXERCISE B

1. Flamingoes can be seen (PASSIVE) in Everglades National Park in southwestern Florida.

2. Roger's father Fred was stunned (PASSIVE) when his car overturned (ACTIVE) on the road, smashing the presents he had purchased (ACTIVE) for his son.

3. The stars were shining (ACTIVE) brightly as we began (ACTIVE) our fireworks display on Canada Day.

4. The marathon was funded (PASSIVE) by friends and family of Ryan, who had been paralyzed (PASSIVE) in a diving accident.

5. When the remote was broken (PASSIVE), the television was turned on (PASSIVE) manually by anyone in the family who was willing (ACTIVE) to get off the couch.

6. The retirement planning session was taught (PASSIVE) by an elderly gentleman whose new book was given (PASSIVE) to audience members.

7. The schools were closed (PASSIVE) when the news of a snowstorm that was coming (ACTIVE) was released (PASSIVE) by the media.

8. The key lime pie was topped (PASSIVE) with whipped cream and garnished with coconut by the pastry chef.

9. My father joked (ACTIVE) that the emerald ring he had purchased (ACTIVE) for me would be delivered (PASSIVE) in an armoured car.

10. The trip on the Greyhound bus, which was arranged (PASSIVE) for the family, was postponed (PASSIVE) by my cousin, who could not take (ACTIVE) time off work.

CHAPTER 26 ACTIVE AND PASSIVE EXERCISE C

The issue of the Mackenzie River Valley has caused great debate in a variety of fields, varying from economics to ecology to politics. All of these groups have come together and fought for what they believed in, whether finances or conservation efforts. Research shows that the pipeline would be economically advantageous for most parties involved, providing employment for native populations and allowing the continental United States access to gas which they need. The economics of the project satisfy native populations, but they always had concerns about the impact the project would have environmentally. These ecological consequences are profound and those who look into the project should not diminish them. Oil consumption, for the sake of the planet and for the reserves, needs to be moderated in order to maintain current function. Although the prospects for the project look gloomy from a biological standpoint, the pipeline's commencement may be a success if we take the right steps from start to finish.

CHAPTER 27 WORDINESS EXERCISE A

1. Amelia has no experience as a composition teacher; so it was difficult to recommend her for that position.
2. If there is a thunderstorm, turn off your computer; we cannot replace the equipment, so we have decided to be cautious.
3. Students who work hard receive excellent grades according to my experience.
4. He thinks Gio and Carmen should not collaborate on the project; whenever they are near each other, they do not accomplish much because they both have bad tempers.
5. I assume I will need a new job because I received a pink slip.
6. Martin studied the fundamentals of kung fu fighting, but his plans for an action movie career were eliminated by his failure to work out regularly.
7. In the court's view, we owed $2000 for refusing to pay the fine on time; we concluded that tickets are to be taken seriously.
8. Rude behaviour will not be tolerated by anyone in contemporary society.
9. Taxes have been raised because the government needs revenues to support the new programs before its term in office ends.
10. Drivers talking on cell phones while driving should remember that those attentive to one task are less likely to have to call their insurance companies.

CHAPTER 27 WORDINESS EXERCISE B

1. The department store offered free complimentary gift wrapping for all customers, and sales have increased dramatically.
2. I suggest hiring a new director if you quit your job.
3. We should respond positively to all complaints.
4. If Christy tries to escape from the backyard, Teagan will do the same.
5. There is nothing in my history that would suggest a physical problem because my medical condition is exceptional.
6. Donna studied basic social work, but destroyed her plans by refusing to adapt to changes in the field.
7. The committee has considered various suggestions, but it has concluded that the accused is untrustworthy.
8. We plan to avoid extreme problems in the future.
9. Married men live longer than unmarried men.
10. Aaron's dentist recommended that he take a trip to Mexico to visit a less expensive dentist to get his teeth fixed after the accident that broke his jaw.

CHAPTER 28 ARTICLES EXERCISE

1. Clark could not remember the names of the cats he was taking care of while he was house-sitting, so he called them Crusty and Fluffyhead.

2. Amanda bought a new dress. The dress was made of silk.

3. I bought a plate of sushi for lunch. It was a plate with eight small pieces of rice and salmon.

4. The work of art was considered a masterpiece and it attracted a number of prospective buyers when it was put on auction.

5. It is frustrating to be the only person in the room who cannot participate in the discussion.

6. I received the book I purchased last week in the mail.

7. I have been in school for most of my life.

8. Mary-Jane wanted the new job because it was more exciting than working at the university as she had been doing, and it was better than joining the army.

9. Banff is a Canadian treasure.

10. If you believe the latest *Globe and Mail*, there is not a more successful songwriter in the country than Leonard Cohen.

11. I work part-time in a local coffee shop downtown for the money to pay my tuition.

12. Deer are mammals.

CHAPTER 28 VERB FORM EXERCISE

1. Many students believe that residences are cheaper to live in than apartments. They have discovered that paying rent is only one cost to having an apartment. There are also groceries that need to be paid for, and appliances that have to be rented or bought. Many young people have been moved out of their apartments because the cost of heat and light has increased too much.

2. Beenish: "Would you like to go out to dinner?"

   Faisal: "I would love to go to dinner."

   Beenish: "Shall we go to our usual place?"

   Faisal: "I am looking forward to it."

   Beenish: "When shall we meet?"

   Faisal: "Six o'clock would be a good time. Did you finish your essay?"

   Beenish. "I have almost finished it."

   Faisal: "It is great to hear that. I will see you."

CHAPTER 28 GERUND OR INFINITIVE EXERCISE

1. The trainer wanted to discuss exercising with his clients.

2. Fred really missed driving when he had his knee surgery.

3. I adored picking vegetables out of my own garden.

4. My shift work required sleeping late in the mornings.

5. She anticipates seeing the wild animals in Zanzibar.

6. My roommate does not enjoy eating meat.

7. When will you finish working on your assignment?

8. Dustin has agreed to be the valedictorian.

9. I expect to spend my vacation in Costa Rica.

10. We sometimes have difficulty thinking of new ways to approach old problems.

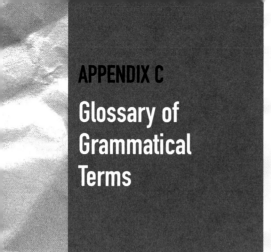

ADJECTIVE A word like "green," "funny," or "glamorous" used to describe a noun.

ADVERB A word like "very" or "quite" used to describe an adjective, or more commonly, a word like "happily" or "sadly" used to describe a verb. Adverbs are hard to categorize, so if you don't know what a word is, it may very well be an adverb, as, for example, the word "not."

APPOSITIVE An appositive is a noun or a phrase that renames the word that comes before it, as in the following sentence:

Michaëlle Jean, the former Governor-General of Canada, was born in Haiti.

ARTICLES There are three articles in English: "a," "an," and "the."

AUXILIARY VERBS Also known as helping verbs, these verbs appear with others. "To be" and "to have" and their forms are often used as helping verbs, as are modal verbs like "may," "might," "shall," "should," and others.

CLAUSE A clause is a group of words that contains both a subject and a verb. A clause that can stand alone as a sentence is a main clause or an independent clause. A clause that cannot stand alone as a sentence is called a subordinate clause or a dependent clause.

COLLECTIVE NOUN A collective noun is one that refers to a group of things and may be treated as a single unit or as a plural, depending on context. Examples are "jury," "family," "group," and "class."

COMPLEMENT A complement completes a sentence that contains a "to be" verb, like "He is an obedient watchdog." "An obedient watchdog" is the complement.

CONJUNCTION A conjunction is a word that joins two clauses together. A coordinating conjunction is one of these seven words: and, or, nor, for (when it means "because"), but, yet, so. A subordinate conjunction also joins two clauses together. Examples include "because," "since," "unless," and "until."

CONJUNCTIVE ADVERB A conjunctive adverb is an adverb used to join two main clauses together as in this example:

I love hockey; however, I hate violence.

COUNT NOUN A count noun is a noun that can be counted as in this example:

She bought three pieces of china. ("pieces" is a count noun)

She bought china. ("china" is a noncount noun)

This distinction is important because you use words like "amount" with noncount nouns and "number" with count nouns. Look at these examples:

There were a large number of people in the room. (not "amount" since "people" can be counted)

There was a large amount of cereal left in the box. (not "number" since "cereal" cannot be counted)

DANGLING MODIFIER A dangling modifier is a common grammatical error that occurs when a modifier is used to refer to a noun or a pronoun that is not actually in the sentence, but just understood. This kind of error impedes clarity and must be corrected.

Eating peanut brittle, his tooth broke.

"He" is missing from the sentence, even though understood. The sentence is incorrect because "eating peanut brittle" has nothing logical to modify. (His tooth was not eating peanut brittle.)

DEFINITE ARTICLE "The" is the definite article in English, used to point specifically to something.

DEMONSTRATIVE ADJECTIVE A word like "this" or "these" that points to a noun.

GERUND A gerund refers to a noun that ends in "ing." See the following example:

Smoking is dangerous to your health. ("Smoking" is a gerund; here it is a noun and the subject of the sentence.)

INDEFINITE ARTICLE "An" and "a" are indefinite articles. "An" is used in front of vowel sounds. Both refer generally to a noun.

INFINITIVE An infinitive is the base form of the verb before it is conjugated. Infinitives begin with the word "to" as in "to be or not to be."

INTRANSITIVE VERB Intransitive verbs are verbs that do not take an object.

The baby is sleeping.

LINKING VERB A linking verb (sometimes called a copula verb) is one that does not involve action, just a state of being.

The suspect appears agitated.

MAIN CLAUSE A main clause has a subject and a verb and can stand alone. In other words, it is a sentence.

MISPLACED MODIFIER A misplaced modifier is a common grammatical error that occurs when a modifier is not placed close enough to the noun or pronoun that it describes.

Yapping and wagging its tail, the baby was amused by the chihuahua.

The sentence should read instead:

Yapping and wagging its tail, the chihuahua amused the baby.

NONCOUNT NOUN A noncount noun is one that cannot be counted like "water," "tea," "soup," and "porridge."

OBJECT An object is the receiver of the action in a sentence.

The car hit the tree. ("Tree" is the object that receives the action of the sentence.)

PARTICIPLES Participles are parts of the verb. All verbs have two participles: a present participle (ending in "ing") and a past participle. In regular verbs, the past participle ends in "-ed." In irregular verbs, past participles vary. For example, "play" is a regular verb; the present participle is "playing" and the past participle is "played." "Sing," however, is an irregular verb; the present participle is "singing," but the past participle is "sung." Participles are used to form different tenses of the verb and can also be used as adjectives to modify nouns or pronouns: "the playing children" and "the singing nun."

PHRASE A phrase is a group of words that does not have both a subject and a verb. A participial phrase contains a participle: "the sleeping infant." A prepositional phrase begins with a preposition: "over the rainbow."

PLURAL Plural is used to indicate more than one. Many words become plural in English by adding "s".

POSSESSIVE ADJECTIVE The possessive adjectives are "my," "your," "his," "her," "its," "our," "their." They indicate ownership.

PREDICATE All sentences have both a subject and a predicate. The subject is the agent or the performer of the action and often—but not always—comes first in a sentence. The predicate begins at the verb and contains everything but the subject.

PREPOSITION A preposition is usually a small word in English that often indicates position. Examples include "after," "behind," "in," "over," "through," "under." Prepositions are always followed by a noun or a pronoun in the objective form.

SINGULAR Singular subjects are "I", "you", "he", "she," or "it." The "number" of the noun is important when choosing the verb that goes with it.

SUBJECT The subject is the performer of the action in a sentence with an action verb.

The subject is what is being discussed in a sentence with a linking verb.

Subjects often come before the verb in English, but not always.

To find the subject, go to the verb and ask "Who or what is doing this?" or "Who or what is being described?"

SUBORDINATE CLAUSE A subordinate clause has a subject and a verb in it, but it cannot stand alone and must be linked to a main clause to form a sentence.

Examples:

Because the dog ate my homework.

Whenever I go to the dentist.

TRANSITIVE VERB A transitive verb takes a direct object.

Fido ate the steak.

Index